BEAUTY BOUND

BEAUTY BOUND

by

RITA FREEDMAN

Lexington Books

D.C. Heath and Company • Lexington, Massachusetts • Toronto

The case studies included in this book have been
altered to protect the identity of the individuals
concerned. Fictitious names have been used, and
composite accounts have been created from the
author's clinical experience.

The author and publisher express their thanks to those
who have granted permission to reproduce
copyrighted text and photographs.
The copyright acknowledgments appear on page 257.

Library of Congress Cataloging-in-Publication Data

Freedman, Rita Jackaway.
Beauty bound.

Bibliography: p.
Includes index.
1. Women—United States.   2. Beauty, Personal.
3. Feminine beauty (Aesthetics)—United States.
4. Feminity (Psychology)   I. Title.
HQ1220.U5F74   1985   305.4'2.   85-45041
ISBN 0-669-11141-4 (alk. paper)

Designed by Peter Carr

Published simultaneously in Canada
Printed in the United States of America
International Standard Book Number: 0-669-11141-4
Library of Congress Catalog Card Number: 85-45041

The paper used in this publication meets
the minimum requirements of American National Standard
for Information Sciences—Permanence of Paper
for Printed Library Materials, ANSI A39.48-1984

ISBN 0-669-11141-4

85 86 87 88 89 90   10 9 8 7 6 5 4 3 2 1

Contents

Acknowledgments

ACKNOWLEDGMENTS are gratefully extended

To the students and patients who have shared with me their problems and experiences with beauty.

To the friends and colleagues who read early drafts and offered valuable suggestions—Howard Bael, Dahlia Berman, Nick Beilenson, Evelyn Beilenson, Allan Duane, Gloria Goldstein, Leon Golub, Sharon Golub, Linda Grossman, Gloria Kahn, and Jacqueline Plumez.

To Judith Handelman, Lucy Werner, and Sharleen Conn, who prepared the manuscript.

To my family who helped me get through the hard times; especially my parents for their continued support; my sisterly friend, Marie Duane, for her comfort and caring; my son Adam, for patiently cooperating with a mother who works at home; my daughter Gwenyth for always being there with encouragement, advice, and insight.

To my editor, Margaret Zusky, and the staff at Lexington Books.

To the teachers and scholars who have taught me to view human behavior from a variety of perspectives, and whose voices echo behind my own.

Introduction

W HEN a sixteen-year-old blonde from Washington, D.C., was crowned in 1921, she launched America's longest running, most popular beauty contest. Despite some display of talent, clearly it was Margaret Gorman's face and form that embodied the national feminine ideal. The Miss America Pageant soon became a national ritual celebrating beauty as woman's noblest achievement.

Nearly half a century later, demonstrators gathered on the Boardwalk of Atlantic City in what many consider the public birth of the current women's movement. There they labored, protesting the beauty pageant, chanting, picketing, and, finally, crowning a sheep as the symbolic winner. A huge trash can was stuffed with items of "women's garbage and female torture"—curlers, wigs, false eyelashes, girdles, and bras.

Reaction to this assault on the worship of beauty was mixed. Some people merely dismissed the protestors as ugly, frustrated women who were proclaiming a politics of sour grapes. Yet those few discarded bras fired the imagination of the media. Headlines describing "Bra Burning" stretched from coast to coast in a grand exposé, and the term *bra burners* became synonymous with *man haters*.

Why was a beauty contest chosen for the site of the first contemporary feminist demonstration? A group of women had discovered that while they outwardly denounced the pageant, they somehow ended up watching it. Even the most "liberated" among them responded at a deep emotional level to the sanctification of female beauty, identifying with the contestants, and crying as the winner descended the runway, gloriously cradling her bouquet. They chose to picket the contest because it seemed to epitomize woman's role as a passive, decorative object. A manifesto was drafted protesting the fact that men are judged by their actions

and given real power while women are judged by their appearance
and given an ermine cape and a bunch of roses. The message was
that all women are hurt by such contests in a culture that substitutes the worship of female beauty for the recognition of female
equality.

Like those of other psychologists, my research interests have
often been motivated by personal needs to understand myself and
my loved ones. For the past decade I have watched a daughter
stumble along the bumpy road of adolescence, with my arms held
out like a safety net. Her body at early puberty is clearly recalled
by Anne Sexton's lines:[1]

> My daughter, at eleven
> (almost twelve), is like a garden.
>
> Oh, darling! Born in that sweet birthday suit
> and having owned it and known it for so long,
> now you must watch high noon enter—
> noon, that ghost hour.

High noon indeed! Bewitched by its own heritage, her body will
betray a young woman unless she can tame it through rites of
passage, through potions and prayers, through cosmetic magic or
the surgeon's scalpel.

I stood vigil over the rituals that marked my daughter's passage
into womanhood, reliving through her my own painful initiation
rites. A first pair of stockings; legs shaved to the knee, then later
to the hip. A first bra to hug budding breasts—which continue
to bloom and blossom. "There's too much of me!" she cries,
pleading to have the burdensome bosom reduced. Next the scale
becomes a dictator; diet regimes are tried and drugstore remedies
are swallowed to dissolve the unwanted self. My own adolescent
agony over acne and overweight flows back in a stream of memories.

Lips painted white, lids powdered green, lobes pierced, once,
twice, three times. "It's the fashion, Mom." Camouflaged in a
cloud of make-believe, her naked face remains hidden. Hair grown
wild and glamourous drapes across her face. "You have no pe-
ripheral vision," I harp in a mother's absurd voice. On strapless

sandals with stiletto heels, she totters through her seventeenth summer. My arms are outstretched, ready for the fall. How I long to play the fairy godmother—to create, by the wave of a hand, such instant loveliness that the world would lay itself at her feet!

She is bright, she is beautiful, and she is not unique. The trials of her adolescent beauty quest are those of the young women who sit in my classes, who read de Beauvoir and ponder their destinies while painting revised self-images again and again. Her fears are those of the patients who sit in my office, who seek to control their lives by remodeling their looks.

The mother in Sexton's poem explains to her child:

> Oh, darling, let your body in,
> let it tie you in,
> in comfort.
>
> . . . .
>
> What I want to say, Linda,
> is that there is nothing in your body that lies.
> All that is new is telling the truth.

Yet the truth proclaimed by an honest young body echoes back to every girl through the chambers of society, where the refrains of nature are mixed with the incantations of culture. I watched my daughter listen to her growing body, saw fear in her eyes, felt pain as she twisted to fit the glass slipper. And I whispered to her in a thousand ways the final lines of Sexton's poem:

> Darling,
> stand still at your door,
> sure of yourself, a white stone, a good stone—
> as exceptional as laughter
> you will strike fire,
> that new thing!

During the years since that first protest against the Miss America Pageant in 1968, psychologists have scrutinized most facets of female behavior, from motherhood to menopause. Physical attractiveness has been largely overlooked, although women's lives are bound up in it. From the toddler flashing her painted toenails to the dowager pulling whiskers from her chin, beauty rituals comprise a major aspect of being female. Textbooks on primates always discuss "attractivity" as a basic part of animal behavior, whereas books on human sexuality and on gender development generally ignore its relevance. Very few of the texts now used in courses on the psychology of women even list beauty or physical attractiveness in the index. Meanwhile, newsstands overflow with magazines devoted to displaying, defining, or attaining it. Week after week the "how to" beauty books are among the top best sellers. How to trim down thighs, how to firm up breasts, how to make Jane less plain, more fit, less fat, and colored just right. Why are these books in such continuous demand? Why are they almost always directed at females? How do they influence women's image?

When questioned about the meaning of beauty, some women say they enjoy its challenge; others say they resent its domination. Most find it hard to admit just how much they value beauty and how much they fear its loss. The triumphs and tragedies of their daily beauty quest are shrouded in silence.

This is why beauty reform remains part of the feminist agenda (although feminists themselves are often confused and threatened by the issue of beauty on a personal level). How *does* beauty influence self-esteem and independence? Is adornment an asset or a liability in achieving equality? Questions of equal pay or equal rights seem clearer and safer. Equal looks are harder to define.

This book is part of the continuous collective effort to question "truth" about women's lives. It examines beauty as a central dimension of femininity. It considers the connection between idealized female beauty and an underlying belief in female inferiority. It explores how beauty increases woman's status while maintaining woman's subordination.

This is not an antibeauty book. Nor is it a critique of those who seek to enhance their attractiveness. Appearance is important and it will continue to be. Beauty is not the enemy. Rather we are all, men and women, bound by a system that encourages obsessive preoccupation with the female body. By calculating the power of beauty to both enhance and undermine human relations, we may achieve a more realistic view of it. Through greater awareness, reform becomes possible.

As women strive to break free of constricting stereotypes of who they are and what they want, idealized feminine beauty must be identified as part of that challenge. It is not merely a decorative diversion. The sense of self resides within the body. False beauty images generate false body parts—remodeled torsos, remade faces—reconstructions that are worn like acquired accessories. As long as women remain hidden behind these distortions, they will be controlled by them, no matter how safe they feel.

New beauty images are needed—comfortable and potent images that will permit uncorseted movement on unbound feet, and that can lead toward unrestricted goals. By peeling off the beauty mystique, like yesterday's makeup mask, we may uncover faint traces beneath, closer to the skin, closer to reality. By cleansing the surface we can reveal hidden images, like pentimento. Who knows? We may even like what we find there.

BEAUTY BOUND

1

The Fair Sex

In olden times when wishing still helped, there lived a king
whose daughters were all beautiful, but the youngest was so
beautiful that the sun itself, which has seen so much, was
astonished whenever it shone in her face.

— Grimm Brothers, *The Frog King*[1]

O N the plains of Asia Minor are found the ancient ruins of
Catal. Excavation reveals that the burial sites of men contain piles of weapons, while the graves of women are filled with
jewelry and elaborate cosmetic sets. Adornment was apparently
so essential to a woman's work that her beauty tools were sent
along with her into the next life.

Women are still considered the fair sex. Among fish and fowl,
it is the male who usually sports the bright colors and fancy
feathers, for he is the one who courts through attraction. But
among humans, in western culture, the female is assigned the
decorative role, as if an added source of beauty was inherited
along with her second X chromosome. This gender difference in
physical attractiveness is widely accepted as a fact of nature.

Beauty is not a gender-neutral trait. There are no televised
pageants in which men parade in bikinis to be crowned Mr. America on the basis of their shapely legs and congenial smiles; no
fairy-tale prince so handsome that the sun is astonished when it
shines on his face. Because beauty is asymmetrically assigned to
the feminine role, women are defined as much by their looks as
by their deeds. To be womanly is to be beautiful, and, conversely,

to be unattractive is to be unwomanly. Good looks are prerequisite for femininity but incidental to masculinity. This asymmetry produces different social expectations and different psychological consequences for each sex.

The link between beauty and gender is embedded in the very meaning of the term *beauty*. One definition of *beauty* is "an attractive well-formed girl . . . as when we say 'she is a beauty.' " Language both reflects and shapes thought. English is one of the few languages that employs different terminology for attractive males and females. Women are *pretty*, a word that primarily refers to physical traits and that means "ornamental beauty without grandeur . . . pleasing in a feminine, childlike way." Calling a man pretty is problematic, for it suggests effeminacy. The Latin word *bellus*, from which *beauty* derived, initially was used to describe women and children only. Even now the word *beauty* rarely is applied to adult men.

Males are *handsome*, a term that derives from the root *hand* and was originally applied to behavior rather than appearance. Handsome connotes strength and accomplishment along with good looks, for "handsome is as handsome does." Males report that they envy other attractive men not for their appearance as much as for their status, possessions, and accomplishments. Handsome people of either sex tend to be doers, while pretty people, like Miss America, are thought to be mainly decorative.

It is a short step from the belief that women are the fair sex to the imperative that they must be. The expectation of feminine beauty inflates its importance, making women more vulnerable to "looksism," a stereotype similar to ageism or racism. Looksism is a form of social control that influences how people see themselves and how they are seen by others. The everyday effects of looksism are described in an essay by Erica Abeel, who observes the following:

> I have this problem. Despite the consciousness revolution of the past five years, I still feel that I have to look beautiful. Men can look any old way. To the world I present a respectable high-tone image, the Professor, sorting out the contradictions of contemporary sensibility. But I have this other round of trivia filling the spaces of my existence. . . . After putting on my shoes, I put on the mask: blusher, eye liner, mascara. . . . Doesn't my naked

face represent me adequately? . . . . Upkeep doesn't stay constant:
It's cumulative. The more you do to yourself the more you *have*
to do. . . . Though my facial rehab is minimal, I realized recently
it is no longer optional.[2]

Again and again in interviews, women mention the impact of
looksism and their efforts to cope with it. Playing the role of fair
lady generates a variety of conflicts, which the following case
illustrates.

Judy describes herself as a rather plain-looking woman of twenty-
nine. A successful advertising executive who is married to a lawyer, she attributes part of her professional success to a dramatic
cosmetic make-over that transformed her from duckling to swan.
Still, she questions its value. Her interview begins with some
early recollections.

"When I was little we each had special roles in the family. My
brother was the athlete, my sister Kate was the pretty one, while
I was the musician. I was proud of my talents and didn't care
much about looks." Parents commonly label their daughters the
cute one, the plain one, the princess, but rarely assign these
particular labels — which evolve into roles — to sons. Girls who
receive such name tags gradually internalize them and start to
enact them.

Judy recalls first feeling self-conscious about appearance in the
fifth grade, when a cousin teased her for wearing glasses. A late
maturer, she became painfully aware of looking babyish in junior
high. While her girlfriends were obsessed with clothes and boys,
she was busy with voice lessons. In high school, she auditioned
for the lead in a musical and was clearly more talented than the
prettier girl who was chosen. "I always knew I wasn't very pretty,
but it never bothered me until I lost that part. My dreams of a
singing career suddenly seemed unrealistic. Gradually I gave them
up. I remember thinking that my brother's acne didn't stop him
from being a track star." Males can acquire attractiveness by
"winning handsomely," while females are expected to *be* beautiful
as well as to perform beautifully.

After finishing college, Judy joined a New York advertising
firm. A colleague advised that although her work was exceptional,
her image was not. "Being well groomed was not enough, she
told me. She thought I could be much more attractive than I gave

myself credit for. At first I resisted. I basically like myself and disliked the idea of pretending to be something I wasn't. But I still remembered the school play and didn't want to miss out again."

On an impulse, Judy rinsed her hair to a strawberry blond. A new kind of contact lens allowed her to step out from behind her glasses. Startled by her own new look, she became intrigued by the reactions of others to it. Beauty is not only expected but is heavily rewarded. People notice and respond to it. Quickly promoted to a position that she well deserved, Judy still wonders whether she would have advanced so fast had she not transformed her appearance. "I certainly enjoy the extra attention, but feel somehow resentful. Inside I'm the same person. In the morning with my glasses on and my makeup off, I'm just ordinary looking. I've always been smart and hardworking and feel that a man with my ability and an average face wouldn't need to remodel himself each day to have his talents recognized."

Judy's job is secure and so is her marriage. She would like to adopt a more natural image but still feels pressured by looksism, not only for her own career but for the social functions required by her husband's law practice. In Judy's case, fulfilling society's expectations for feminine beauty has sometimes been painful, other times rewarding, and frequently confusing. The challenge of combining physical attractiveness with psychological integrity is not only different but more difficult for her than for her husband. Moreover, the essence of feminine beauty is ever changing and therefore hard to define.

Defining Beauty

Beauty is many things—an external radiance, an inner tranquillity, a sexual allure, a fact of social exchange. Contradictory definitions of the nature of beauty abound, indicating widespread ambivalence about its meaning.

On the one hand, beauty is dismissed as mere facade, a superficial trait of little consequence. On the other hand, it is infused with supernatural power: a spellbinding, dazzling, irresistible princess can capture hearts and control kingdoms. Beauty is sometimes equated with the fresh innocence of a country maiden, but other times it is fraught with the dangers of a femme fatale. It is noble but suspect, pure but corrupting. The stereotypic gorgeous blonde is dumb, yet sexy; passive, yet exciting. At one moment her beauty is coveted as an asset; the next moment it may be shunned as a liability.

First beauty is worshiped as an innate quality that cannot be artificially contrived; next it is packaged and peddled as an illusion that anyone can cultivate. Princesses are born but they also give birth to themselves. (Debra Sue Maffett remodeled her nose before capturing the 1983 Miss America title.) To look as natural as possible, a woman hides the fact of her face-lift. To look as glamourous as possible, she flaunts her platinum curls and crimson nails. Precise definitions of beauty dissolve in such contradictions.

Fifty contestants bearing geographic names parade before a panel of judges, who rank them as finalists and runners-up. Fifty million viewers, through their passive participation, approve this method of judging who is the fairest in the land. Meanwhile, a computer blends the profiles of the past fifty Miss Americas and predicts that the next winner will be a curvaceous five-foot-eight-inch twenty-one-year-old with blue eyes.

Do these statistics accurately define the essence of beauty? The queens who reign over rodeos and homecoming proms seem to embody the idea that feminine beauty is external and quantifiable. Yet when people are asked to define attractiveness, they mention a range of subtle qualities that are abstract and highly personal.

As a psychological experience, beauty is an interactive process. It derives as much from the beliefs and perceptions of the beholder as from the image of the beheld. This is why its definition is so elusive and its influence so hard to determine. We can never be sure where it comes from or who possesses it. Does it depend on physical dimensions or on psychological ones? Is it housed in the flesh or created through fantasy? Who owns and controls it, the beholder or the beheld? Was Schopenhauer right in declaring that "only the man whose intellect is clouded by sexual impulses could give the name of 'the fair sex' to that undersized, narrow-shouldered, broad-hipped and short-legged race" called woman?

A century ago, Sir Francis Galton constructed a model of beauty by summing together the features of the population. He super-imposed hundreds of faces, one upon the other, and concluded that the composite result did indeed portray the ideal of beauty that was fashionable at that time. A lovely face, he believed, had regular, average features, while an ugly one was "full of sur-prises." However, the concept of beauty does connote something beyond the average. Defined as "a combination of rare or unusual qualities," beauty has an exclusionary function that divides those who have it from those who don't. If the majority succeed in transforming themselves into the ideal, then the standard must change, for the value of beauty as an ideal depends on its re-maining extraordinary. Thus, the odds are fixed so that only a few can win.

Beauty norms are in constant flux as new standards are adopted and abandoned. Worship of curves gives way to admiration of muscles; kinky hair gives way to straight hair; legs replace breasts, and vice versa, as the fashion focus moves down or up. When beauty images change, bodies are expected to change as well, for nature cannot satisfy culture's ideal. Lashes must be longer, hair silkier, cheeks rosier.

Perhaps, as some biologists suggest, we are born with an un-conscious ability to recognize signals of youth, fertility, and strength because these traits offer a reproductive advantage. Cul-tured beauty norms are then superimposed upon this natural capacity to discriminate attractiveness. In fact, there is a sur-prisingly high level of agreement about who is beautiful and who is not. Ratings among judges are consistent regardless of age, socioeconomic level, and ethnic differences.[3] Within a given cul-ture, a consensus prevails despite the fact that beauty standards constantly change and that individuals who look vastly different are judged equally attractive. People may have difficulty in de-fining the essence of beauty, but they seem to recognize it when they see it.

Concepts of beauty are established quite early in life. Children's ratings of the attractiveness of kindergarten classmates correlate highly with adult judgments of the same youngsters.[4] A high level of social agreement indicates the pervasive nature of ap-pearance stereotypes. Even the pleasure of admiring one's own pretty face depends on standards acquired through others. Judy's case illustrates how self-concept can be undermined when success or failure is attributed to appearance. As a child, she felt content with her average face until she was passed over for the lead part in a musical. She again suffered self-doubt when she was told that good grooming was not enough to get ahead.

One popular misconception about beauty is that it counts most at initial encounters and becomes less important with familiarity. In fact, evidence suggests just the opposite. Appearance continues to have a significant influence even on long-standing relationships.[5] Another common misconception is that beauty is democratically distributed so that every person is considered attractive by someone or other. Again the data suggest the opposite conclusion. Certain faces are consistently admired, while others are consistently rejected. Appearance therefore makes a real difference over the course of hundreds of daily encounters. Herein lies the power of beauty to define us.

The ancient Greek term *kalos* and the Latin term *bellus* meant both beautiful and good. An association between these two qualities remains strong to this day. Beautiful people are seen as a joy—if not forever, at least in a multitude of dimensions. As judged in numerous studies, attractive people are thought to have greater warmth and poise, to be more sensitive, kind, sincere, and successful, and to lead more fulfilled lives.[6] A pleasing exterior is assumed to cover an equally pleasing interior.

It is clearly untrue that we regard beauty as merely skin-deep, concludes Ellen Berscheid, a leading pioneer in beauty research. There is a strong belief that what is beautiful is also good. We may give lip service to so-called higher moral values and dutifully insist that beauty lies within, that looks are superficial, and that character is what counts. But such sanctimonious maxims only cover up a strong unconscious worship of appearance.

Until recently, the significance of physical attractiveness remained largely unexplored by social scientists. Now it is proving to be a potent force in personal relationships—something poets and artists have long understood. Not only are good-looking people associated with good things; they are also treated better. Cute babies are cuddled more than homely ones; attractive toddlers are punished less often.[7] Teachers give special attention to better-looking pupils, strangers offer help more readily to attractive

people, and jurors show more sympathy to good-looking victims.[8]
Female patients in mental hospitals receive more private therapy
if they are young and pretty;[9] attractive applicants are more readily hired for many although not all, jobs. As in Judy's life, attractive people get ahead faster.

And the preferential treatment attractive people receive has
long-term effects. They actually seem to be better adjusted socially, to have healthier personalities, and to possess a wide range
of interpersonal skills that help them to influence others.[10] Perhaps
they feel more confident because they anticipate good treatment.
Or perhaps the good treatment they receive brings out the best
in them. Beauty generates positive feedback. Since good things
are expected from good-looking people, they seem to grow into
the qualities they are thought to possess. One study showed that
beauty bias can even affect telephone conversations between
strangers.[11] Males were asked to call unknown females who had
been described to them as either attractive or unattractive. The
females were not told that this information had been given to the
callers. Somehow the men unconsciously encouraged the "attractive" women to respond in a friendlier, more expansive way,
whereas the "unattractive" women were correspondingly less effective on the phone.

Beauty bias is real. It is even more powerful than people realize
or are willing to admit, concludes Berscheid. It reflects the broader
aspects of our gender roles and is applied more strongly to women
than to men. Furthermore, the association of beauty with goodness and of beauty with women tends to elevate females as a class,
which is one benefit women derive from the role of fair lady.
What is beautiful is not only good but also sex-typed.

The Facts of Beauty Bias

> O woman, you are not merely the handiwork of God, but
> also of men; these are ever endowing you with beauty from
> their own hearts. You are one-half woman and one-half dream.
>
> — Rabindranath Tagore[12]

Is there empirical evidence that females are considered the fair sex? What facts support the premise that beauty is gender bound? Although few studies have specifically focused on beauty as a masculine or feminine trait, gender differences have emerged nevertheless. Research indicates that attitudes about attractiveness are applied differently to each sex. Beauty counts for everyone, but more so for women.[13]

From the moment of birth, beauty is sought, perceived, and projected onto girls. When parents were asked within twenty-four hours after delivery to rate their first-born infants on a variety of characteristics, daughters were described as beautiful, soft, pretty, cute, delicate, and little. Sons were rated as firm, strong, large-featured, well coordinated, and hardy. The baby boys and girls in this study had been carefully matched for equivalent length, weight, and level of responsiveness.[14] Despite the physical similarities of these infants, their parents nevertheless brought home "beautiful" daughters and "strong" sons. A baby dressed in blue was described in another study as bouncy, strong, active; the same baby dressed in pink was called sweet and lovely. Studies confirm that throughout childhood girls receive more attention for their appearance than do boys.[15]

Some of the early research on physical attractiveness focused exclusively on female subjects. For example, the diverse physical characteristics considered beautiful in women by men of many societies were cataloged, but no data were gathered on women's preferences regarding men's features. Male attractiveness was simply not deemed worthy of investigation. By omitting male controls, such studies reflect the bias that female appearance is more interesting and important than male appearance.[16]

Women's photographs are judged as significantly more attractive than men's in numerous studies in which subjects are asked to rate pictures.[17] Facial beauty is considered more characteristic of females and of young children than of males or older people.[18] (Linking women and children together within the concept of beauty supports the belief that childlike qualities, such as wide eyes, smooth skin, and rosy cheeks, are essential to female attractiveness.) Since most women use a variety of cosmetic adornments and most men use few, the standard for female beauty is shifted artificially upward in these photos. Women are then judged against an inflated norm, while men are judged against a more realistic one.

Attractiveness has been found to correlate with ratings of masculinity in men and femininity in women. However, the correlations are significantly higher for women, suggesting that beauty is more salient in the perception of femininity than masculinity. In addition, both sexes are judged less attractive with age, but older men are still viewed as highly masculine, whereas older women are considered less feminine as well as less attractive.[19]

In young women, beauty correlates positively with their degree of happiness and self-esteem and correlates negatively with their degree of neuroticism. For men, however, no relationship is found between personality traits and physical appearance, which indicates that looks have less impact on the mental health of males.[20] Moreover, unattractive men are deemed better able to compensate for their appearance than are unattractive women. As one psychologist concluded, "If a person must be homely, it is [a] better fate to be male than female."[21]

These studies touch only the surface of a growing body of evidence confirming that beauty is a gender-related trait. At every age, appearance is emphasized and valued more highly in females than in males. Women are more critically judged for attractiveness and more severely rejected when they lack it. A woman's beauty is constantly anticipated, encouraged, sought, and rewarded in a wide range of situations. However, its greatest impact may be in the romantic arena.

Bertrand Russell observed that "on the whole, women tend to love men for their character while men tend to love women for their appearance." And he was right. When it comes to romance, beauty counts much more for women than for men.

Like a chimp in heat, a pretty gal gets actively pursued. Frequency of dating correlates highly with attractiveness in females but not in males. Unattractive college women go out less often than their pretty roommates, but unattractive men date just as often as handsome ones.[22] In a computer dating study, subjects were randomly assigned partners and later asked how much they liked their dates. Appearance was the only characteristic that accurately predicted degree of satisfaction for both sexes, but correlations were significantly higher with respect to female appearance.[23]

Males consistently place greater emphasis on good looks when choosing dates than females do. When five hundred couples were matched on the basis of the qualities each desired in a date, it turned out that each sex was looking for different things. Women were seeking guys with good grades who were popular, danced well, and were of their own religion. For men, it was imperative that their dates be pretty.[24] A substantial number of males in another study said that beauty was the most essential characteristic they sought not only in a date but also in a potential mate. Not one of the females in that sample rated appearance as the primary factor she used when choosing a date. Moreover, college women felt that it was less socially acceptable for them to admit their interest in male attractiveness.[25]

Women are aware that beauty counts heavily with men and they therefore work hard to achieve it. Similarly, homosexual males often are equally preoccupied with their looks because they face problems similar to those of women. Gay men realize all too well that males initially assess dates mainly on the basis of appearance. Like women, gay men regard their bodies as objects of courtship much more than straight men do. Homosexuals stress physical attractiveness in their personal ads, and they complain, as do women, that they become sexually obsolete at a younger age than straight men do.[26]

Dustin Hoffman described as "shattering" his realization that although he could successfully portray Dorothy in the film *Tootsie*, he could never turn himself into a beautiful woman. Life as a plain-looking woman felt quite different than life as a plain-looking man. "I'd never been related to that way before in my life—having men meet me, say hello, and immediately start looking over my shoulder trying to find an attractive woman. I could feel that number printed on me, that I was a 4 or maybe a 6, and I would get very hostile—But I also realized I wouldn't ask myself out—I wasn't attractive enough, as Dorothy, for me to want to go to bed with myself." Hoffman reasoned that men want to feel more attractive themselves, and so "we try to get a good-looking girl next to us, to get rid of the Dorothy feeling."[27]

In a way, men can reclaim beauty vicariously. The status one gains by association with an attractive mate or date has been called the "rub-off effect." Because female beauty has great value, men get some of it rubbed off on them. When an unattractive man is seen coupled with a beautiful woman, he is judged to be more intelligent and more successful than when seen with a plain one.[28] The woman's beauty does not increase perceptions of the man's attractiveness but elevates perceptions of his character, likability, and competence. It is as though people think he must be doing something right in order to get such a dandy prize. In contrast, an unattractive woman paired with a handsome man gains little in social advantage. Why don't women gain as much as men do from the rub-off effect? One explanation is that while beauty serves as a strong signal of a woman's ability to fulfill the feminine role (that is, to be beautiful is to be womanly), attractiveness in a man tells less about his ability to fulfill the masculine role and, consequently, has less of a rub-off value for his mate.

Like the curvy lines of a sports car or yacht, a lovely date or mate proclaims a man's virility to the world. "His" woman is an extension of himself and becomes another asset. Since men are aware that a woman's beauty can increase their status, they offer social rewards in exchange for it. Trading female beauty for male power (the so-called Jackie–Ari phenomenon) pairs glamourous women with unattractive but important men. Preoccupation with female appearance stems in part from this asymmetrical rub-off effect. Attractiveness might be less important to women if it were not so unequally transferable.

Attractive women tend to marry men with higher occupational levels than their own. For lower- and middle-class women, ratings of beauty are good predictors of marriage to a higher-status mate.[29] Analysis of personal advertisements shows that women are more likely to offer physical attractiveness, while men are more likely to seek it, and that the reverse holds true for financial security, which men are more likely to offer and women are more likely to seek.[30]

Clearly, the link between beauty and femininity influences dating and mating preferences. It is not merely an abstract concept but a reality that has social importance. Subsequent chapters will explore its effects on self-image, adolescent development, adjustment to aging, and feelings of power. In Judy's case, a plain face limited her social life in college and discouraged her goal of becoming a singer. She reports that her husband was initially attracted to her strawberry-blond hair and admits that she spent a small fortune when first dating him in order to look as chic as possible. The effect of Judy's cosmetic transformations rub off onto her husband's career as well as her own. He considers her an asset at business affairs because she embodies a combination of beauty plus brains.

The belief that females are the fair sex is rooted in the larger social system. It supports other misconceptions that "explain" the nature of beauty as well as the nature of women. Such myths serve to perpetuate gender differences and to justify gender inequalities.

The Role of Myths

The beauty of woman is naught but a delusion of the masculine brain clouded by the fumes of instinct.

— Schopenhauer

There are as many contradictory myths about the nature of women as there are about the nature of beauty, and myths about both have much in common. Like beauty, women are viewed as both good and evil. Both beauty and women are considered dangerous and seductive. Both are seen as a mysterious enigma, feared as powerful but dismissed as ineffectual. Parallel myths about beauty and women bind the two together in a single construct.

Myths are collective beliefs that seem self-evident. A mixture of logical half-truths distorted by personal feelings, they stand outside the usual process of reality testing. Like the giant breasts that chase the hero in a Woody Allen film, myths become inflated by fantasy. Blown up by the fears and longings of childhood, they help meet basic needs for safety and security. Myths serve to demystify experiences that feel threatening; they pretend to enlighten even as they confuse.

If society believes, for instance, that meat spoils when touched by a menstruating woman, evidence will be generated for hundreds of years to confirm the truth of that myth. Like the pigeons in B. F. Skinner's laboratory who danced in superstitious circles because they believed that their twirling produced pellets of food, people work hard to confirm false connections between two factors; menstruation and rotten meat, bra burners and man haters, women and beauty. Myths are thereby "proven" as fact and adamantly defended as truth.

Just as menstrual taboos alter the experience of menstruation, myths about beauty alter its impact. They are used as yardsticks for self-evaluation. People measure themselves against a mythical ideal and then remodel themselves to fit that pattern, becoming what they believe they should be. Having been taught that feminine beauty means having full, softly rounded breasts, women judge themselves against this standard. Missing the mark, they put on padded bras or suffer silicone implants. As flat chests disappear, reality is replaced with a replica, and the truth of the myth is confirmed. Myths thus function as self-fulfilling prophecy and are therefore dangerously self-perpetuating.

Learned men debated for centuries about whether females had souls, whether the clitoris was a vestigial organ, whether women should be educated or granted constitutional equality. Defined by such beliefs, females enact their prescribed role. Once you sincerely believe, for example, that women are mentally inferior, you can logically conclude that they do not need to be educated. They in turn will conveniently demonstrate their intellectual incompetence. If you believe that women are by nature passive homebodies, you can feel justified in binding their feet in the name of beauty and can later observe how contentedly they sit near the hearth. Once you assume that women are the fair sex, you can reward them from infancy for cultivating the attributes of beauty, and their appearance will eventually confirm the initial premise as truth.

The evolution of myths can be understood in terms of overall mental development. From the moment of birth, children face the difficult task of trying to make sense of the world. Jean Piaget compares intellectual growth to a system of file cards, each one representing a notion about distance, pain, or mother's face. Early in life, cards are constructed about masculinity, femininity, beauty, and body image. No card is ever perfectly accurate, explains Piaget. Children have wide conceptual gaps. With experience, their mental file cards are amended to describe reality more accurately.

Cultures grow and mature as do children. Myths are to culture what cognitive errors are to children's thought. Like religion or science, myths help us explain perplexing events such as the shape of the earth, the origin of life, or the meaning of sexual differences. They evolve through the fusion of hundreds of mental file cards. The distortions inherent in gender myths parallel the errors of children's thinking. Both derive from a partial understanding of reality. For example, a four-year-old will respond to Piaget's famous water jar problem by declaring that a tall thin glass holds more water than a short wide one. You can pour the water from one glass to the other in front of her, showing that they both hold the same amount. Still she clings to her initial answer; her eyes see the "truth" that the water is higher in the taller glass. She is not ready to amend her file card that says higher water level means more water. Until she is ready, new evidence falls on unseeing eyes. Tearing up an old file card means having to view the world in a new way. To question the belief that women are the fair sex requires a reinterpretation of gender roles. Thus, myths change slowly, if at all, only when enough people are ready collectively to rewrite their gender file cards.

When demonstrators tossed their bras into a trash can in Atlantic City, the response of outrage was disproportionate to the sight of a few sagging bosoms. Bras were correctly identified as part of a crucial support system, as props for a much larger social issue. At stake was not the shape of the breast but the shape of the myth that women are specially endowed with beauty. The unbound liberated breast (like the unbound foot) was quickly recognized as a threat to the idea that feminine beauty should be cultivated and displayed within certain bounds. At risk was the belief that women are objects of visual pleasure, that their breasts ought to be contained and reshaped to look pleasing, that they are unaesthetic and unacceptable as they are. When great attention is paid to preserving such customs as opening doors, putting on makeup, or wearing bras, it is because these simple acts symbolize more important values. If bras, as symbols, are allowed to be stripped away, then woman's role as a beautiful object may come undone as well.

According to Piaget, innate processes drive us toward intellectual growth, but it is experience which ultimately fills out our mental file cards. Similarly, the belief in beauty as a feminine trait is culturally programmed. Society teaches us to suspend logic, to ignore contrary evidence, and to accept half-truths about women's bodies. Through socialization, myths that connect beauty with women survive the passage of time and resist periodic attempts to challenge them.

Beauty and Deviance—A Delicate Balance

> Implicitly adopting the male life as the norm, they have tried to fashion women out of a masculine cloth. It all goes back, of course, to Adam and Eve—a story which shows among other things that if you make a woman out of a man, you are bound to get into trouble. In the life cycle, as in the garden of Eden, woman has been the deviant.
>
> — Carol Gilligan[31]

Humans tend to organize ideas into simple binary concepts. Mental file cards get separated into neat piles of black and white, good and bad, male and female. This tendency is imposed by the world as well as imposed on it. Day differs from night, up from down. Anatomy itself divides humanity in half: men here, women there. Furthermore, language encourages us to think of gender in binary terms—he/she, his/hers, mommy/daddy—transforming a world that was originally more unified. Categories of language in turn create categories of people, as when the generic *he* generates *she* as an exception.

Binary concepts help us cope with diversity. They permit either/ or decisions, which have a comfortable finality. To think of men as powerful, women as beautiful, is convenient. However, such dichotomies lead to stereotypes that compress gender roles into symbols and that misclassify people into narrow slots. In an essay,

Nora Ephron recalls her adolescent belief that "the way you sat, crossed your legs, held a cigarette, looked at your nails . . . was absolute proof of your sex. . . . I thought that just one slip, just one incorrect cross of my legs . . . would turn me from whatever I was into the other thing."[32]

Binary categories often combine into complex chains. Concepts of masculine and feminine become infused with notions of good and evil, weak and strong, pretty and ugly. Like magnetic fields, they attract positive and negative charges. The process of evolution did not fashion one sex as a superior version of the other. Yet almost universally the masculine pole of the gender dichotomy enjoys higher status. Once masculine traits acquire greater value, they set the standard for the human ideal. Women find it hard to measure up to a masculine norm. Biologically distinct from males, females become culturally distinguished from what is considered normal. This is how the anatomy of difference can dictate the anatomy of destiny.

Historical documentation that women have been categorized as a deviant and inadequate form of human being is familiar but still sobering. Aristotle proclaimed, "The female is a female by virtue of a certain lack of qualities . . . a deformity which occurs in the ordinary course of nature." A millenium later, St. Thomas Aquinas described woman as "an imperfect man . . . an incidental being." A century ago, Le Bon, the founder of social psychology, called woman "the most inferior form of human evolution—closer to children . . . than to an adult civilized man." Freud offered a twentieth-century version of this enduring theme, describing woman's "mutilated genitalia" and her "deficient superego."

In a now classic piece of research, often referred to as the Broverman study, mental health clinicians were asked in the early 1970s to rate a list of adjectives reflecting their views of a healthy personality.[33] Some therapists rated the traits for a "normal male," others for a "normal female," and still others for a "normal adult." Results showed that those characteristics assigned to the healthy male were identical with those attributed to a healthy adult. In contrast, characteristics assigned to a healthy female differed from those of a healthy adult. For instance, mentally healthy women were rated as more submissive, less independent, less objective, and more emotional than healthy adults. Moreover, preoccupation with one's appearance was considered normal for a healthy woman but not for a healthy person. If a well-adjusted female differs from a well-adjusted person, it is impossible to be well adjusted both as a woman and as a person at the same time. These results confirm that the "male as normative" principle continues to shape and perpetuate a belief in female deviance. Evaluated in terms of man's experience, woman's reality becomes enigmatic. She stands as an outsider whose body is exotic but alien, whose voice is different.

When gender is viewed as a dichotomy, with the norm fixed at the masculine end, female "otherness" becomes inevitable. The small step from duality to deficiency creates a great gap. Within such a model, women always seem to deviate from the accepted standard. If masculine equals normal equals valued, then feminine equals abnormal equals devalued. As Simone de Beauvoir observes in *The Second Sex*, the fact of being a man is no peculiarity. "He thinks of his body as a direct and normal connection with the world . . . whereas he sees the body of a woman as a hindrance, a prison, weighted down by everything peculiar to it."[34] The second sex is born from this binary model of gender. And so is female beauty.

How can woman be glorified as the fair sex while at the same time be demeaned as "the other sex"? How can a myth that equates woman with beauty survive alongside a myth that brands woman as deficient?

In fact, myths about gender, like myths about beauty, are often linked in just such counterbalanced pairs. Together, contrary myths create an equilibrium that helps preserve them both. Women are crowned with beauty precisely because they are cloaked in difference. The idealization of female appearance camouflages an underlying belief in female inferiority. Just as excessive narcissism has its roots in self-loathing, the myth of female beauty grows from the myth of female deviance. Beauty helps to balance woman as a misbegotten person. It disguises her inadequacies and justifies her presence.

Paired myths often appear so contradictory that we fail to recognize them as integrally connected. The ritual crowning of Miss America and the ritual isolation of women in a menstrual taboo may not seem like branches of the same ideology. Yet both are grounded in the soil of gender duality, both relegate women to a special place, and both encourage a distorted perception of the female body. Through contradictory myths woman is first deified as a mother goddess, then burned as an evil witch; first worshiped for her purity, then disdained as corrupting; first pursued for her beauty, then isolated as unclean. Witches and fairies, Snow White and the wicked stepmother—each requires the other to remain believable. The myth of female beauty and the myth of female deviance form a mutually supporting union, a strange marriage that is delicately balanced.

Why are masculine attributes revered, thereby creating female deviance as a corollary and female beauty as a by-product? Many people believe that patriarchy is anchored in biology—that women are naturally subordinate because they are smaller, weaker, and more childlike. (In fact beauty images often emphasize childish traits in females.) Furthermore, women's reproductive role sets them apart from men. Females are destined to create and preserve life at the basic level of the flesh. Hence they are defined (and tend to define themselves) in relationship to bodies: their own bodies, their husbands' and their children's bodies. Motherhood links women to the so-called "profane" realms of nature, so that men take over the more "sacred" realms of culture.

Maternity ties female bodies to nature in another way. An infant first experiences the mother as part of the self. Her face, her voice, her smells are initially fused with a baby's self-awareness. Mother's body is the primary source of security and pleasure, but at the same time it has the frightening power to deny gratification. It is not always there when needed. To the helpless infant, the maternal body assumes gigantic proportions and evokes enormous ambivalence. Therefore female flesh is both feared and idealized. As adults we still long for its love, while we tremble at its power to carry us back to the terrible dependent state of infancy.

Kim Chernin concludes in her book *The Obsession* that cultural preoccupation with controlling women's bodies and their appearance is motivated by a memory of the primordial mother who had power over life and death. Out of the ecstasy and frustration of early experiences with the mother we develop an obsession with female flesh, explains Chernin. Women's bodies become a focus for the problems of human existence. Longing for security translates into longing for mother, which sustains the myth of female goodness and beauty. Anger at life translates into anger at mother, which generates the myth of female deficiency.

Never quite what she should be, woman must be revalued. She is, after all, needed for the very life-giving functions that make her so profane. Although assigned a separate and unequal place in society—generally excluded from the world of politics and power—woman cannot be exiled too far or too long. In the end, she is needed to do the work of nature. Therefore, she must be drawn back into man's world for mating and mothering, for lunch and laundry. Beauty confers added value on the devalued sex. It makes woman worthy of joining man's life, of sharing his bed, bearing his children, and wearing his name.

In *The Dialectic of Sex*, Shulamith Firestone describes these dynamics on the personal level of romantic love. A man must elevate a particular woman over all others to justify his "descent to a lower caste," she writes. Falling in love, therefore, depends on the temporary "alteration of male vision." Through mystification and glorification, a woman's class inferiority is overcome.[35] Idealized beauty is essential to this romantic vision. Brides must be, and are, gorgeous in the groom's eyes. Mythical beauty elevates women as a class, compensating for their lower status. Quite simply, female beauty helps turn deviance into delight.

At the same time, beauty clearly distinguishes woman as different, as a member of the other half of humanity. A bride senses that idealized love is ephemeral; that it is only a matter of time before she will be discovered as just another woman. Similarly, beauty is only a temporary equalizer. Ultimately, it exposes the fair sex once again as the other sex. For the symbols of contrived beauty—the lacquered nails, the crimson lips, the strawberry-blond hair—exaggerate gender differences. They elevate woman onto a pedestal while paradoxically defining her separate role. In lieu of equality, beauty serves as a kind of prop, or consolation prize. In the end, props and pedestals make poor equalizers. They cannot substitute for full personhood.

The conflicting attitudes that result from contradictory myths are revealed in a study that found two major types of prejudices in men. One form of bias stereotyped women as fragile, naive, and pure. Men holding this attitude placed women on a pedestal and wanted to be chivalrously protective of them. The second form of bias defined women as emotionally and intellectually inferior, therefore deserving of subordination. Many men expressed both these attitudes at once, for in this case contradictory biases support each other.[36]

Women internalize the same conflicting attitudes and often feel confused. Judy, for example, knows that her contrived beauty image contributes to career success. At the same time, she resents having to pretend to be something she is not. While she enjoys the added attention that beauty brings, she feels deserving of recognition "as is." She wants to please her husband, yet she questions her role as a "blond asset at his business affairs."

In search of self, Judy faces the dilemma of enacting conflicting myths. Demeaned in deviance while idealized in beauty, she is tossed on a sea of ambiguity, and suffers the chronic malady of insecurity. Caught between incompatible concepts, woman hesitates "between one and the other without being adapted to either and from this comes a lack of equilibrium," writes de Beauvoir.[37] From this comes the vacillation between vanity and self-rejection, and the terror that perhaps drove a beauty idol like Marilyn Monroe to destroy that crowned and coveted body with an overdose of Nembutals.

When myths are conflicting, they portray woman as mysterious and indefinable. Throughout history people have "knocked their heads against the nature of femininity and failed to understand it," claimed Freud. The "enigma of woman" remained Freud's great unsolved puzzle, perhaps because preserving the enigma was essential to preserving his concept of female deviance. As long as woman remains a faceless enigma, distanced by difference, she is harder to know but easier to ignore. As long as woman wears her beauty as a disguise, she can be seen as both more and less than she really is, more beautiful and less normal. Attempts to discover the secret essence of femininity will invariably fail, explains de Beauvoir, because it simply does not exist.

The myth of woman as the fair sex perpetuates the feminine mystique. Petticoats and veils, padded bras and packaged bodies, everything that accentuates difference confirms woman as the "other." Recall the scene when Cinderella arrives at the ball. Even her stepsisters fail to know her, so blinding is her beauty. Camouflaged as a lovely enigma, she becomes unrecognizable. Unknown and unknowable, she is all the more desirable. Like Venus, a goddess of beauty but also a planet wrapped in steamy clouds, her core is hidden in a romantic mist. Beauty maintains the erotic mystery of a woman by concealing the human being beneath.

2

Looking Good
and Feeling Bad

"The only time I ever think I'm beautiful," said Sascha . . .
"Is when some man is staring into my face in broad daylight
and telling me I'm beautiful. And then as soon as he turns
away for a minute I think he changed his mind. And if he
doesn't turn away or change his mind, I start thinking he's
one of those idiots with no taste."

— Judith Rossner[1]

B ELIEF in one's own attractiveness can be as hard to achieve
as physical beauty itself. Members of the fair sex tend to
view themselves unfairly. Ashamed of cellulite, limp hair, and
age spots, plagued by self-consciousness, distorted body image,
and appearance anxiety, women judge their bodies as unworthy
of self-love. Many equate what they look like with who they are.

A forty-year-old is being interviewed. "Please describe yourself
in some way that would give a good sense of who and what you
are." She sits for a moment in silent confusion and then says
tentatively, "Do you mean physically, or what?" When told that
she is free to choose, she begins her response with a list of physical
characteristics: "I'm short and blond, a bit overweight." Sociologist Lillian Rubin conducted dozens of these interviews and
found again and again that women started by describing their
bodies. Although more than half of that sample worked outside
the home, some in high-paying professional jobs, not even one
began by discussing herself in relation to her career.[2]

This attests to the primacy of appearance in women's self-image, concludes Rubin, "which is not surprising in a culture where women have learned that beauty is their most highly valued commodity." Poor body image was the rule rather than the exception among her subjects. The greatest unhappiness was expressed by those who had been the most attractive and were now struggling to adjust to the physical changes of mid-life. For these women, appearance served not only as the primary source of their self-identity, but as a serious threat to it as well.

Although females have long been stereotyped, like Narcissus, as being enchanted with their own reflections, just the opposite seems true. Asked to evaluate photographs of themselves, more women voice criticism than satisfaction. When psychologist Marcia Hutchinson selected over one hundred subjects for a project on body image, she carefully chose women who were of normal weight, with no history of eating disorders or of mental illness. Further assessment, however, showed that only one out of the entire sample was not "actively waging war against fat." None of these women was seriously overweight, none was emotionally disturbed, yet all were dieting, all were self-rejecting, and all suffered from poor body image. Hutchinson was forced to conclude that " 'flesh loathing' exists in epidemic proportions among women."[3]

The problem is quite evident by the time of adolescence, when teenage girls say they feel relatively less attractive in comparison to their peers than do boys. More women than men describe persistent feelings of physical inferiority. One out of three report feeling anxious, depressed, or repulsed when they look at their nude bodies in the mirror. In polls conducted by *Glamour* magazine, young women under the age of twenty-five said they feel increasingly concerned about their attractiveness with every passing year.[4]

Nora Ephron describes her fascination with the book *Conundrum*, an account of the difficult adjustments required during a transsexual change. The metamorphosis from male to female portrayed there seemed identical to Ephron's own painful struggles to transform from female into feminine. "I too felt that I was born into the wrong body," she writes, "a body that refused, in spite of every imprecation and exercise I could manage, to become anything but the boyish lean thing it was. . . . I wanted more than anything to be something I will never be—feminine, and feminine in the worst way."[5]

In *Women and Self-Esteem*, Linda Sanford and Mary Ellen Donovan report that the majority of females studied in therapy groups over a five-year period habitually downgraded their worth, and poor body image was a central factor in their self-rejection. When asked to name something they liked about themselves, most had trouble coming up with even one response. Pressed to describe their feelings, they made strong negative statements bordering on self-hatred.

> I guess the feeling I most often have toward myself is this nagging loathing, a kind of disgust . . . sometimes everything about me, especially my body, seems disgusting . . . there are times when I look in the mirror and want to smash it. Lots of times I feel I'm not worth walking out the door.[6]

Nearly every woman in these therapy groups suffered from negative body image. Some were conscious of the connection between a lack of self-esteem and poor body image, while others were not. Most viewed their bodies inaccurately. They distorted reality in two particular ways: either they saw themselves as having the wrong size and shape (fatter, wider, rounder than they really were), or they saw a certain body part as grossly abnormal. They spoke of their "thunder thighs," "tree-trunk legs," or "mammoth breasts," and these distortions dominated and transformed their whole body image into a caricature.[7] Women generalize from one bad feature to their whole appearance, while ignoring the ways they are attractive.

Sanford and Donovan assert that one reason so many women experience their bodies as a problem is that our culture teaches women that they must be pretty to be worthy, and sets up beauty standards that are unhealthy and unattainable. The poor body image that underlies a variety of adjustment problems is largely a product of social conditioning. These authors conclude that "we weren't born believing we had to be attractive to be worthy, nor born with the idea that being pretty means being thin or blond." Women are taught the standards currently worshiped as ideal and taught to equate self-worth with appearance.

The mind does not remain a blank slate for very long. An idealized image of feminine beauty is soon etched upon it. In our culture, this image is built on a Caucasian model. Fairy-tale princesses and Miss Americas have traditionally been white. This fair image weighs most heavily on the brown shoulders of minority women who bear a special beauty burden. They too are taught that beauty is a feminine imperative. They too set out in search of it, only to discover that failure is built in for those whose lips smile too thickly, whose eyelids fold improperly, whose hair will not relax enough to toss in the wind, whose skin never glows in rosy shades.

Looksism joins with sexism and racism to exclude those who are unwelcome in the dominant domain. All three combine to stigmatize nonwhite women as triply jeopardized, triply deviant. Black women, even more poignantly than white women, speak of feeling downright ugly at some point in their lives. Lorraine admits in an interview the deep shame she and her sister felt about being the darkest ones in the family—"much blacker than Mama, who was openly disappointed that we girls didn't take after her. Because she was light, we couldn't even blame Mama for our skin, the way some other girls blamed their mothers."

The media constantly reminds minority women of their non-conforming features. Lorraine developed a defensive habit of blocking out the commercial images that hurt so much. "As a teenager I would look away when a blond model came on TV selling creme rinse, so I wouldn't have to see what I wanted so badly but could never have."

"White beauty" continues to influence the black ideal, even after two decades of "Black is beautiful." Marrying light still means marrying up—a caste system that lingers as a legacy of life in a racist culture. Light-skinned women have a special rub-off value to black men, who are socialized to admire and covet the white norm. Lorraine comments that some of her most painful experiences with beauty have resulted from the way she was judged and rejected by black men because of her dark skin and "bad" hair.

To be human is to reflect on oneself. Like amateur artists, we draw on the canvas of our minds self-portraits of our bodies. As the subjective reality, these mental images can feel as real as the flesh itself. Infancy provides the first lessons in the anatomy of self-image. During childhood we gradually learn that some parts of the body are admired as lovely, and other parts are rejected as shameful and ugly. Acceptance and rejection, satisfaction and dissatisfaction, become attached to body parts and to their internal images. The transition from body awareness to body image to body acceptance is a critical sequence, since the accuracy of the image and its positive or negative value determines how we later experience ourselves and others. Reflection on oneself gradually leads to a feeling of "me" as distinct from others, and body image is central to that enduring self-concept.

Body image is in constant flux, growing larger when we are inflated with pride, growing smaller when we are diminished by failure. It is also influenced by how closely the real body conforms to the prevailing beauty norm. If there is a great discrepancy between the ideal and the real (for instance, if a cult of thinness defines most women as overweight), then the majority of women will see themselves as misfits and will feel pressured to remodel themselves to fit into the popular mold. A psychological reorganization must occur when one's appearance is incongruent with the current vogue, or when a changing body becomes incongruent with a former body image.[8]

In every era, a dominant beauty standard exists alongside alternative modes that pull women in opposite directions. There is a constant shift in emphasis between erotic sophistication and adolescent innocence. For example, in the 1920s, the flappers proclaimed their sexual freedom through short skirts and bobbed hair but bound their breasts to convey a youthful boyish look. Similarly, in the 1960s, beauty idols like Monroe and Bardot projected a curvaceous eroticism combined with a childlike naïveté. Currently, a delicate ideal is admired alongside a worship of muscles and athleticism. These shifting and conflicting components of the beauty ideal make schizophrenic demands on women to maintain opposite body types at the same time. No wonder women find it hard to sustain a positive body image.

Regardless of how extreme a beauty norm may be, it still acts as a social imperative. Once a certain look is sanctioned by enough people, it redefines normal appearance, even if society has crossed over the borderline of sanity. Our current obsession with slimness has been described as a form of cultural neurosis. While a personal delusion sets an individual apart as mentally ill, the opposite occurs in the case of a mass delusion. What can one say about the mental health of a culture that defines the ideal female body as grossly emaciated? Or the ideal female foot as the size of a doll's? Or the ideal waist as small enough to be encircled by a man's hands? Or the ideal face as being unlined forever? These examples of social pathology derive from the beauty myth. Negative body image is the internalization of such social neuroses.

Body image is so intimately linked with self-concept that distortion of one literally deforms the other. Trying to determine the direction of influence between them is difficult, however. Feelings of inadequacy may stem from an underlying body loathing. On the other hand, perceptions of the body as loathsome are just as likely to derive from low self-esteem.

Because beauty is linked with femininity, the influence of body image on self-concept is greater for females than for males. A woman is more likely than a man to equate herself with what she looks like, or what she thinks she looks like, or what she believes others think she looks like. Studies show that women's self-concepts are correlated with their own perceptions of their attractiveness, whereas men's self-concepts relate more closely to perceptions of their effectiveness and their physical fitness.[9] In other words, men tend to judge themselves in terms of what they can do, whereas women tend to equate self-worth with good looks. Males view a competent self as also attractive, whereas a competent woman may or may not see herself as pretty. Furthermore, men's evaluations of their own attractiveness correlate more highly than women's with other people's ratings. That is, men are more realistic and accurate in seeing themselves as others see them. Among women especially, there seems to be very little connection between actual physical attractiveness and their degree of contentment with their own body image.[10]

Hutchinson concludes that the interaction between negative body image and low self-esteem has been undervalued as a mental health issue. Despite the preponderance of females who suffer from distorted body image, clinicians tend either to ignore the phenomenon or to interpret it as evidence of serious psychopathology rather than as the product of a sick social system. Distorted body image inhibits sexual expression, contributes to psychosomatic symptoms, and increases stress, shame, and guilt. It is implicated in such "female" disorders as anorexia, obesity, agoraphobia, and depression. Anorectics, for instance, cannot see their emaciated condition and vehemently deny that they look too thin. Obese women report feeling that body boundaries have been lost and that the self merges with the environment. Some continue to see themselves as fat even after dramatic weight loss. Agoraphobics hide at home, afraid to expose themselves to public scrutiny.

When rigid cultural expectations set up impossible standards, then failure to reach perfection contributes to depression. Females outnumber males by an estimated three to one in the incidence of clinical depression. Women tend to distort perception of their bodies in the negative direction, just as depressed people do. In contrast, men tend to distort body image in a more positive, self-aggrandizing way, just as nondepressed people do.[11] Furthermore, people who see themselves as less attractive than they really are seem to be more prone to depression.

Failure to achieve beauty or to retain it contributes to women's sense of helplessness. They feel impotent with regard to controlling a fundamental aspect of their feminine identity. The burden of idealized beauty is added to women's system of "shoulds," increasing their vulnerability to depressive disorders. Female patients commonly attach feelings of anxiety to a particular body problem. Instead of saying "I'm unhappy," a patient may say "I'm fat," or "My skin is ugly." In this way she gains a false sense of potential control by isolating the depression. Identifying the problem as ten pounds of extra fat, she can believe that things would be better "if only I were thinner." Body image thus becomes confounded with disorders that are actually unrelated to it.

Appearance is so closely tied to women's mental health that cosmetics are proving a useful adjunct to therapy. Hospitalized patients have shown dramatic improvement when given daily

makeup or weekly facials. Even deeply depressed women who
have been unresponsive to other forms of therapy sometimes "return to life" when brought into a beauty salon.[12] Cosmetics have
a healing effect because a woman who looks better starts to feel
better about herself.

In another instance of cosmetic therapy, delinquent teenage
girls (truants, prostitutes, and drug abusers) were enrolled in a
rehabilitation program that taught them good grooming to help
them reduce self-destructive behavior and to restore self-confidence. Delinquent boys in the same program were taught a trade.[13]
Such differences in treatment stem from the idea that if only a
female becomes attractive enough, her problems will be solved.

Recall the Broverman study, in which clinicians rated mentally
healthy men as being similar to healthy people but described
healthy women quite differently. Socially desirable characteristics
were generally assigned to males, whereas a number of traits
judged undesirable for well-adjusted adults were considered appropriate for females. Healthy women, for instance, were described as more submissive, more dependent, and more concerned
with their appearance than healthy men. In other words, clinicians *expect* sane women to be somewhat neurotically obsessed
with their looks.[14]

For a woman to be well adjusted, she must adopt the behavioral
norms for her sex even though these may be considered undesirable for mentally healthy people. She is thus caught in a bind: if
she refuses the role, she will be viewed as less feminine, but if
she conforms to the role, she will be considered maladjusted in
terms of healthy adult behavior.

Not only is a woman socialized to act differently than a normal
adult, but to look different as well—more like a female than a
person. Her lips must be redder, lashes longer, waist smaller,
skin smoother. She is already deviant because of her gender, and
the made-up image demanded by feminine fashion signals to an
even greater degree the "normality of her otherness." Just as the
female role requires a distortion of healthy adult behavior, a feminized body likewise requires distortion of a healthy adult body.
In a sense, women normalize themselves by signaling their ab-
normality.

The pathology that is built into the feminine role (including excessive demands for physical attractiveness) remains invisible as long as culture defines it as healthy. To enact femininity through preoccupation with appearance, for example, fosters excessive narcissism. Yet failure to cultivate good looks causes insecurity and self-rejection. This damned-if-she-does-and-damned-if-she-doesn't situation ultimately leads a woman to her own personal body conflicts.

The Broverman study showed that many undesirable traits, are considered part of the normal feminine role. In the long run, submissive and dependent behavior do not build confidence, even when viewed as appropriately feminine. While thirty-seven different positive attributes were rated as characteristics of healthy men, a mere eleven traits (some of them socially undesirable) were attributed to healthy women. Adoption of femininity requires contraction into a few narrow dimensions—two of them being appearance and neatness. Women who aspire beyond these eleven approved areas—those who cultivate traits found on the longer masculine list—run the risk of seeming unfeminine both to themselves and to others. This risk further undermines confidence in their own femininity.

Preoccupation with appearance is considered both normal and healthy in women. However, Sanford and Donovan report an alarming number of patients suffering from obsessive self-consciousness. Focused on the smallest details of appearance, these women constantly turn to their mirrors for a "fix" of self-reflection. Sometimes called image addicts or mirror junkies, they are seen holding up compacts in restaurants or peering into rearview mirrors at red lights. Many report that they feel like an observer watching a stranger move through the day. One admits:

> I'm constantly checking on my face, a hundred times a day, especially if I'm nervous. Even when I know I look OK, I have to make sure, once again. I'm never certain what I'll see, as if some ugly pimple will suddenly pop out. I can't pass a mirror without turning my head for a critical glance. Sometimes I do like my face, but more often it just makes me anxious.

Chronic self-consciousness leads to compulsive comparison with others. Not only do these women scrutinize themselves mercilessly, but some turn the same microscope on everyone else.

Searching for differences by which to judge their own relative worth, they put themselves to the test over and over. In fact, they are unconsciously identified with the flaws of other women:

> . . . and here we are again folks, a table of women, seven of us, and the first thing I do to assess my coworkers . . . is look around at all of you to see who is prettier than I. . . . my lover used to say how I was prettier than the other women in my women's liberation group and I would feel better while feeling worse. . . . it drives me crazy and actually prevents me from enjoying social situations. . . . I got so that I could count on being the second prettiest woman in any given situation! . . . I would always be able to find one woman who was prettier and usually not more than one . . . even on buses, even in classes, doctors' offices, restaurants.[15]

Vanity Fair and Unfair

The following case illustrates how heightened self-consciousness and chronic comparison to others can lead to psychological maladjustment. Here, a lifetime search for identity through beauty resulted in a phobic obsession. At forty-two, Elizabeth is a stunning green-eyed blond with a model's face and figure. Yet she is paralyzed with anxiety whenever she sees another woman who seems more attractive than she. Whether this happens at work, in a store, or on the street, Elizabeth feels suddenly "reduced to nothing, a zero, a totally worthless human being." At these moments she may try to escape by running to her car or to the ladies' room. Disgusted with herself, she then becomes depressed.

When an attractive new worker was hired at her office, Elizabeth stayed home for several days, unable to face the situation. Recently, she has begun to anticipate and avoid places where the presence of pretty women is likely to threaten her. She has been turning down invitations and refusing to go on business trips with her husband. The future seems quite bleak as she imagines a time when she may be too frightened to go out at all. In therapy, Elizabeth confides:

> I feel so sick—crippled by these horrible thoughts. I just dread one customer who comes to the office. If she stands near me, even

for a minute, I begin to sweat and tremble. I can't even think about her without feeling awful. It can happen anywhere. Some woman will come along who I know is better looking and she kind of erases me, cancels me out. Next to her, no one even sees me. If I'm not the best, I'm just nothing. These thoughts have been tormenting me for years, but now it's getting worse because I see myself shriveling up with age, just like my mother. Every morning when I put on my makeup, I see her face staring up at me. I find a new wrinkle and wonder how many more years I have. It's ridiculous, wanting to be the prettiest one forever, although I used to be, really I was a 10, now . . . maybe just a 5.

Elizabeth traces her beauty obsession to the sixth grade when she first began to use her appearance to compete with other girls. A plain child and a poor student, she had always felt like an outcast, even within her own family. But at puberty her beauty blossomed. Her parents seemed proud of her for the first time, and people told her she was as pretty as an older sister whom she had always envied. Beauty had made her both visible and valuable.

By the time she entered junior high school, Elizabeth had discovered peroxide and makeup, which brought greater popularity. However, her father began to tell her she looked like a clown when she dressed up. He even called her a tramp—but at least he continued to notice rather than ignore her. Though her grades were low in high school, she was voted football queen and offered several jobs at graduation, "mainly because I was pretty, since I was never very good at anything."

Eventually Elizabeth married "a truly handsome man. . . . Together we were a fabulous-looking couple. People would stare wherever we went." Now he too is aging and she doesn't get the same kick out of being seen with him. Though he reassures her that she is still beautiful, she thinks he is merely trying to make her feel better. Recently she had her eyelids done and her face peeled. "I'll go back for more as often as I can. It's the one thing that keeps me sane, knowing that surgery can preserve whatever good looks are left." While she recognizes how destructive her obsession is and wants to be free of it, she still pursues every remedy that promises to stop the clock.

As long as she continues to believe that appearance is her primary asset, Elizabeth will remain unsure of the thinking, feeling self within. Her case is certainly not unique in clinical practice, nor is it very different from what healthier women experience, although with less intensity.

The oppression of poor body image plagues even the prettiest women, for, as we have seen earlier, myths cannot be proven or disproven by objective evidence. A twenty-two-year-old actress, Nastassia Kinski, appeared on the cover of *Time* magazine. (She was one of only three females featured there in the previous fifty-six issues. Another lovely twenty-year-old, Princess Diana, was one of the few women ever to appear on *Time*'s cover more than twice in its entire fifty-year history—and Diana merely had to charm a prince.) Nastassia was obviously chosen for her lovely face, but a photographer reported that "she doesn't like her looks, although the very things she doesn't like—her lips, her nose, her legs—are what make her so attractive." He confidently predicted that one day Nastassia will wake up and realize that she's a beautiful woman.[16] How long will it take? Will she, like Elizabeth or like Marilyn Monroe, spend years tormented by doubt despite her obvious beauty?

Film stars and pageant winners who personify the myth continue to suffer, for they too are worshiped from inside someone else's head. They too remain vulnerable as they strive for a permanent state that is impossible to preserve. In fact, part of their very allure, ironically, is the fact that beauty is ephemeral, that one day the rose will wilt.

"They say it's worse to be ugly. I think it must only be different. If you're pretty, you are subject to one set of assaults; if you're plain, you are subject to another," writes Alix Kates Shulman in her novel *Memoirs of an Ex-Prom Queen.*[17] Are beautiful women any more self-accepting than their less attractive sisters? The answer is unclear. In some studies, prettier women express greater confidence in their appearance and describe themselves as more feminine and more likable.[18] Yet other studies find no relationship between appearance and self-esteem. When judged from their photographs, pretty females are stereotyped in some studies as more intelligent and more liberated, wanting to marry later and have fewer children, and desiring sex more often and enjoying it more than plain-looking women. In other studies, prettier women are labeled vain, self-centered, egotistical, untrustworthy, and "fickle lovers."[19]

Beauty can be problematic. Positive pleasures are confounded with negative pitfalls. In fact, one complaint voiced by pretty women is that no one takes the problems of being pretty very seriously. Since beauty is associated with goodness, its advantages are assumed to outweigh its disadvantages. But this is not always the case.

The contrasting pros and cons are evident in Elizabeth's life. Beauty initially brought parental recognition, which she had always wanted. But soon her father rejected her for looking too seductive. Beauty brought popularity and the joy of a handsome husband. In its wake it left her anxious about her looks and about their gradual loss. Highly dependent on appearance as her major asset, Elizabeth failed to establish a broader base of self-esteem and failed to recognize or cultivate other strengths. Herein lies one common problem of being pretty. Looks can be an all too easy source of unearned admiration. Because family and friends are socialized to view females in terms of this narrow dimension, pretty women may get less encouragement to pursue other talents. Beauty is considered the appropriate vehicle for their success. The flip side of this problem is described by one exceptionally attractive and highly successful executive who never feels sure that her accomplishments are truly merited. Afraid of being judged as mere facade, this woman tries again and again to prove her worth by pursuing one difficult goal after another. She is driven by a need to show herself and others that she is not getting ahead on the basis of looks alone.

Beautiful women do attract more attention, but some of it is unwelcome and some of it—for example, sexual harassment on the job, street hassling, incest, and rape—is quite destructive. Pretty women are more likely to become targets for the anger of men who fear the power of their beauty. A man who resents female domination of any kind will fear being captivated, bowled over, or smitten by an irresistible knockout. He may consciously or unconsciously try to demean or possess a woman whose beauty threatens to take him over. A delectable dish off the *Cosmopolitan* menu stimulates fear as well as appetite. In fact, fear is an essential part of the romantic obsession with beauty. Empowered by good looks, a pretty woman can seduce men, treacherously deceive or desert them. Therefore she is a challenge to overcome, something worth possessing, controlling, devouring. Beauty affords not only a reason to pursue a woman but to conquer her as well. The more beautiful she is, the more dangerous, and therefore the greater is the challenge of the pursuit. (This desire to overpower beautiful women is an essential element of pornography, where sexual violence conquers sexual glamour.)

A final pitfall that trips up pretty women is the very transiency of their attractiveness. Loss of beauty is one of the hazards of having it. A woman accustomed to instant admiration can be devastated to find herself suddenly unnoticed. When the happiness of middle-aged people was compared with their attractiveness in college, those women who had been prettiest when young were found to be less satisfied with their lives and less well adjusted in middle age than those judged plain looking in college. Not surprisingly, the men's level of satisfaction was unrelated to their former attractiveness, again confirming the greater impact of appearance on women's lives.[20] Females find themselves in a no-win situation. Without beauty, they feel unfeminine. Having acquired it, often through painful transformations, they must pay the price of its inevitable loss. Clearly, looking good is not a guaranteed inoculation against feeling bad.

Alien Objects

For who can hate her half so well
as she hates herself?
And who can match the finesse
of her self-abuse?

Years of training
are required for this.
Twenty years of subtle self-indulgence,
self denial;
until the subject
thinks herself a queen,
and yet a beggar—
both at the same time.

.   .   .   .

She must refer all moral questions
to her mirror.

. . . . .

She must never go out of the house
unless veiled in paint.
She must wear tight shoes
so she always remembers her bondage.
She must never forget
she is rooted in the ground.

— Erica Jong[21]

Girls are socialized to seek the approval of parents and peers from earliest childhood. Conditioned to use an external frame of reference, their self-awareness is heavily "filtered through others." Minority groups commonly share this other-directedness. In order to survive, subordinates must be sensitive to what others want and expect them to be. Like other minorities, women internalize the social myths that define them.

While many roles are denied to females, that of beauty object is subtly as well as overtly encouraged. To enact femininity is to become a kind of exhibitionist, to display oneself as a decorative object. Few women are consciously aware of their objectification. Even fewer are concerned about it. After all, adornment is fun. Dressing up and showing off are ways of pleasing oneself and others. It seems a lot easier to be a sex object than a surgeon; certainly better to be looked at than overlooked. Attention, admiration, and compliments are ego enhancing. Yet, as Elizabeth's case illustrates, there are insidious side effects to feeling constantly on display.

Objectification changes body image and erodes self-esteem. To be objectified means to be seen as a thing that exists for the viewer. As object rather than subject, a woman suffers a kind of "psychic annihilation." As object, her existence depends on the observer, who can either bring her to life by recognizing her or snuff her out by ignoring her.

Girl-watching is a prime example of female objectification. Televised beauty contests legitmize the sport as a form of recreation, like bridge or bowling. We even have special words like *ogling* and *leering*, used specifically to describe the activity of males staring at females. Girl-watching and street harassment are found in virtually every Western culture. Unwritten custom invites males to inspect, admire or humiliate females who pass by, freely offering judgment through shrill whistles, threatening stares, or animal sounds, the equivalent of a verbal pat on the rear.

Secretaries and saleswomen who crowd city streets at noon are all fair game. Many are also active participants. Carefully groomed for the public arena, they peer from behind powdered lids, hoping to be acknowledged. Women react in different ways to street hassling. Some say they thrive on it as genuine praise. Some pretend not to notice. None can fully ignore it. Most experience a mixture of pride, fear, anger, and embarrassment. They walk on feeling flattered, insulted, confused, sensing that the underlying judgment was not simply toward the body. A mere whistle inserts a wedge between mind and body, reducing a person to an object. Street hassling is generally not intended to make women feel good about themselves but to make them uneasy. Those males who hassle are not motivated simply to compliment, but to assert their right to judge a woman, to invade her awareness, to make her self-conscious, to force her to see herself as an object in their eyes. Girl-watching and street hassling perpetuate the belief that female appearance is public property and that female objectification is legitimate.[22]

Once objectified, women's bodies can be reduced to a collection of parts through visual dissection. In one survey, 90 percent of the men questioned said they focus first on a woman's legs as she passes, 8 percent focus on her breasts, and a mere 2 percent begin with the face.[23] Visually dismembered, a woman is then rated piece by piece, like chicken quarters—thighs firm, breasts full, light or dark meat. She can be succinctly summed up as "a piece." Some males glibly categorize themselves as tit, ass, or ankle men, for the process of objectification dehumanizes the observer along with the observed.

As people watch women, women become preoccupied with being watched and become obsessed with whatever body part they think needs correction. The results of one experiment in which subjects could experience the situation either as the observer or the observed showed that females were more likely than males to feel observed (as well as subordinate). This sex difference was interpreted as stemming from women's cultural role as performer and men's role as audience. Nancy Henley concludes that:

> In a society in which women's clothing is designed explicitly to reveal the body and its contours; in which women are ogled, whistled at, pinched while simply going about their business; in which they see ads . . . showing revealingly clad women . . . their bodies accessible to touch like community property . . . in such a society it is little wonder that women feel observed. They are.[24]

The myth of female beauty encourages objectification, escalates self-consciousness, and contributes to a crippling phobia that is found almost exclusively in women. As women are scrutinized, ogled, and harassed, it is not surprising that some of them start to dread public places. These are the agoraphobics who become so paralyzed by fear that they cannot leave their houses. Nine out of ten agoraphobics are young women, usually shy, dependent, and overprotected. They embody the belief that woman's place is at home. Agoraphobia has been called an extreme product of female sex-role socialization. Multiple factors contribute to this phobia, for it exemplifies the complex interactions between body image, self-concept, gender role, and mental illness in women.

Joan was a classic agoraphobic, referred for therapy at age twenty-five. Afraid of going outside alone because she might "fall or have an accident," she suffered severe panic attacks when shopping or traveling in public. Her activities had become more and more limited each year. She reached the point when she would go out only if someone held on to her, and eventually even that support was not enough. By the time her husband insisted she seek help, Joan had become a virtual prisoner in her own home. It was, she said, the only place she really felt safe.

Although Elizabeth was not a typical agoraphobic, her beauty obsession likewise inhibited her from functioning in public. Recall her increasing fear of going places where a more attractive woman might "cancel her out." Elizabeth avoided hotels or airports in anticipation of an anxiety attack and worried that loss of beauty with age would lead to complete isolation.

The term *agoraphobia* derives from the Greek word *agora*, meaning the public plaza, a place that was prohibited for women of ancient Athens. "A decent woman must stay at home; the streets are for low women," wrote Menander in 300 B.C. Now legally free to walk where she wishes, the agoraphobic is fettered by fears, as if caught in a residue of anxiety built up over centuries of female harassment. To walk alone in public makes her a "street walker," a woman of the world, where she, too, becomes "one of the girls going by" to be scrutinized and visually disrobed. Or perhaps symbolically to become a "fallen woman," as Joan feared.

The everyday objectification of women on Main Street, in the media, and in the mind supports the multimillion-dollar pornography industry. Pornography is a mixture of objectification and sexual hostility that is carried to the extreme. Like the myth of female beauty, pornography also masquerades under the pretense of admiration. It too displays woman as vision while disguising woman as victim. In both cases, the victim in the vision is hidden behind her makeup and her twisted smile.

Pornography is bought and enjoyed almost exclusively by men. Women generally react to it with anger, shame, disgust, or disinterest, for pornography is based on a sexual double standard that precludes equality and mutuality. Lack of mutuality is the crucial element that distinguishes pornography from erotica, and lack of mutuality likewise is an essential aspect of the myth that assymetrically assigns beauty to the female role.

In *Pornography and Silence*, Susan Griffin examines the hidden meaning of pornography as it relates to women's everyday experience with beauty.

> A woman's body forms the center of a magazine . . . She is ornamented, fixed, made pretty. Except for her decorations, she is nude. But her face is masked in lipstick, eye shadow, eyebrows plucked and shaped in perfect arches. Now she spreads herself out under the camera on blue satin like a jewel . . . And yet at each turn of her body, at each face or curvature exposed, we see nothing. For there is no person there. No character, no woman recognizable as someone we might *know*. For the pornographic camera performs a miracle in reverse. Looking on a living being,

a person with a soul, it produces an image of a thing. She plays the part of an object. And rather than an accidental quality of pornography, this objectification of a whole being into a thing is the central metaphor of the form.[25]

The centerfold figure is held out like a ripe fruit ready to be plucked and devoured. Her cheeks are luscious, her cleavage is compelling, and she seems powerful in her airbrushed beauty. Yet, in the end, the pornographic image shows that "a woman's mysterious beauty is simply nothing. . . . Her glamourized strength is stripped away through objectification; she belongs to the voyeur, not to herself, and she is degraded," writes Griffin. By infusing woman's body with an added mystical element, the myth of female beauty enhances the meaning of pornography. Without the beauty mask, there would be less mystique to strip away. A centerfold model, a Miss America, and an everyday woman all share a similar role, for all are seen in a similar way, Griffin explains. A woman who is ogled on the street is being visually "had," much like a pornographic model. She too is split off from herself, reduced to a facade, seen as prettier but less human than she really is. In a sense, the everyday environment is transformed into a pornographic arena where fashion-bound figures parade on display and where street-walking women are worshiped and demeaned in public rituals.

Though we may deny that a sex goddess like Monroe has anything to do with our daily experience of beauty, her image becomes an archetype that alters vision. Like Monroe, ordinary women strive to impersonate a contrived caricature; they, too, suffer the confusion of feeling insecure even when idolized; they, too, construct a false self whom they mistrust; and they artfully package the exterior in order to confirm their presence only to watch themselves disappear in the process. "If I can just be pretty enough, then I'll be seen as someone important," Elizabeth insists. She clings to the delusion that being looked at means being seen, when in fact objectification (like pornography) results in the opposite: being looked at but remaining unseen. Thus, physical enhancement can lead to psychological effacement; looking good sets the stage for feeling bad.

Pornography has much in common with the beauty mystique: both depend on secret props and ritual sacrifices. Both use woman's body to idolize her as angelic, confine her as dangerous, or degrade her as shameful. Both glorify the presence of body but demand the absence of mind. As Griffin points out, both reflect an underlying sadomasochistic relationship between men and women. Objectifying another person, whether consciously or unconsciously, is a sadistic act that inflicts pain on someone else. Allowing oneself to be objectified by participating in the process is a masochistic act that inflicts pain on oneself.

A fine line divides the legitimate display of beauty from the illegitimate display of pornography. Those who seek admiration as a beauty object but fear exploitation as a sex object must be careful not to cross the line. The demands of beauty and the taboos of pornography require a balancing act that often throws women off balance. Vanessa Williams, Miss America 1984, was loudly applauded on the pageant runway but promptly censured when runaway exploitation carried her across the border into pornographic territory.

Miss America must be provocative but wholesome—a pretty but pure vestal virgin, like Cinderella. Her message is, "Look but don't touch." Similarly, in Elizabeth's case, her father first admired her fresh, nubile beauty but later called her a made-up clown and a tramp. Even *Playboy* magazine will not feature models who have done hard-core pornography. They too try not to cross the line, maintaining an illusion of purity to titillate the voyeur. The fake wholesomeness of beauty pageants has been called the flip side of pornography. Like a pair of contradictory myths, each side of the image depends on the other. Both distort the female body, making it harder for women to sustain a positive view of themselves.

When banner headlines exposed Miss America as Miss Penthouse, Miss Williams's crown toppled off. Beauty elevates but pornography degrades. The higher the pedestal, the farther the fall. Banner headlines likewise exposed feminist protestors as "bra burners." The same message was delivered in both instances: that beauty must be exhibited within the proper domain, and those who ignore the borders of propriety can expect reprisals.

Mythical Discourse

Twentieth-century technology has had a dramatic impact on self-image. Glamourized faces bounce off the mirrored walls of urban life. Perfect profiles are captured and magnified by the glass eye of the Instamatic. Throughout history, idealized models of female beauty have been fashioned and worshiped, but the impact of today's visual media is different from the effect of Botticelli's *Venus,* for example. Renaissance Venus figures were romanticized and glorified as unattainable, but modern technology blurs the boundaries between romanticism and realism. Film creates optical illusions that encourage Ms. Main Street to aspire to Miss Universe.

Television injects a potent dose of beauty imagery into the mainstream of life. Because it is experienced at home as part of the daily routine of dusting and dining, TV's carefully contrived stereotypes seem all the more authentic. Women turn unconsciously to the television set to confirm current beauty norms, only to be given further evidence of their own flaws. Staged characters create unrealistic expectations. In one study, men gave lower ratings of attractiveness to average women after watching an episode of "Charlie's Angels."[26]

Television's barrage of commercials spawn the newest "miracle" products that promise to bridge the gap between the real and the ideal. Advertisements have been called a form of "mythical discourse." They predispose the viewer to accept the commercial message as truth rather than as construct. They sell not only the product but also the prevailing social standards and thereby reinforce attitudes about feminine beauty. A United Nations report on the status of women called advertising the worst offender in perpetuating the stereotype of women as sex objects and as an inferior class through the constant degradation of women's bodies.

Billions of dollars are spent annually on beautification: $3 billion on makeup alone, $2 billion on hair products, and a mere $800 million on "feminine hygiene" products. (Critics note that more is spent on self-adornment than on education or social services.) Cosmetic companies invest over half their budgets on promotions, thereby creating markets for vaginal sprays, lip gloss, and fade creams.

These industries thrive on personal doubt. To be successful they must not only motivate a desire for the product but must also convince a woman that without it she is undesirable. First, an obscure problem is defined ("Unfortunately, the trickiest deo-dorant problem a girl *(sic)* has, isn't under her pretty little arms"); then a cure is offered that allows the buyer to become her own fairy godmother. Advertisements create a climate that questions the normality of the female body. At government hearings on feminine-hygiene sprays, one doctor testified that ads for these products present the "horrendous image that females are inher-ently smelly creatures."

In search of self-acceptance, a woman becomes prey to the subtle web spun by clever ad makers, whose message is loud and clear. No matter how hard she tries to attain acceptability, she remains unfinished or imperfect. No matter how good she looks or smells, something is always missing.

In an essay entitled "The Mask of Beauty," Una Stannard writes:

> Every day in every way, the billion dollar beauty business tells women they are monsters in disguise. Every ad for bras tells women that her breasts need lifting . . . every ad for high heels that her legs need propping, every ad for cosmetics that her skin is too dry, too pale, or too ruddy, or her lips are not bright enough. . . . In this culture women are told they are the fair sex, but at the same time that their "beauty" needs lifting, shaping, dyeing, painting, curling, padding. Women are really being told that "the beauty" is a beast.[27]

Thus the bright light of Madison Avenue exposes females as unfit—as hags, dogs, beasts, zeroes, uglies, losers—an embar-rassing affront to true femininity. Viewers buy the message as well as the product.

Despite rapid changes in gender roles, women's image has be-come more, not less, objectified in advertisements during the past two decades. One study found that in the forties and fifties most magazine ads depicted women working either within or away from the home. In the eighties, more ads showed them simply

sitting around looking pretty but doing nothing. This was particularly true in women's magazines, where the numbers showed
a decrease in ads depicting females in a family role, no change in
those showing an occupational role, and an increase in those where
no clear activity was portrayed.[28]

The latest media pitch is to the "twenty-four-hour super-
woman." Engaged in a whirlwind of professional, maternal, social, and domestic activities, this superstar always looks smashing
while racing from one role to another. An ad executive comments,
"This is the first major campaign built around the working mother.
We showed her as wanting to succeed but also wanting reassurance that she is still her beautiful self."[29] Cosmetics for the super-
woman are packaged in pseudoscientific hype. Experts in lab coats
offer her computerized analysis of hair follicles, acupressure and
ultraviolet treatments, skin vacuuming and collagen protein mas-
ques. The cures are certainly contemporary, but the nature of
the disease does not change. Well-worn stereotypes give way to
updated forms of the same old myth. In some ways the so-called
new narcissism may be even more insidious than the old, for it
appeals to a well-educated woman who is striving to develop
herself as a total person.

Feminists have been protesting against pornographic and commercial images that degrade women ever since the demonstration
in Atlantic City in 1968. But paradoxically, the women's movement may have increased appearance anxiety even while trying
to combat it. Feminism encourages reexamination of one's identity. It fosters an active approach to problem solving and teaches
personal control through assertive behavior. Sometimes this message has been misconstrued as a new mandate for physical make-
over. Eager to reshape their lives, some women focus excessively
on reshaping their bodies. Ultimately, they become trapped in a
cycle of narcissistic self-absorption and masochistic self-rejection.
These dynamics are evident in such disorders as anorexia, weight
obsession, and compulsive fitness training (which are discussed
in a later chapter)—disorders which have all increased in a climate
of feminist reform. Patients describe feeling tossed between traditional feminine images and liberated feminist models. As one
observed, "It's scarier to be a woman these days . . . because we
are still expected to be svelte, beautiful, and downright delicate

while we're running huge corporations with an iron hand. It's a schizophrenic kind of existence."[30]

Members of the fair sex are caught in a current of rapidly shifting beauty standards, judged against neurotic norms, bombarded by demeaning advertisements, and confronted by new feminist models. It is not surprising that they are so often troubled by negative body image. Mind-body alienation is fostered by numerous aspects of the female experience. Hutchinson identifies this alienation as a physical phenomenon derived from body sensations; a psychological phenomenon that weaves through personal history and distorts imagination; a cultural phenomenon that perpetuates the myth that females must look a certain way; a political phenomenon that oppresses women in a struggle against their own bodies; a philosophical-spiritual phenomenon that sets mind against body as enemies.[31]

The conflict between being a normal person and a normal woman persists, and mind-body alienation adds to this feeling of social deviance. The transformations of beauty rituals beckon as a possible solution to the dilemma.

3

Props and Paint

It is not easy to create a myth and to emulate it at the same time. . . . What is ultimately clear is that even the attempted myth must be made a model for imitating, a drama to be tried on for fit. . . . It is a mold, a prescription of characters, a plot.

— Jerome Bruner[1]

WOMEN are not really fairer than men. Their special beauty is not innate but an acquired disguise. To act out a myth is to impersonate a caricature. And so the ladies' room becomes the powder room, where the costumes of femininity are applied.

Props and paint are essential elements of the female role, as basic to the culture as to the economy. Though a woman may feel powerless in many ways, her body is an arena she can try to control. Cosmetic rituals serve as a source of salvation. Involving technology that would astound a fairy godmother, they combat appearance anxiety and provide an avenue of self-expression. They change the person as well as her image. As Jean Cocteau once observed, "A defect of the soul cannot be corrected on the face, but a defect of the face, if you can correct it, may correct a soul."[2]

And so women visit the "repair shops" for overhaul and fine tuning. Fabricating flesh into fantasy is not easy. What does feminized beauty currently entail? Faces are toned, moisturized, massaged, masked, peeled, lifted, and plastered with foundation, powder, base, and blush. Ears are pierced, pinned back. Brows are tweezed, penciled, dyed. Lashes are curled, and dressed with mascara. Lids are lined, shadowed, and surgically "done." Lips

are glossed, frosted, plumped. Nose and chin are implanted, reduced, turned up or down. Hair is permed, rinsed, straightened,
curled, dyed, teased, sprayed, wigged, greased, gelled. Teeth are
capped, and removed to accent cheekbones. Nails are manicured,
polished, wrapped. Body hair is removed by depilatories, waxing,
tweezing, shaving of the upper lip, chin, brows, underarms, and
legs. Breasts are augmented, reduced, lifted, padded. Torsos are
corseted and girdled. Rumps are plumped. Tummies are tucked.
Hips and thighs are firmed, reduced. Cellulite is "dissolved." Feet
are reshaped by high-heeled, pointed shoes, and toes are ampu-
tated to fit them. To this partial list add a plethora of diet and
exercise programs and a variety of fashions that constrict flesh or
inhibit movement.

While make-overs are practiced by both sexes, men in Western
cultures engage in them less often, less universally, and less fran-
tically. Although few women indulge in all of the above rituals,
virtually every woman interviewed felt that at least a few of them
were imperative to her basic beauty routine.

What motivates females to transform themselves? The answer
is a strong human need to conform to social norms. A personal
decision—to have a perm or a face-lift for example—is dictated
partly by group pressure. Women enact the popular image for
the pleasure of being like others and of being liked by others.
Beauty transformations produce the security of group acceptance
while they reduce the fear of social rejection.

Cosmetic rituals are also valuable in legitimizing the purchase
of human touch. Chimps groom each other for hours for the
simple pleasure of physical contact. We have few rituals that
encourage body contact in American culture, but manicurists,
hairdressers, and body groomers are permitted to lay their hands
on us. They know the workings of our flesh as well as the secrets
of our heart. And they are not easily replaced. A few days after
Nancy Reagan moved into the White House, her favorite manicurist was flown in from California for an emergency nail repair
(a cross-continental manicure that reportedly cost $1,500 in travel
expenses).

Beauty rituals often become "functionally autonomous." This

means that the process takes on more importance than the end product. Like other daily habits, these rituals prove satisfying through mere repetition. "If it's Thursday, I must be having my nails done." The daily beauty fix can be as addictive, compelling, and expensive as some drug habits, and the withdrawal process just as painful.

For ladies of leisure, the pursuit of beauty has historically served as a kind of career, a central focus of existence quite as demanding as any full-time job. Busy making appointments and keeping them, having facials, pedicures, and body waxings, such women have been compared to the heroines of Russian plays who are really mourning their lives but try to conceal the mourning by devotion to their images.[3]

Commitment to beauty can continue even beyond the grave. Funeral outfits are sometimes prepared in advance of dying and instructions left with hairdressers. After taking the sacrament, Madame de Pompadour's final act before death was to rouge her face. In a clever essay, Nancy Henley compares beauty parlors to funeral parlors and the work of beauticians to that of morticians. Both promise (if you pay enough) to produce a totally natural look; both carefully guard the secrets of their trade; and both use cosmetics to turn people into "unreal images and inhuman spectacles."[4] While funeral parlors mask death with the look of life, beauty parlors mask women with the look of loveliness. After the funeral of Princess Grace of Monaco, reporters were quick to reassure us that she looked as magnificent in death as in life ("perhaps even more so"). Do a fair face and a dead face really have so much in common? Is a sleeping princess, frozen in passive splendor, the ultimate model of femininity?

The symptoms of a comatose state are all too common among depressed women. Barbara, for example, was withdrawn and silent when she returned to therapy after her sophomore year at college. She spent much of the day either sleeping or weeping, waiting for something to shake her out of her depression. The shyness that had plagued her since childhood became much worse during college, and she was feeling extremely isolated.

Barbara had been my patient several years earlier, but I hardly recognized her. The awkward, unattractive teenager that I remembered had grown into a very pretty young woman. When I commented about the change in her appearance, she explained that her nose and chin had been remodeled right after high school graduation.

> I had expected to have my nose fixed for years. It's almost a ritual in our family. My mom and aunt had the same ethnic nose—my grandfather's. We always joked about it. Everyone just assumed that I'd have mine redone someday like they had. And so I did. Besides, Mom would never have left me alone until I got rid of that bump. She's so concerned about mixing with the right crowd and constantly talked about "The Nose" like some huge liability.

Since childhood, Barbara had felt overshadowed by an elegant and extroverted mother. This socially ambitious mother found her quiet and plain-looking daughter both a disappointment and a cosmetic challenge. Barbara described her own feelings after the surgery:

> In a way, I "came out" that summer after high school—sort of like a ceremony where I presented my new face to the world. Mom was very excited. I guess we both thought I'd be suddenly happier. But the shy part of me was still there. I felt proud but also ashamed. I didn't know what to say to people. And I still don't know whether to tell friends at school about my nose job. I look much better now, and I'm more confident about my appearance. But still so terribly self-conscious in new situations.

At the next therapy session I suggested that Barbara bring in a picture of herself before and after the surgery. We looked at the two photos and I asked if she ever wanted her old self back. Definitely not, she replied.

> It's not that I want to go back to that other person. She doesn't exist anymore. But I just can't figure out which parts of me are acceptable. I don't have to hide my face, but the rest of me doesn't feel pretty enough. I don't know whether I can safely reveal myself to others without being rejected.

Barbara's depression was not caused directly by her cosmetic make-over, nor was her personality dramatically altered by it.

Yet the psychodynamics of her depression changed as the problem of feeling unacceptable shifted from the outside to the inside.

People play out social scripts by sending subtle messages that conceal as much as they reveal. Like Barbara, we all try to defend "the territory of the self" from unwanted scrutiny. Like her, we discreetly guard secrets of our nose jobs and our electrolysis treatments. Gray hair is quietly washed away and body parts are veiled away. (The agoraphobic completely screens herself from public view.) While primitive people paint their faces to ward off evil spirits, Western women feel exposed without at least a dash of lipstick to protect them from the social forces that threaten. Few dare to venture out even to the corner grocery without putting on a touch of makeup as defensive fabrication. The more important the event, the more elaborate the defense.

Why must the territory of a woman's body be so carefully guarded? What is there about her that requires so much concealment and fabrication? Why must she use her body to tell so many social lies?

Cosmetic Strategies

Abused and scolded, blamed for every disaster when the going got tough, [women] have nevertheless come up smiling, lipstick in hand.

— H.R. Hays[5]

Aware of their dual roles as the fair sex and the other sex, females use a number of different strategies to normalize their social position. First, beauty transformations are used to help women look more womanly and, therefore, more acceptable. Makeup and stylish clothes demonstrate that a woman is committed to femininity, cares enough to look her very best, wants to be attractive to others, and is willing to take pains to prove it.

A totally opposite cosmetic strategy is used by those who seek to cast off their otherness by boycotting beauty rituals. A woman who rejects makeup, stops shaving her legs, or stops wearing a bra redefines herself and is relegated to a special category. Her pale lips or hairy limbs pronounce her an anomaly. Anonymity is shed by omitting a ritual required to confirm membership in the fair sex. Obesity can be another representation of this gesture.

But a woman who fails to play her proper part, even through a trivial act like the omission of a bra, will soon be seen as a threat to the whole system. Refusing to correct the "flaw" of her drooping breasts, she is in effect rejecting its meaning and its power to define her as the other. Sociologist Erving Goffman concludes that for females, gender has the effect of a stigma, and he notes that the reaction aimed at those women who step out of place is similar to the reaction shown toward cripples, who likewise bear a social stigma, for "the cripple has to play the part of the cripple, just as many women have to be what men expect them to be."[6] Goffman adds that women are likely to be derogated if they fail to assume their "correct" place. When they violate their scripts by not cultivating beauty (or by not remaining passive), they lose social support and hence become isolated. An unresponsive social environment undermines their self-confidence and leads, in Goffman's words, to the "stigmatized mentality" common among members of minority groups.

The protestors who picketed the Miss America Pageant were initially explained away as unattractive "broads," embittered by their ugliness, who were using feminism for solace. Actually, the reverse may be closer to the truth. Feminism in effect generates the ugliness, by negating the value of cosmetic rituals. When women challenge their subordinate role by abandoning beauty signals, they in effect discard the crutches that mark them as cripples. Consequently, they become less attractive, less recognizable as women. To be a "true woman," explains de Beauvoir, one must accept herself as the Other.

As a final strategy to normalize themselves, some women cultivate "masculine" traits, thereby gaining entry into the real world of men. Here is the adult version of the tomboy; see how smart she is, how she thinks like a man; see how strong she is, how she plays on a man's team; see how capable she is, how she works in a man's world. Striving for acceptance as one of the boys, a woman may succeed in nudging her way into their club, to frolic for a while in the mainstream of life. But the "tag of female" remains in the hyphenated titles of woman-judge, female-astronaut, lady-doctor, police-woman.[7]

The door leading into the boardroom of the male world is a revolving one. It can suddenly sweep a woman out unless she justifies her presence within. She will be tolerated longer in the club by acknowledging that her membership is special. This can be accomplished through beauty signals that confirm her underlying femininity. As Elizabeth Janeway notes:

> Women who move into a man's world expect to have to legitimize our presence there. A whole repertory of transitional behavior is being invented for this purpose, but what is interesting is that it differs from masculine behavior, in the same situation. What is required of women is not a demonstration of successfully learned masculinity, but of remaining and residual femininity. We are being asked to admit that we can't get rid of it.[8]

The earrings worn by Chris Evert Lloyd at Wimbledon or the ruffled collars at Justice Sandra Day O'Connor's throat are such signals of residual femininity. They are put on like badges, no matter how lovely they look or how feminine they feel. Some professional women admit that they flash their femininity in much the same way as a chimp presents her rump in a gesture of submission. These flashes are intended to show that she is not really so threatening, precisely because there is a mere woman underneath. The day of my doctoral defense is well remembered years later not only for the academic challenge but also for the care taken in creating the right image for my all-male dissertation committee: a seductive sweater to capture attention, and long hair draped as a softening backdrop for my solid presentation. The men who judge must be reassured of the compliant woman beneath the competent scholar.

Cosmetic strategies do help to normalize women. But they insidiously confirm female deviance even while counterbalancing it. Paradoxically, the more attractive a woman makes herself, the more deviant she often looks in her feminine drag.

This works in several ways. First, props and paint accentuate gender differences, creating some that have no basis in nature (blue eyelids) and exaggerating others that are minimal (hairless legs). Shape of brows, contour of feet, style of hair become potent substitutes for natural sex differences. Lacquered nails and frosted lips flash like neon signs instantly advertising femininity. They transform abstract notions of beauty into something tangible, something we can see and feel. Once grounded in anatomy, these beauty symbols acquire the illusion of biological truth, and we start to think of them as fixed and permanent gender differences. While blue eyelids are pretty and feminine, they are peculiar distortions that affirm female otherness in the flesh.

Props and paint add cosmetic boundaries to women's distinct world. They separate the sexes actually and psychologically through rituals of segregation. Historians have often focused on household chores or child care as components of women's separate sphere while overlooking beauty rituals, which are central to the female experience and which bind together women of different classes, regions, and ethnic groups.[9] Shared experiences, whether at the makeup counter or in the dressing room, create commonality. Shaped by the same myths, adorned in the same fashions, women recognize themselves in each other and are recognized as isomorphic by men. Cosmetic rituals create a framework for the female world while at the same time producing uniformity within it. The faces smiling from the covers of women's magazines or from the centerfolds of men's magazines reflect this sameness, a rubber stamp of the prevailing beauty ideal. "Young and pretty, the slaves of the harem are always the same in the sultan's embrace."[10] In molding themselves into the image, women lose their individuality even while seeking to establish it. Barbara liked her new face. She did not long for the old self who no longer existed. But she had not been able to establish a new sense of identity that fit her reconstructed image.

Finally, beauty transformations maintain female deviance by associating femininity with phoniness. Props and paint undermine credibility, evoke suspicion and mistrust. Cellophane nails, silicone breasts, bottled blush, all link women with the false and the trivial. When a woman resembles a mannequin, she is not taken very seriously. Nietzsche associated deception with the feminine nature and wrote, "What is truth to woman? . . . her great art is the lie, her highest concern is mere appearance and beauty."

The artifice inherent in cosmetic rituals has been used as proof of female inferiority. For example, with the revival of corsets in the nineteenth century, critics labeled women not only deceptive but also stupid. Anyone who would subject herself to the senseless torment of corsets was considered "brainless and inferior." Victorian magazines like *Punch* ridiculed tight lacers and concluded that women's demands for education were equally ridiculous. "Woman asks for education but she usually arrays herself in a style that suggests either the infantile or the idiotic."[11] Their fashions proved that females could not think rationally. Notice the counterbalancing of myths. On the one hand, a corseted waist was viewed as the essence of femininity and reason enough to love a woman madly. On the other hand, it was proof of a woman's mental deficiency. The contemporary equation of blondness with both glamour and dumbness reflects similar dynamics.

The same beauty rituals that help women compensate also condemn them. As Una Stannard observes:

> The very cause of woman's glorification, her presumptive beauty, is at the same time the stigma of her inferiority. . . . Women are not free to stop playing the beauty game, because the woman who stops would be afraid of exposing herself for what she is—not the fair sex. And yet the woman who does play the beauty game proves the same thing.[12]

"What's a woman to do?" If she ignores the demands of the beauty myth, she feels like an outsider, for unadorned means unattractive. If she capitalizes on cosmetics to normalize herself, she only exaggerates her caricature as the other sex. A sense of balance is hard to achieve. In Barbara's case, the various cosmetic alternatives left her feeling uncertain, unworthy, and unhealthy.

Social Organs

Humans are social animals. Since appearance communicates, nature has dressed us up with special organs that send social messages. Just as wedding rings signal marital status, social organs give a quick printout on how old, sexy, or dominant we are at a given moment.

Social organs, or "Body Hot Spots," as R. Dale Guthrie calls them, enhance our chances for survival.[13] The more we know about each other, the better we can separate friend from foe. For instance, the evolution of the male beard is explained as an exaggeration of a powerful biting jaw. Beards give the illusion of jutting out the jaw, which is a gesture of belligerence. We speak of strong- or weak-chinned men. Women with large jaws are considered unattractive because they look "too aggressive." Cosmetic transformations often increase or diminish natural body hot spots. Japanese women at one time blackened their front teeth, creating the helpless toothless look of a baby. Similarly, western women paint the mouth, "making up" or mimicking the swollen lips of a nursing infant (or perhaps as some theorists suggest, the swollen labia of a chimp in heat).

Males and females *are* different. Yet our differences are not always as natural as we suppose. Structural and functional differences between the sexes are called dimorphisms. These can change during the life cycle (for instance, as males become progressively balder than females). Dimorphisms are relatively less extreme in humans than in other primates, which may explain why we go to such trouble to alter them. Some sex differences are primarily biological, while others are not. Moreover, genes can express themselves in various ways, depending on the environment. Oysters, for example, shift back and forth from male to female as water temperature rises and falls. Sex differences in lifestyle tend to create sex differences in social organs. When men shave their faces, a highly obvious dimorphism is reduced. When women wear high heels, the sex difference in height decreases but the differences in posture and gait increase.

Just as environment alters genetic expression, genes likewise alter the social system. Blond hair, a bountiful bosom or a balding head changes a person's social reception. By bleaching hair or padding breasts we can reset the social stage. In effect, we reshape our destiny as we remake our anatomy. Altering appearance also changes the way we see ourselves, and this is a crucial consequence of cosmetic change.

Ironically, some of the most indigenous female characteristics that *are* biologically based, such as menstruation, pregnancy, and lactation, are not highly valued in terms of aesthetic beauty. The swollen belly of pregnancy and the smells of menstruation are not considered very attractive—which shows that it is not the dimorphism, per se, but the way society values it that counts. Whatever the biological components of beauty, it is culture that confers meaning on them. "What does make a difference is that a difference is made," observes Jessie Bernard.[14] Culture labels woman the fair sex and then assumes that nature designed her that way. It is culture not nature that declares the bound foot lovelier than the unbound foot; culture that first covers the female breast and then covets it.

Social organs create nonverbal dialogues between people. A rounded bosom in a tight sweater evokes a stare from an observer. The stare in turn prompts the sweater wearer to change her posture, to look away in embarrassment, or to smile invitingly. Such dialogues feed back into her self-evaluation, resulting in a feeling of pride or shame.

A basic ingredient in these dialogues are the thoughts inside the head of the beholder. Human perceptions are not simply instinctive. Expectations are learned, and they influence our sensitivity to body hot spots. We become more likely to see what we have been taught to seek. Culture edits nature's script, for myths alter expectations along with anatomy. Once taught that crimson lips, uplifted breasts, or tiny feet are signals of beauty, people will notice and react to them more intensely. Social organs also have different meanings, depending on the time and place. Cleavage may be an asset on a Saturday night, but a liability on a Monday morning. Therefore, optimal social strategies require constant signal change.

Humans have invented ingenious ways to alter body hot spots, shifting the meaning of social organs from instinct toward intellect. Blondes emerge from bottles. Bosoms bloom overnight. Cosmetic transformations are powerful precisely because the origins of dimorphisms are unclear, and because cultured beauty creates the illusion of greater natural fitness. In the struggle for survival of self and progeny, the less fit can pretend greater fitness than they actually possess. Today, not only the wealthy but the masses as well can afford to put on a false fitness front, and look younger, sexier, more virile than nature intended. As more and more people create contrived body signals, the competitive pressure increases. Beauty standards are elevated by cosmetic transformations. Those who remain unadorned look progressively less attractive. Phony social messages from phony social organs lead to phony social systems, which in turn maintain gender myths.

Dialogues between people exist on two levels. The words them-selves form the surface structure, while the more important un-derlying meaning is found at a deeper level. Like language, beauty is a form of communication. Just as good conversation requires a common vocabulary, beauty dialogues require shared beliefs. The active eye of the viewer is as important to beauty as the face of the model, for the observer defines beauty by responding to it. It takes two, both beholder and beheld, to turn women into beauty objects. Socialized to view females as the fair sex, men have learned to respond to contrived symbols of beauty and women have become bound up in the process of producing them.

Casting the Role

Witchcraft was hung in History,
But History and I
Find all the Witchcraft that we need
Around us, every Day.
— Emily Dickinson[15]

Body beautification is a universal social gesture apparently stemming from a deep human need. Practiced by both males and females in virtually every culture, it traces back to ancient civi-lizations. A staggering variety of decorative rituals are found worldwide. To the western eye, some of them—such as the stretched necks of the Burmese, the filed teeth of the Sumatrans, or the elongated heads of the Senegalese—seem quite grotesque.

None of these cosmetic transformations are inherently more pleasing than others. Their aesthetic value depends on their social context. Black teeth or red nails seem attractive to someone con-ditioned to appreciate them as such. Who can say whether scarring one's face is elegant or hideous? Whether stretching one's lips with bone or implanting one's breasts with silicone is an aesthetic improvement or a monstrous mutilation?

Remember that beauty is defined as a unique and unusual quality—something beyond the ordinary. The distortions fash-ioned through cosmetic transformations produce an unnatural extreme. Redder lips, longer necks, blonder hair, flatter heads are loud signals that go beyond the boundaries of nature. And pain is often part of the decorative process. Pain signals an extreme commitment; the greater the pain, the more unique the end product.

Adornment serves as a kind of coded dialogue spoken through hair styles, jewelry, or body painting. Its vocabulary conveys subtle messages. In *The Decorated Body*, Robert Brain presents a fascinating review of cross-cultural cosmetic rituals. He explains that body decorating is concerned with questions both of self-identity and group identity: "Who am I and who are we together?" Cosmetics are more than simply a decorative mask, he writes; they imprint on body and mind the traditions and philosophy of the social group.[16]

Props and paint are used by both sexes to create a greater contrast between feminine and masculine characteristics. Brain concludes that in most societies males and females decorate differently but equally, whereas in western cultures women adorn "to a far greater extent and in a greater variety of ways than men. . . . Body decoration has become primarily associated with female vanity." According to his analysis, the current western preoccupation with female beauty grows from fundamental cultural values and reflects a strange denial of female sexuality. Beauty rituals are used primarily to make women "socially acceptable," he concludes. "A woman turns herself into a lady and her strongest motivation is to pursue social, not sexual, satisfaction." For example, Brain suggests that cosmetics call attention to the face as a way of distracting the eye from other erogenous areas.[17]

Our western tradition linking body adornment with female vanity is long but by no means consistent. The Greek conception of beauty encompassed the total person, outer form as well as inner qualities. The male body was revered and considered more attractive than the female body. Early Christian teachings challenged the idea of beauty as mind-body unity, and "set beauty adrift—as an alienated, arbitrary, superficial enchantment."[18] The mind was associated with the higher values of culture and of men, while the body was relegated to the lower realms of nature and of women. Separated from the inner spirit, flesh was rejected as a narcissistic object, the proper concern of women but a dangerous temptation for men.

Fear of female beauty became part of religious asceticism. Tertullian, a second-century theologian, warned women never to enhance their appearance and to "neglect, conceal and veil their natural beauty," lest men be tempted to sin by seeing it. Consequently, female beauty took on exaggerated meaning and power. The British Parliament joined the Church in trying to restrain women from beautifying themselves. A bill passed in 1650, entitled "The Vice of Painting and Wearing Black Patches and Immodest Dresses of Women," was designed to protect men against "the false adornments of the painted, patched, plumped out, marriage hungry female."[19]

Religious injunctions against sexuality connected the female body with sorcery, so that beauty became linked with power and with evil. Part of the power of beauty stems from fear of the supernatural. A glamourized woman combines charm with enchantment. She bewitches, bothers, and bewilders. One drinks her in like a visual potion that captures and corrupts the soul. The Malleus Maleficarum, an infamous church document of 1486 that officially condoned the burning of witches, described woman as:

> Beautiful to look on, contaminating to the touch and deadly to keep. . . . A natural temptation, a desirable calamity, a delectable detriment, an evil of nature . . . painted with fair colors.[20]

Hundreds of thousands who were sacrificed as witches over several centuries were considered deviant in some way—too smart, too old, too bold, too long unwed. And some were condemned to burn merely for their faces alone—judged either too beautiful or too ugly to be endured. Erica Jong reflects on the faces of witches and ponders:

> What does a witch look like? . . . She is either exceedingly beautiful or horribly ugly, bewitching in her physical graces or terrifyingly hideous. In either case she menaces men, for her beauty both blinds and binds, and her ugliness assaults and astounds the senses. Whether he meets an ugly witch or a beautiful one, man is victimized by female power.[21]

Legends like those of Eve and Pandora connect woman with contamination and sin. Eve corrupts a perfect Eden by opening her mouth to the apple; Pandora pollutes the world by opening her "box" and exposing its contents. The bodies of these women go out of control, threatening the very downfall of "mankind." Therefore, they must be constrained for man's protection, and God takes the lead by punishing Eve with the travails of child-birth. The suffering of womankind becomes an extension of Eve's punishment, and an inherent part of womanhood. Cosmetic traditions that require female suffering, subordination, and self-sacrifice are justified through myths that portray women as threatening creatures who need constraint.

Beauty safely conceals woman's frightening dimensions, while compensating for her deficiencies. The adornments of feminine fashion—the painted ubiquitous smile, the dainty sandaled foot—are ingratiating symbols. They reassure a man that this particular woman is not Pandora's sister, not a devilish witch or a castrating bitch. Even as a glamourous vamp she at least does not resemble his dominating Mom. The trivia of lipstick and lace reassure him of her impotence. By donning the disguise of a doll, she signals her willingness to be "his little woman." And her mythical beauty serves as a survival tactic for them both.

Whenever sex was considered a weakness to which men succombed, women were feared as seductive and corrupting. Consequently, codes of dress and veiling were enacted to hold their power in check. St. Thomas decreed self-adornment of females a mortal sin because it evoked lust. Yet he encouraged married women to look pretty purely to please their husbands "lest through despising her he fall into adultery." A contemporary update on this advice is found in such books as Helen Andelin's *Fascinating Womanhood*, and Marabel Morgan's *The Total Woman*, which urge a good Christian wife "to spruce up in order to keep your man."[22] (The exhortation to be both provocative and pure at the same time remains a central paradox of the beauty myth.)

Medieval chivalry was built on the adoration of female beauty as the symbol of chastity, purity, truth, and all else that was virtuous. Italian and Western European art depicted very little beauty bias until the time of the Renaissance, when females started to predominate in the work of Botticelli and Rubens. With Raphael, woman's body became glorified as the "essence of human beauty." An eighteenth-century painter suggested that a curved line was more naturally interesting than a straight one; hence,

women's curves represented the true "line of beauty." The small-
ness, smoothness, and delicacy of the female nude were considered inherently lovely. Female models still far outnumber male
models in contemporary figure-drawing classes.

For most of the eighteenth century, Western European men
vied with women in adorning and displaying their bodies. No-
blemen, as heavily turned out as the ladies, paraded in powdered
wigs and satin pumps, showing off their shapely legs. Men's
fashions were like women's: constantly changing and used to signal sex and status. Then came the French Revolution, which not
only changed the social roles of men but dramatically altered
men's appearance. This shift has been called "The Great Masculine Renunciation," during which males rejected most cosmetic
rituals as effeminate.[23]

Along with the new ideals of the French republic came the
belief that a man's most important function was not in the salon
but in the office or factory. Tight breeches and codpieces were
abandoned, silk stockings were replaced by loose trousers, and
wigs were discarded for close-cropped hair. For the past two
centuries, men in western cultures generally have dressed mod-
estly, shunned cosmetics, and worn utilitarian clothes. They have
stopped displaying wealth overtly on their own bodies, adorning
their wives instead with jewels or fur, making beauty woman's
birthright and her burden.

In the United States, adornment became increasingly associated
with women's lives and women's bodies in the early nineteenth
century. Historian Lois Banner concludes in her book *American
Beauty* that the social and work roles of men and women became
more differentiated with the industrial revolution. Americans began to view the cultivation of beauty, along with the preservation
of religious and spiritual values, as the special concern of women.
Banner cites nineteenth-century poems, sermons, and manuals
which assert that "It is woman's business to be beautiful," "Woman
is the beauty principle," and "Beauty is unquestionably the mas-
tercharm of that sex."[24]

Pictures of pinups, nymphs, and Gibson girls began to appear
on streetcar posters, in barrooms, on packs of cards—a phenomenon that was later described as "the cult of women." By the turn
of this century, the commercialism of female beauty was evident

in the burgeoning fashion industry, the growing numbers of salons, the increasing use of cosmetics, and the marketing efforts that accompanied all of these.

A "Cinderella Mythology" developed for women in the nineteenth century as a counterpart to the "self-made-man" image, reports Banner. Young women in the antebellum years worked to turn themselves into elegant ladies while their mates worked to become men of property. Together they represented the essence of capitalist values. To "be a belle" was nothing other than a profession, wrote Harriet Beecher Stowe.[25] When a wife could spend her day pursuing beauty, it indicated leisure and thereby proclaimed her husband's success. Fashion represented fun and self-indulgence—the way elite life was meant to be.

Ironically, the Protestant work ethic, so basic to our American value system, indirectly promoted the pursuit of beauty as woman's work by preaching that diligence pays off and that no sacrifice is too great to achieve a worthy goal. For women who had few achievement arenas open to them, the work ethic easily translated into a mandate for personal make-over. Ambitious ladies poured their energy into beautification (which did not violate the traditional feminine role). And so the road to success took a detour through the beauty salon, making narcissism and Puritanism rather peculiar partners.

Meanwhile, nineteenth-century Darwinists predicted that all women eventually would be attractive, because men were selecting good-looking wives and passing this trait on to their children. The idea that beauty could (and therefore should) belong to every woman was soon adapted to commercial ends. Good looks were promoted as a "natural right" of all ladies. Since cosmetics can be sold to anyone who can afford them, they serve to democratize beauty by spreading it around. Buying and selling attractiveness fits nicely with the American values of egalitarianism, materialism, and rugged individualism, notes Banner.[26]

Ever since the turn of the century, women's magazines have featured "before and after" shots. The testimonials of ordinary housewives prove that nature needs only a gentle prod. Responsible women are told they owe it to themselves and to their families to make the effort. Those who ignore their potential have only themselves to blame. Once unattractiveness is equated with la-

ziness, guilt is added to the stigma of looking plain or fat or old.
As Zsa Zsa Gabor once quipped, "There are no ugly women,
just lazy ones." When Barbara considers her before and after
photos, she voices no regrets. Like most women, she is pleased
with the results and feels a sense of accomplishment in her remade
image.

It is only a short step from deceiving others to deceiving oneself.
Beauty rituals, initially used to disguise a defect, eventually screen
us from self-scrutiny. When constantly masked by make-over,
one's own naked face can seem alien. This is why beauty products
are marketed as if the changes they create are quite natural. The
myth asserts that female beauty is innate, needing only to be
brought to the surface and displayed. So-called pure products
made of lemon balm, fresh milk or honey, pure wheat germ oil,
with balanced pH maintain the illusion that nature remains in
command. In the 1970s women responded to a decade of the
"natural look" by buying more cosmetics than ever before to
achieve an unmade-up image. As the real face becomes fused with
fantasy and myth gives the illusion of truth, women end up feeling
ashamed when caught unadorned. They learn their parts so well
that they forget they are impersonating the role of fairy princess.

Playing the Part

> All women that shall . . . seduce and betray into matrimony
> any of his majesty's subjects, by the scents, paints, cosmetics,
> washes, artificial teeth, false hair . . . hoops, high heeled
> shoes and bolstered hips, shall incur the penalty of the law
> in force against witchcraft . . . and upon conviction, the
> marriage shall stand null and void.
> (From an act of British Parliament, 1659.)[27]

When Barbara initially came for therapy at age fifteen, she was
insecure and self-deprecating. I asked if there was anything she
really liked about herself. Glancing down and extending her pretty
sandal, she replied, "One thing I do have is a beautiful tiny foot."
"Yes, but what else is special about you?" I prompted, knowing
her many talents and trying to expand her feelings of worth. A
long silence followed. Looking down once more, she finally added,

"I guess I also have a nice high arch." Sadly, I wondered how often Barbara had heard the happily-ever-after ending of Cinderella, whose equally tiny foot had reshaped her destiny.

The story of Cinderella has much to teach about beauty transformations: how they incite envy, how they can be magically acquired, and how they attract and deceive men. Perhaps this tale has survived for over a thousand years in hundreds of versions because it socializes children so well to the special meaning of female beauty. Cinderella is a tale of rivalry. Women use deception, body mutilation, and witchcraft to compete for male attention. Bonds between women are strained while men are pursued, and the competition is fierce because there are not enough princes to go around.

In the beginning of his book on the role of fairy tales, Bruno Bettelheim writes that a child's greatest need is to find meaning in life above and beyond the events of the moment.[28] Piaget describes this search for meaning as a continuous adaptation to reality. Knowledge grows in small steps, says Piaget, as children try to construct a mental conception of events by asking over and over, "What is the world really like and how can I live in it?" Fairy-tale fantasy serves to fill the gaps in children's concepts. As simplified models, these stories and their characters reinforce the ways in which men and women relate to each other. They convey our social heritage, including cultural myths about gender roles.

All fairy tales are stories of personal transformation. In many of them, a part of the body is used to resolve some difficulty. Rapunzel's strong hair, Snow White's blood-red lips, Cinderella's unique foot, reassure children that even when they feel isolated or rejected by others, they can turn to their own bodies for strength and solace. In fact, fairy-tale figures—such as Goldilocks, Snow White, and Red Riding Hood—are often named for their appearance.

Fairy-tale characters are polarized as either good or evil, thus making identification easier for children, who view the world through primitive concepts. (Research shows that 80 percent of female fairy-tale characters are evil and ugly, and the remaining 20 percent are beautiful young girls.) Good = beauty = clean = love on the one side; while on the other, bad = ugly =

dirty = rejection. Cinderella was "as good as she was beautiful," we are told, and thus the two qualities become fused. When the stepsisters rename Ella "Cinderella," they "dirty" her name to correspond with her looks. (In some versions she is called Cinderslut, associating loss of virtue with loss of beauty.)

Once goodness and beauty are fused, virtue becomes harder to recognize under a soiled face. Eventually Cinderella must be made over, transformed so that goodness and beauty are reunited. According to Bettelheim, one moral of this tale is that virtue will be rewarded regardless of appearance. But even the most naive child knows intuitively that Cinderella could never have been loved by the Prince while dressed in rags. The hidden message, which children clearly hear, is that packaging counts, no matter how worthy the inner woman.

Cinderella has two mothers, a common fairy-tale device that appeals to our ambivalence about our own mothers. The dead natural mother is the good and loving one, who later returns in the form of a godmother. She is allied with men and with nature; she bestows beauty as a reward for purity. The bad mother (safely placed one step removed) is a cruel and jealous one who strips Cinderella of her finery and her father's love. She is insecure and dominating with men, and destroys the beauty of other women to reduce competition.

A closer look at these two mothers shows they both have a common goal that mothers have shared for centuries: marketing their daughters as brides. As in real life, fairy-tale mothers encourage the beauty rituals, model the fashions, and provide the motivation and means that turn their girls into marriage material. It is Barbara's mother who translates the acceptable images of femininity, pointing out the defects of Barbara's body and helping her to "correct" them. It was Victorian mothers who laced corsets ever tighter, Chinese mothers who initiated the rituals of foot-binding, African mothers who even today watch a tiny clitoris being excised, black mothers who burn hair while ironing it straight, white mothers who arrange for nose jobs and lift five-year-olds onto the runways of beauty pageants. I remember my own mother taking me to the electrologist when I was twelve. It was a secret we shared with no one else, a mother-daughter conspiracy to "normalize" my face. I recall a young patient, barely fifteen, whose breasts were surgically reduced with her mother's consent.

When Cinderella's stepsisters struggle unsuccessfully to fit into the shoe, their mother holds out a knife, urging them to cut off a toe or slice down a heel. (Bettelheim notes that this is one of the few instances of self-mutilation in fairy tales.) The mother provides the means, gives the instructions, and ignores the pain and the crippling consequences. "Cut off your toes," she cries. "Once you are Queen you won't have to walk anymore"—an all too familiar refrain, echoed by our culture. "Cut off your education; once you are wed you won't need to work anymore." Or, more universally, "Cut off your name; once you are his you won't need your identity anymore."

Beauty transformations are not passed down by mothers to victimize their daughters. Most mothers, whether good ones or bad ones, are simply fulfilling their role as socializers. They sense only too well that good looks may be the most important legacy they can pass on to a young girl. It is the mother's magic wand, an insurance policy to guarantee happiness ever after.

In conveying beauty rituals to their daughters, mothers also teach conformity to the feminine role. This process further strains the ambivalent love-hate relationship between mother and daughter. As a mother tries to coerce compliance to traditional beauty standards, tensions are increased. When a daughter rejects her mother's ideas about proper feminine appearance, she rejects her mother as well. For this very reason, girls may consciously choose beauty or body issues as a symbol of their struggle for independence (as tragically exemplified in young anorectic women, for instance). At age thirteen, Barbara pleaded to have a second hole put in her already pierced ears. When her mother firmly denied permission, Barbara took a needle and in a difficult and defiant act, pierced the earlobes herself, thereby using a conflict over a beauty issue to proclaim her adolescent independence.

On the surface, one message of *Cinderella* is that cosmetic transformations fail. The stepsisters in their contrived finery are ridiculous figures, mocked and humiliated. Not so for the heroine, however. Cinderella's artifice is as great as her sisters', but she has been made over by the "good mother." Her transformation comes unsolicited, a reward for virtue and servitude. And she is beautified in secrecy, reminding us of the contemporary assurance that "Only her hairdresser knows for sure." Often the private nature of beauty rituals further isolates a woman, who believes that she alone has a false bosom or a lifted face.

Rituals of cosmetic transformation create rivalry among women. When the palace ball in *Cinderella* is first announced, there is a flurry of activity, diets, dressmakers, and lessons in elocution and curtsying as contestants struggle to put on their disguises. Remember, however, that beauty is an exclusionary concept, attainable only by the few. The stepsisters (along with the waitresses and secretaries) who flock hopefully to the ball leave empty-handed, their self-esteem diminished along with their resources. This is the fairy-tale version of a beauty pageant, where young bodies are displayed, paraded, then divided into winners and losers.

The witchcraft provided by a godmother makes Cinderella not just pretty but spectacular. "The-Most-Beautiful-Girl-in-the-Land," we are told; "100 times, nay 1,000 times more beautiful than her sisters"; so beautiful that even those who know her best fail to recognize her. A hush falls as she enters the palace, followed by murmurs of astonishment. The prince finds her irresistible (and so does his father!); "even the fiddlers are amazed at her beauty."

Here, in fairy-tale form, is the magical power of female beauty: the power to attract crowds and control kings; the power of Miss America, of Marilyn M., Jackie O., and Princess Di—a power that women can rarely match in any other way. Hard at work in her clogs, Cinderella was ignored; transformed by her satins and slippers, she conquered the world.

There is a potent message here for the children who listen, the little ones who Piaget and Bettelheim tell us are testing reality in stories and searching for meaning in life. What do they learn? That without beauty, virtue goes unnoticed; that a girl's looks can be quickly and miraculously made over; that cosmetic transformation is the key to love and attention. Children also learn that power and happiness do not come to women through active pursuit and assertive engagement with life, but rather through obedience, servitude, patience, and, ultimately, through the magic of cosmetic make-over.

Cinderella's conquest at the ball is paradoxically a product of her passivity. Compliant and uncomplaining, she has denied anger, lived virtuously, been a good girl. Yet she seems incapable of meeting her own needs. When the messenger comes searching for the owner of the slipper, she stands mute, not daring to whisper "Here I am, my foot will fit." True to her nature, she waits to be discovered.

In the end, it is not her efforts but her unique body that resolves the conflict. Unable to act intentionally, she accidentally stumbles while fleeing in the dark, with the Prince in hot pursuit. Has she become a fallen woman, losing that "tiny receptacle into which some part of the body can slip and fit tightly?" asks Bettelheim.[29] With such marvelous erotic imagery, it is not surprising that this tale has survived for 1,000 years! As a vaginal symbol, the shoe is always made of glass or gold so that it cannot "stretch to fit another." (Glass also shatters, like a virgin's hymen.) Cinderella's childlike foot symbolizes purity and uniqueness. No other woman has one quite like it, the perfect size for this prince. Notice how one part of the female body becomes symbolic of the entire woman. Cinderella's beauty, innocence, and destiny are embodied in her tiny foot (in the same way that Barbara measured her value in terms of that one special trait).

Objectification and preoccupation with isolated body parts dehumanizes women, but it also degrades men when they become so obsessed with ankles or breasts they forget the person within. Bettelheim suggests that Cinderella would be loved no matter what she looked like. However the story's resolution rests on her foot size. This prince has developed a fetish. So preoccupied is he with finding the right foot that the stepsisters are able to trick him. By slicing down a heel or toe (in Grimm's account), they squeeze into the slipper and therefore into his life. He starts to carry off first one then the other to be wed, but blood is seen through the glass, exposing the sisters as imposters, as bleeding "nonvirgins." Their mutilations are symbolic of castration, for these aggressive women will stop at nothing, even cutting off flesh, to trap a man. In contrast, when Cinderella puts on the slipper (like a wedding ring), no blood flows. She remains virginal. Sexually passive, she does not threaten a man but waits to be taken by him.

The sexual symbolism of a tiny foot with its elegant slipper reflects the Far Eastern origins of this ancient tale. Crystal or embroidered shoes were often given to Chinese girls in reward for the agony of foot-binding, and to display their most precious body part. A bound foot in its elegant shoe is of course *the* classic example of the high price demanded by the myth of female beauty.

Fairy tales always end happily. Though we never know whether Cinderella loves the Prince (or whether he is even lovable), we believe in happiness ever after. The perfect fit of the shoe symbolizes her willingness to shape her life around his. However, the slipper can also be seen as a symbol of bondage. By conforming to the tiny dimensions of the feminine role, she is no longer free to grow. A pathetically stunted foot, the smallest in the land, is really only fit for a doll's life.

We are all fed a gourmet diet of Cinderella sagas and Miss America pageants, in which passivity is richly rewarded and beauty transformations buy security and love. As women now strive toward independence, there lingers the longing for a prince whose life can be slipped into and who can lift the burden of shaping one's own destiny. Colette Dowling calls this dilemma the "Cinderella Complex." Those of us suffering from this syndrome, she says, vacillate between the wish to achieve an authentic identity and the temptation to hold back and let a man confer one on us. Dowling believes that the unconscious wish to remain dependent prevents us from moving ahead in life. "We have been taught to believe that as females we cannot stand alone, that we are too fragile, too delicate, and too needful of protection," writes Dowling.[30] Like Cinderella, we wait for something external to change our lives. In effect, our feet feel too small to fill the shoes of a full-grown person. Like Cinderella, we stumble in our efforts to step out into the world, and like her, we turn to beauty transformations as a defense against unhappiness.

But the Cinderella Complex is not only reflected in ambivalence over independence. It is etched in a woman's flesh as well, from her reshaped nose to her frosted smile and platformed feet. Dowling describes the cosmetic disguise as a "counter phobic facade." aressed up in an exterior of assertive self-confidence, many women remain internally vulnerable and self-doubting. Though looking powerfully beautiful, they feel essentially powerless. They are like Barbara who, at age fifteen, offered her pretty little foot and her nice high arch as the things she valued most in herself.

Women yearn for recognition. Uncertain of their place in the world, they struggle to determine what they want and more basically who they are. Attempts to attract attention through props and paint are part of this longing for confirmation of worth. Women are shouting, "Look at me, not through me. Acknowledge my presence." The Cinderella Complex translates into a mandate for beauty transformations. These further increase dependency by diverting a woman's energy, depleting her resources, and diminishing her self-esteem.

4

Acting and Attracting

Women have served all these centuries as looking glasses possessing the magic and delicious power of reflecting the figure of man at twice its natural size. . . . If she begins to tell the truth, the figure in the looking glass shrinks.

— Virginia Woolf[1]

B EAUTY enhances the power of women even while diminishing it. As a primary source of social influence, appearance is paradoxically a major cause of female weakness. Males and females experience and express power differently. Aggressive action is considered masculine and consequently unfeminine. The use of direct overt power tends to masculinize a woman, whereas it is lack of strength that feminizes a man. Beauty, not dominance, is woman's domain. For signals of power are confounded with signals of gender, creating a dominance hierarchy that rests on sex differences. As women learn to channel energy into being seen rather than into being strong, attracting becomes a substitute for acting.

Power can take many forms: the capacity to implement ideas, to command attention, to act autonomously, to compel obedience. It involves subtle dynamics based on people's perceptions of each other and on the resources they control. Studies indicate that men and boys consider themselves more powerful than women and girls. Males are more concerned with controlling others and more likely to take a dominant role when dealing with females.[2] When college students were asked to name the most powerful person they knew, over half the subjects of both sexes named their fathers. In contrast, only 2 percent of the men and 16 percent of the women named their mothers.[3] Analysis of media images indicates that males are generally portrayed as active and authoritative, while females are portrayed as attractive and submissive. Such images both reflect and influence the prevailing social standards.

Leaders must look the part as well as act it, for leadership depends on recognition by others. Stereotypes of how men differ from women are almost identical to stereotypes of how leaders differ from followers. Leadership is associated with expertise, independence, and assertiveness, qualities that are judged to be more masculine than feminine.

A dominant man of high-status may relate to lower-ranking men in much the same manner as he relates to women—ordering the drinks, picking up the check, controlling the conversation. If a woman takes over such activities when a man is present, she signals power, in effect, by adopting "masculine" behavior. The perceived status of males is rated as consistently higher than that of females. Consequently, those women who do manage to acquire and to use certain forms of power find themselves in a position of "status incongruity." Their high-power rank conflicts with the lower status of the feminine role.[4]

A dual system of power has been distinguished in animal behavior.[5] First, the agonic mode, which involves threat or direct use of force. Agonic power has aggressive overtones. It typically leads to fight-or-flight reactions. Second, the hedonic mode, which involves indirect or covert influence. Hedonic power is often achieved through display. By becoming more conspicuous, flashing bright colors, dancing, howling, or somehow exhibiting oneself, an animal or person can command attention and take over a situation. A cheerleader, for example, controls the spectators hedonically by charming them with song and dance. In contrast, the football player dominates the rival team agonically by hitting hard. (Cheerleaders add color and help sell tickets, but they have little influence over the game's outcome.) Agonic power is commonly enhanced through weaponry, while hedonic power is enhanced through adornment.

One important effect of the beauty myth is to shift hedonic

power into the feminine role. Studies indicate that the exercise of direct power by women continues to be seen as disruptive and illegitimate in most cultures.[6] In fact, females are subtly distinguished as either good or bad according to the forms of power that they employ. Agonic power threatens femininity and is therefore associated with ugly, bad women: dangerous witches, castrating bitches, homely "libbers." Such women act aggressively (agonically) and therefore unattractively. In contrast, hedonic power modes enhance femininity and are associated with beautiful, virtuous women, or glamourous seductive ones.

In *Women, Men, and the Psychology of Power*, Hilary Lips explains that agonic power flows from sources not readily available to females—physical strength, education, money, and expertise. She adds that women often lack either the legal rights or the self-confidence to use such resources effectively. Since males and females differ in their access to power, they approach the process of social influence from contrasting points. Men generally start from a stronger position and therefore use economic or physical force more readily; women usually start from a weaker position and so turn to indirect forms of control such as charm, dependency, or love withdrawal. Reviewing the research, Lips concludes that the power derived from "attractiveness, charisma and personal magnetism" is readily available to women and that only in these areas does women's power equal or exceed men's. Consequently, beauty and hedonic display, rather than direct assertion, become primary sources of female strength. Lips notes further that although women have rarely achieved high positions in business or politics, they frequently reach top levels in the performing arts, where good looks often are an essential component of success.[7]

The modes of power a person uses affect how powerful he or she feels. Since hedonic power often goes unacknowledged or is deemed manipulative and so is mistrusted, it does little to enhance the user's status or confidence. Heavy reliance on beauty and charm can leave a person feeling insecure even after success. Moreover, a modest, self-effacing attitude is encouraged in women, which further deprives them of feeling responsible for their own achievements. Hedonic power strategies contribute the least to self-esteem, and these are precisely the ones most readily available to women, concludes Lips.

Feeling powerful and feeling good about oneself are closely connected. Confidence in one's potency bolsters ego strength. Socialized to use indirect modes, women may fail to recognize agonic modes of power (such as authority or money) as being essential to maintaining their self-esteem. Having relatively little direct power to begin with, females tend to deny its value and unconsciously abdicate it to others. They fear direct action and hesitate to use it.

If a woman equates the power to act with masculinity, then it becomes difficult for her to use such power without feeling ambivalent. She will turn instead to hedonic modes of influence, even when these are inappropriate or ineffective. She may cry, go on a diet, change her clothes, or powder her nose instead of demanding a raise or hiring a lawyer. Consider the following scene from Nora Ephron's novel *Heartburn:* "I'm suggesting that you make a wild and permanent gesture of size," said Richard, "and mine was to ask you to marry me. . . . Yours can be anything you want." She replied, "The only wild and permanent gesture of size that has ever crossed my mind is to have my hair cut."[8] Women learn repeatedly that direct, self-initiated action is viewed with suspicion; that it may lead to social rejection, economic reprisal, or even a label of neurosis (such as "masculinity complex").

The following case illustrates the kinds of problems that arise from conflicts over the use of direct power in controlling others. Emily sought therapy because she felt unable to cope with her son. She described Bobby as "a loud, active, and stubborn four-year-old who is very tough . . . much stronger than I am . . . a real powerhouse." Unable to get him to bathe or go to bed on time, she was clearly dominated by him and felt quite helpless. "Bobby's all boy. Loud, rough, constantly moving and fighting. . . . I often wish I'd had a daughter instead," she admitted. "I think I could have handled a quiet little girl much better." Notice how stereotypes of dominant males and passive females influence the mother-child relationship, making it hard for some women to believe they have the strength or the right to take charge of a demanding male—even one who is only four years old.

When asked how she felt about power, Emily said she rarely thought of people in terms of it and was uncomfortable using it. Power conflicted with her concept of a close mother-child bond.

In this case, ambivalence over power led to a sense of ineffectiveness as a parent. At the same time, Emily was a competent and successful saleswoman who was ambitiously undertaking a new career. Always fashionably dressed, she had her hair done several times a week. While still in her thirties, she had cosmetic surgery to "get rid of those little eye lines." The hedonic modes of power—attractiveness, seduction, charm, which she successfully used in her work and in her marriage—proved of little value with her son.

In therapy, Emily explored how her perceptions of Bobby as an aggressive, dominant male and of herself as a passive female influenced her feelings as a mother. She gradually realized that Bobby really was not bigger, stronger, or tougher than she was. By acknowledging her legitimate need for privacy and rest, and by accepting her right to assert direct control, she was able to set limits on her son's behavior. Slowly she regained her position as the strong parent he needed. However, as Bobby grew older and bigger, Emily experienced continued difficulty in retaining her image of herself as a potent mother.

Size and strength certainly influence social power. American men are about 7 percent taller and 30 percent stronger than women. The dimorphism in size places females in the deferential position of looking up to males, as an inferior looks up to a superior or as a child looks up to an adult. To stand above confers an inherent power advantage.

Emily once vacationed in Arizona, where Bobby was given a pair of high-heeled Western boots and a cowboy hat for his birthday. Dressed as a classy macho dude, he gained several inches of illusory height. Seeing the peak of his hat level with the top of her head, Emily felt a subtle shift in the dynamics between them.

Big females and little males are socially mismatched. During adolescence, tall girls may slouch in order to look less imposing. Tall women seek "appropriately" taller mates and report feeling not only awkward but also vaguely guilty about undermining men's rightful place "above them." Susan Brownmiller describes her reactions when face to face with a shorter man:

> Even though I'm not quite five feet six, a lucky size for feminine appearance, I usually feel lumbering in relation to a smaller man.

The familiar ratios are out of kilter; the level of eye contact is oddly reversed. Perhaps with an unwitting, forceful gesture I might accidentally tip him over. I suffer for his shortness and feel guilty for the unalterable fact of my height. I slouch, I twist, I tilt my head. I reach into my little bag of feminine tricks, anything to diffuse my apparent solidity, my relative strength.[9]

The Prince and Princess of Wales are nearly the same height. As we can see in their engagement photograph, taken on the steps of Buckingham Palace, he was placed one step above her, creating the illusion of a more dominant-looking figure. Imagine a reverse pose, with him a step below, his head nestled in her neck.

The more successful a person is, the taller he or she is judged to be, and conversely, tall people are assumed to be more successful than short people. Short men are treated more like subordinates and also more like women. Lacking "stature," they too are physically touched more often and passed over for leadership positions. While the psychological burden suffered by short males is well recognized, the effect of being smaller on women's sense of social power has generally been overlooked.

Animal research confirms that male dominance in primates derives partly from sex differences in size, strength, and aggressive tendencies. In species where sexual dimorphisms are extensive, there tends to be greater dominance asymmetry. Human power hierarchies stem from similar underlying biological factors but become modified or exaggerated through culture. Margaret Mead reported that societies with minimal aggression also have minimal sex typing, while societies that encourage aggression have the most male dominance and the greatest gender-role divergence. (It seems that competitive cultures subordinate the weak, which usually includes women.) Cosmetic rituals that increase dimorphisms therefore tend to increase gender differences in the dominance hierarchy.

For example, fashions that enhance feminine beauty often alter women's physical proportions. Hairstyle and clothing can create the illusion of a more dominant figure or a more diminutive one. High heels elevate females to new levels of importance, and a woman who wears flats finds herself coming up short, not only to most men but also to well-heeled women who look down on her. Wedding gowns with lengthy trains, feathered hats, and billowing petticoats all stretch apparent size and aggrandize appearance. However fashions that confer the power of added size nearly always inhibit movement. A gain in the hedonic power of display is generally offset by a loss in the agonic power to act.

Moreover, the beauty ideal frequently requires women to reduce certain proportions (illustrated by the photograph of Marilyn Monroe wearing a corset). A three-inch foot, an eighteen-inch waist, a one-hundred-pound body, have each been admired at one time or other as the epitome of feminine beauty. Fear of castration and of impotence causes men endless doubts about their size. (Male genitals can never be too big, just as Cinderella's foot could never be too small.) Corseted waists, girdled hips, narrowed feet, diet-bound bodies, help create "his little woman." Of course, a constricted body in turn dictates an equally constricted life.

Status hierarchies have been called the vertical dimension of human relations. When Stokely Carmichael proclaimed the correct position for women in the civil rights movement as "prone," he was describing not only a sexual posture but the proper place of any subordinate, looking up from lower down in the social system. To walk tall is to convey confidence; to stoop indicates insecurity. We speak of reaching new heights or of coming up short; feeling upbeat or beaten down; rising to the occasion or lowering oneself.

Bowing and kneeling are gestures of respect that acknowledge subordination. The high-society debutante meets the ultimate challenge of hedonic display by performing the grand curtsy. As reported in the *New York Times*, "A Texas debutante in a long white gown, with a gold-embroidered sunburst on the bodice and carrying a bouquet of red roses, approaches the spotlight, bends her right knee, lowers herself gingerly to the floor and to the collective holding of breaths gracefully executes the Dallas court bow."[10] (This in 1984.) Like Cinderella's stepsisters, the debutante has spent weeks perfecting the bow's graceful execution. Costumed as a pseudo-bride, a debutante prostrates herself before society in a humble gesture of feminine submission, then smiles up from her position below.

The many parallels between nonverbal gestures of gender and those of power are explored in Nancy Henley's book, *Body Politics*. Henley explains that signals of femininity often are tantamount to those of submission, whereas signals of masculinity are equivalent to those of dominance. For example, women as well as other subordinates tend to break eye contact as a sign of submission, while men and other dominants are more likely to continue to stare. Dominants command greater territory, while subordinates back away to make room for them. Likewise, women yield public space more quickly than men, stepping aside when someone walks directly toward them on the street. Larger people can dominate a situation simply by taking over more room. Men tend to sit sprawled out in a commanding position; women and subordinates typically adopt postures that are more constricted and take up less space.[11]

These are just a few of the many examples of "status identifiers" cited by Henley which serve as the nonverbal equivalents of "Yes, sir." Status identifiers clearly overlap with gender identifiers to maintain power differences between the sexes. Henley cautions that if we ascribe difference in nonverbal behavior (such as choice of clothing and hairstyle, or posture and gait) to "sex roles alone" without considering the power factors that underlie them, we are likely to miss their full meaning.

When subordinates (females) do try to adopt direct power gestures, they may be subjected to so-called taming strategies. For instance, if a woman sends a signal of dominance, it may be consciously or unconsciously misread in order to temper its meaning. Her aggressive stare may be interpreted as a sexual invitation. Or she may be told in the middle of an argument that she looks cute when she's mad, or that her mascara is running. She can be trivialized and effectively disarmed of dominance gestures when they are reinterpreted as signs of femininity, explains Henley. Such taming strategies are likely to inhibit her from future attempts to dominate.

On the other hand, a woman sometimes gets away with audacious acts by embedding them in the trappings of adornment, which is one reason feminine beauty serves as a useful source of power. For example, high heels, which bring her eye-to-eye with a man, makes staring more effective. Or the jangle of bracelets and the flash of diamonds can continuously intrude her presence, even though she knows better than to interrupt verbally.

Status hierarchies are maintained as much by the appeasement signals of subordinates as by the aggressive gestures of dominants. Those who are or who feel weaker cannot risk being attacked, so they must send clear messages of "no offense." A gesture of appeasement translates into an appeal for peace. Woman's ubiquitous smile is a classic appeasement gesture, sometimes called the feminine version of the "Uncle Tom shuffle." Research shows that women do smile more than men, especially when they are angry.[12] Putting on a smile is as natural to a woman as putting on makeup. When a man calls out "Hey babe, give us a smile," he is asking not only for a flash of femininity but for one of deference as well. And a splash of bright lipstick gives this appeasement gesture added potency even from afar.

Beauty transformations serve to amplify gestures of submission. Makeup, fashion, and footwear all confirm that a female knows her proper role and is ready to play it. When used as a signal of appeasement, cosmetic adornment becomes self-protective body language, a disarming defense. Winston Churchill once remarked that "it is hard if not impossible to snub a beautiful woman—she remains beautiful and the rebuke recoils." Female executives report that they consciously use a variety of visual and verbal strategies to temper signals of status and to reduce the real threat of their high rank. Some admit they actively try to convey deference, helplessness, and even motherliness through clothes, posture, and voice tone. Their goal is to put people at ease and especially to help men feel comfortable, despite the actual reversal in the power hierarchy.[13] These softening touches camouflage agonic power behind a facade of feminine deference.

Feminized beauty dresses appeasement gestures in lace panties, pink angora sweaters, and strapless sandals. These not only convey a helpless look but may actually create a helpless person, both physically and psychologically. In time, subordinate behavior, whether real or contrived, eventually produces a habitual sense of internal vulnerability. Describing the psychological conversion of a transsexual, Jan Morris calls such adaptations the "symptoms of womanhood."

The more I was treated as a woman, the more woman I became. I adapted willy nilly. If I was assumed to be incompetent at reversing cars or opening bottles, oddly incompetent I found myself

becoming. . . . I discovered that even now men prefer women
to be less informed, less able, less talkative, and certainly less self-
centered than they are themselves; so I generally obliged them. . . .
I know it is nonsense, but I cannot help it.[14]

Decorated and displayed like a doll, a person begins to feel internally helpless. What starts as posturing and pretense soon feels
automatic and authentic.

These are precisely the strategies recommended in such best-
sellers as Marabel Morgan's *The Total Woman* or Helen Andelin's
Fascinating Womanhood, which sold millions of copies in the past
two decades (even while feminism flourished). In essence, these
are cookbooks for cultivating signals of subordination.

If you are a large, tall or strong woman, you will have to work to
disguise these features so men will see you as little and delicate.
No matter what your size . . . you can appear fragile to a man
if you follow certain rules. . . . It is not important that you
actually be little and delicate, but that *you seem so* to the man. . . .
Get rid of an air of strength, ability, competence or fearlessness,
and instead try to develop an attitude of frail dependency so that
men will want to take care of you . . . and if you are efficient
and capable in masculine things you will have to "unlearn" these
traits.[15]

Note the paradox of climbing onto a pedestal to gain power by
perfecting the art of signaling submission. Dependency is a useful
and available source of strength for someone who feels cut off
from other more direct power modes. Most women are, in fact,
smaller, weaker, and poorer, with lower earning capacity and less
authority than their mates. Moreover, they are rewarded from
early childhood for using hedonic display rather than agonic action. The following section looks at feminine clothing, hair, and
shoe styles as power signals that alter human relations.

Tresses and Dresses: The Long and Short of It

Never shall a young man,
Thrown into despair
By those great honey-coloured
Ramparts at your ear,
Love you for yourself alone
And not your yellow hair.

— W.B. Yeats[16]

Hair serves as a source of hedonic power that can be used to attract attention. Barbara, the troubled adolescent who was discussed in the previous chapter, arrived for therapy one day quite upset, her head covered with a scarf. It seems that her boyfriend had acquired a taste for blondes and had threatened to break up with her unless she dyed her hair. Willing to do almost anything to hold on to him, Barbara cut school and tried to bleach her black hair a brassy gold. "It's hideous and Mark hated it," she wept, unveiling the sad results. Then, in the next breath, she completely forgave him, explaining how embarrassed he would feel to be seen with her when she looked so awful. "If only my hair had turned out better," she rationalized, "I know he'd still love me." Like many women, Barbara had turned to the magic power of a new hairdo to salvage a faltering relationship, only to end up feeling unsightly and unlovable. Searching for a source of strength, she was left sadly weakened.

When it is highly styled and ritualized, hair heightens the hedonic power of display but also causes insecurity and self-consciousness. The burden of tending to a glamourized head weighs most heavily on the shoulders of females. What's *on* a woman's head may be judged as critically as what's *in* it—which explains why nearly half of every dollar spent on beauty goes toward hair care, as females work to crown themselves the fair sex.

Hair piled high adds height and therefore power. Whether coiled in a nest of braids, wound in a round chignon, teased into a beehive, or gelled into space-age spikes, feminine hair styles swell the head and stack on stature, as shown in the photo of Farrah Fawcett. In the days of Marie Antoinette and Madame de

"I could never turn myself into a beautiful woman," remarked Dustin Hoffman after he appeared in the film *Tootsie*. "I was a 4 or maybe a 6...and I couldn't get used to it—having men meet me, say hello and immediately start looking over my shoulder to find some more attractive woman to talk to."

Sixteen-year-old Margaret Gorman, the first Miss America (1921), poses in a swimsuit and flat heels. Her ample costume easily conceals any underlying flaws.

A model displays the string bikini, which first appeared in 1974. Note her high heels and her slim proportions compared to the first Miss America. Current fashions are so revealing that women are forced into surgery or chronic dieting to remold flesh that in times past was laced into corsets or hidden under petticoats.

Demonstrators picket at the Miss America Pageant in 1968. This public rally launched a new wave of feminist reform in the United States and rekindled the age-old controversy between fashion and feminism.

Vanessa Williams, Miss America of 1984, discovered that a fine line divides the legitimate display of beauty from the illegitimate display of pornography. The demands of beauty and the taboos of pornography require a balancing act that often throws women off balance as admiration turns into exploitation.

The wedding gown, with its grand but cumbersome proportions, illustrates the power and constraint of women's clothing.

A 1985 fashion designer presents the bride of the future. During the twentieth century, women's legs were liberated from the lengthy skirts that had hobbled them for centuries. But as the hemlines rose, so did the value and vulnerability of the naked leg.

The first time Lady Diana Spencer appeared in public with Prince Charles, she was caught by photographers holding up the front of her black strapless gown. Feminine fashions often create precarious moments when women feel hampered or overexposed.

Even before they reach school age, children clearly know that being pretty is an important part of being female. Little girls like these are being rated for their beauty, charm, poise, and personality.

Thirty-nine-year-old Diane Atkinson holds her trophy along with her grandson, having just won the "Most Glamorous Grandmother" contest at Coney Island.

1ough the majority of young women say they feel dissatisfied with their ·earance, the number of participants in beauty contests has been increasing 1 year. On the average, contest winners are tall, blue-eyed, and under nty-two years of age.

Adorned as a pseudo-bride, this debutante executes the deep court bow. She prostrates herself before society in an elegant but humble gesture of submission.

Debutante balls are making a comeback in the 1980s. Adolescent girls often feel conflicted between a desire for social approval and a need for achievement, which creates a fear of success. Cosmetic rituals help pull them safely back onto feminine ground.

The Dallas Cowboys' cheerleaders provide an attractive foreground for the real action, which takes place on the playing field beyond. They convey the message that good-looking girls belong one step out of bounds, cheering the guys on to victory.

Pompadour, women's hairdos reached such ridiculous heights that cartoonists depicted birds nesting on top of them.

Historically, both men and women have worn elaborate coiffures as a uniform of rank. Ancient Egyptian rulers shaved their heads, then covered them with towering hairpieces. In the eighteenth century, wealthy men owned as many wigs as women did and set them in elaborate styles. English judges still preside with the authority of their weighty wigs. But the ornate hairdos that were once a status symbol for both sexes are now linked primarily with feminine beauty. For most of the twentieth century, western men have worn their hair short and simple. This asymmetry in fashion perpetuates the myth of female beauty, linking signals of gender with those of hedonic power.

One third of American women dye their hair. Just as many visit a salon every week. The hair appointment serves as a landmark on the calendar, a ritual that precedes almost every important life event. To be well dressed requires dressing one's head. Hairdressers and clients alike regard a pretty hairdo as a prime virtue, essential for social success. In a study of the attitudes of beauticians, not one of them ever questioned the value or meaning of the beautification process.[17]

Hair care represents a major investment, one that must be protected from sun, sweat, wind, water . . . and the disarray of passion. Glamourized hair drains power even while conferring it. The annual cost of maintaining a platinum blonde, professionally styled each week, can run into thousands. Hair care is sometimes painful as well as expensive. Women who wear their heavy hair pinned up suffer headaches and sigh in relief when they can let it down. Long-haired little girls remain dependent much longer on others to keep them well groomed. Flowing hair can block vision, like a pair of blinders. In the 1930s, when Veronica Lake popularized the peek-a-boo cut that cascaded over one eye, accident rates soared as loose hair got caught in machinery. This problem is illustrated by the photo of the young athlete who is veiled by her long hair.

Shorn short, men are spared the endless daily struggle with a dead issue . . . the clips, pins, curling irons, bands, bows, rollers, nets, lotions for wetting and setting, sprays for holding and molding. The hedonic power of luxurious hair is mainly reserved for females as a sexual lure and a status symbol. On men, long hair is considered effeminate. No politician or corporate executive can risk having it. In the 1960s, pony-tailed male hippies were expelled from schools as a threat to decorum; and long before then, in the 1660s, Harvard had prohibited the wearing of "long locks and foretops . . . and the use of curling, crisping or powdering." Religious fundamentalists consider it a "deformity against God" and cite the biblical injunction that "the Lord hath forbidden long hair unto men". Judeo-Christian tradition warns of the femme fatale whose seductive curls are a special obstacle which God placed in man's way. Wives were thus required to veil this dangerous temptation. Orthodox Jewish women still cover their hair after marriage.

Letting hair down means freeing inhibitions and sharing intimacies. To undo one's hair is to come undone, for loose hair may signal a loose woman, (as the photograph of Cher suggests). Rapunzel hung down her tresses to haul in a lover, while the sexually repressed Victorian wife slept with a tightly coiled braid. Hindu brides were chosen for their long locks (just as Chinese brides were selected for their small feet).

Long hair on little girls represents childish innocence as well as feminine glamour. Fathers reportedly pressure wives into keeping their daughters' hair long. They describe the pleasure of seeing, touching, playing with it. Long hair thus enhances the Oedipal attachment by providing a sensuous bond between father and daughter.

One patient who is over forty admits that during most of her adult life she straightened her kinky hair before going to visit her rather proper high-society father. He never failed to compliment her nice hairdo or to criticize her when she left it naturally curly. This woman recently stopped straightening her hair for daddy and realized that she was finally ready to live without her father's approval.

Another woman recounts a childhood struggle for permission to cut off the babyish braids that her father adored. At age twelve, with one swift stroke, Jane dramatically declared a new stage of independence. Thirty years later, Jane's father recounted to her his shock at seeing her as a short-haired rebellious adolescent whom he somehow never felt as close to again. This case illustrates how hair as a sexual symbol can carry a growing girl first toward and then away from her father. Jane again cut her long hair just prior to divorce. By separating from her hair as she had in child-hood, she unconsciously severed her dependency on her husband, who loved it. Using the power invested in hair as a beauty symbol, women attach themselves to men and can then "wash men out of their hair," or "cut men out of their lives."

Since long hair symbolizes sexuality, cutting it back can be used to renounce the traditional feminine role. During the 1920s, women agonized over whether to bob, and husbands threatened to divorce them if they did. Guthrie lists "suffragettes, flappers, lesbians, nuns and high-powered business women" as examples of short-haired rebels.[18] Until the sixties, very short hair was still a sign of liberation or tomboyishness. Even today career women are advised to wear their hair neither too long nor too short, neither too curly nor too straight, thus reducing the connotations of gender, power, and sexuality associated with extremes of hair style.

Hair can provide a great deal of sensuous pleasure. Fondling or brushing it gives the same kind of tactile joy as petting a cat or snuggling up in mink. Among primates, tending fur is an important grooming ritual that creates social bonds between troop members. Hair care provides good strokes and an excuse for intimacy. A hairdresser is not merely a technician but a friend who delivers loving care and reassurance. Cropped close, men miss many of these pleasures. Their hair lacks the power of glam-our, the status of added height, the sexual allure of flowing move-ment, the novelty of variety. Rinsed in style, feminized hair gains an extra coat of erotic strength. Does the gain in women's power balance the loss? That depends. Most women choose to pay a certain price for the pleasure they derive. For feminine hair is also great fun. A brand new hairdo can lift the spirits better than almost anything—except perhaps a new dress.

Dressed to Kill

Female beauty has been hung on a clothesline of fashion. As a signal of gender and power, clothing is as important in defining woman's world as the body beneath it. Despite the apparent caprices of designers, fashion is not really arbitrary. Experts ad-vise us to dress for success because clothes convey authority, competence, and rank. They channel activity into proper masculine or feminine patterns, as seen for example in the seductive gait of the high-heeled lady. "Clothes make the man" is not merely a cliché. "It is clothes that wear us, and not we them," wrote Virginia Woolf. Each new wave of feminism includes some aspect of dress reform, for a woman's role is costumed and dictated by her robes.

Gender distinctions in clothing have such a long tradition that we take them for granted as being natural and desirable. The Bible decrees that "woman shall not wear that which pertaineth unto a man, neither shall a man put on a woman's garment."[19] Sumptuary laws that were designed to preserve class privilege sometimes required women to wear more clothes to demonstrate modesty, sometimes fewer clothes to indicate subordination.

Ever since the end of the eighteenth century, when western males gave up most forms of decorative display, their clothes have generally been dark, drab, and simply cut. Culture dresses one sex in hot pinks, the other in navy blues. Loosely fitted trousers allow men free movement; broad-shouldered jackets convey strength and substance. Individuality is underplayed, and there is a dull sameness about a group of businessmen all draped in professional drag. Since changes occur more slowly in men's styles than in women's and are relatively minor when they do occur, men's clothes do not make them appear instantly obsolete each season.

In contrast, fashions for women are more colorful and more frivolous. Transparent fabrics like silk and chiffon sensuously display the female body as soft and fragile. Greater variety of color and style allows women to put on a whole new image each day. Novelty fuels interest, thereby conferring hedonic power. Rapid changes in fashion also reflect cultural ambivalence over woman's proper role.

Sex differences in clothing tend to be greatest at times when gender roles are also separate. For example, the stark black-and-white contrast of bride and groom symbolizes the role divergence of husband and wife. The greater amount spent on adorning the bride attests to the greater importance of female appearance. In a culture quite impoverished of rites and rituals, the wedding gown remains a singular relic. One of the last ceremonial robes left to us, it is an elegant example of the power and constraint of female clothing. In my own case,

> I spent the last few months of college working on my wedding dress. My bridal fantasies were first outlined on paper, then lovingly cut from the antique lace train of my mother's marriage gown. For months I sewed and dreamed through classes while the future groom studied surgical techniques. The dress began to embody the event, a kind of beauty pageant with me the sole contestant. Washed in white and sterile as snow, I arrived at my wedding and melted down the aisle in the christening robe of a newborn wife. Long and full, it framed me larger than life. With the measured steps of a bound-footed bride, I awkwardly trailed it behind. One false move and I was undone. Modestly shrouded in illusion lace, I witnessed the ceremony through a white cloud, waiting like a newly poured statue to be unveiled.

A bridal gown is often a woman's costliest garment—her once-in-a-lifetime investment in a moment of glory. It can become a media event, first kept secret, then photographed from every angle, next described in detail on the society pages, and finally passed on to heirs. Its proportions are huge, as seen in the illustration of Princess Diana on her wedding day. Bound and veiled in lace, infused with the show-stopping power of Cinderella at the ball, a bride is crowned queen for a day.

Conflicts between modesty and mobility, between revealment and concealment, remain central issues in women's fashions. Concealment increases the hedonic power of the hidden part, but generally reduces agonic power by inhibiting movement. On the other hand, clothes that are highly revealing frequently permit freer action but increase vulnerability (as breast or thigh comes into view). Street harassment, for instance, escalates in the spring, when coats are shed and bodies move more freely.

Erogenous zones constantly shift between ankle, neck, and hair. As one area is uncovered, another is covered up. Taboos of concealment can complicate even the simplest activity. Victorian women wore gloves both indoors and out. The covered hand (like the bound foot) signaled leisure even while requiring it. Victorian gowns had such tight sleeves that lifting the arm was almost impossible.

The first time Lady Diana Spencer appeared in public with Prince Charles, she was caught by photographers holding up the front of her black strapless gown as she bent forward to step from a car. Moments later she was seen tripping over its hem while climbing a steep staircase. Here was a sexy Cinderella, as shown in that photograph, losing her modesty along with her footing in full view of the camera. These kinds of precarious moments are produced by the trappings of fashions; they render women vulnerable and thereby grant men an opportunity for gallantry. A prince to the rescue first requires a princess in distress, one who needs to be helped out of cars, up stairs or into chairs. Men commonly direct women's movements, steering them gently but firmly across streets and through doorways. The withdrawal of such gallantries at critical moments can poignantly remind a woman of her real helplessness.

For instance, a patient related the following incident with her husband:

> All week I had been trying to talk with Jim about the trust fund. Finally on Saturday night as we drove to the city I managed to say some of the things on my mind. At first he was very defensive, but then he just gave me the angry silent treatment. After we parked he started walking rapidly ahead of me to the theatre. I was already very upset over Jim's reaction but found myself slipping along the icy sidewalk in a long dress and heels. I was furious at him for walking so fast that I couldn't keep up. It was as if he abandoned me. . . . But I also felt quite helpless and realized how much I needed him to lean on.

Women often experience the interplay between psychological and sartorial powerlessness, though they may not always recognize the connection. A therapist who is using dreams to help women become more aware of their feelings of vulnerability has found an interesting theme emerging from dream analysis. Women of all socioeconomic levels report being tripped, hampered, and restricted by the clothes they wear in their dreams.[20]

Clothing conceals flaws and creates illusions. To drape beauty over one's body is easier than refashioning the body itself. Current styles are so revealing that women must turn to surgery or chronic dieting to mold flesh that in former times was more easily laced into corsets or hidden under petticoats and veils, (as illustrated by the first Miss America's bathing suit, compared with a contemporary version). The freedom to wear a mini-bikini or a skin-tight tank suit feels liberating only to someone with a skin-tight body. In *The Psychology of Clothes*, John Carl Flügel concludes that greater freedom and flexibility in women's fashions during this century have produced a loss along with a gain. "In asserting her right as a human being, woman has lost some of the erotic privilege which she formerly enjoyed in virtue of her specific femininity," he writes. "There has been an accentuation of the body rather than of clothes, an idealization of youth rather than of maturity, and a displacement of eroticism from the trunk to the limbs."[21]

For a thousand years men have worn garments with a divided leg that allows free movement. During that millennium, women's legs have been hidden and hampered by skirts that until this century reached to the ground. Long garments do increase power through stature, and are still worn by judges and clergymen as a symbol of authority. Yet a regal robe, like a peacock's tail, grounds its owner. In one way or other women's skirts have hemmed them in or tripped them up. The Dolly Varden dress of the 1840s had a long train that dragged in the mud. The ballooned crinolines of 1860 were so inflated they could not fit through doorways. The bustle back of 1890 turned sitting into a precarious balancing act. The hobble skirt of 1915 bound the legs in a veritable straitjacket. The pencil-slim version of the 1950s made girdles imperative. The miniskirt of 1970 turned reaching or bending into a grand exposé. The wrap version flies open unpredictably. The ball gown turns stairs into a treacherous challenge. And so forth and so on as reforms in fashion "progress."

Remember that until 1970, women in pants were prohibited both by law and custom from classrooms, restaurants, and offices. Pants still have a masculine connotation, and the trend in the 1980s is back to skirts for business, social, and serious occasions on which women want to signal their proper feminine role. Fashion reforms that initially increase personal freedom and power invariably seem to lead back to some new variation of constraint. Loose pants are liberating but they lack sexual allure. Tight ones are erotic but restrict movement. Jeans, which first stood as a democratic symbol of gender and status equality, today must be both sexy and classy. Tightened up by designers, they can be as restricting as a hobble skirt.

The twentieth century has witnessed the Chinese foot released from its bindings and the western leg freed from its floor-length skirt. A liberated leg is an overt sign of physical, economic, and social power. It proclaims a woman's right to come and go, to run a business, run for office, or run around. Flügel calls the shortened skirt a triumphant gesture of freedom for the modern woman. However, shorter skirts have encouraged a new preoccupation with the limb as a symbol of femininity. As hemlines rose, so did the value and vulnerability of the naked leg.

Toeing the Mark

> We fit our sphere as a Chinese woman fits her shoe, exactly as though God had made both; and yet He knows nothing of either.
>
> — Olive Schreiner, 1883[22]

Nancy Reagan's foot is a size 7A. This vital fact was cited in the *New York Times*, beneath a photo of the shoe she would wear to the 1981 inaugural ball. Two different pairs were fashioned for that gala: "cream-colored satin evening pumps with hand-embroidered crystal beads and rhinestones, and an ivory satin pair with heels encrusted in jewels." Men's feet are not so newsworthy. The president's inaugural footwear goes unreported, for the toes of the commander in chief never twinkle with rhinestones.

Glamourized feet are a classic example of how femininity, beauty, sexuality, and power are fused and then confused. "I don't love you cuz your feets too big," goes an old jazz song. A big-footed clodhopper is considered crude and unattractive, whereas the dainty unblemished foot of an infant is aesthetically pleasing. A small foot is youthful and aristocratic. Imperial families of ancient China began to stamp the female body with permanent proof of gentility. Ladies' feet were first infantilized, then displayed in the satin and pearls of an inaugural slipper. In time, the tiny golden lotus foot (with its deep cleft as shown in the photograph) grew into a new erogenous zone. To touch or smell it was considered an act of great intimacy.

The enhanced erotic power of the bound foot was achieved by concealment as well as by distortion. Only a husband could see or handle this treasured private part. Starting in childhood, girls were taught always to keep their feet covered (just as girls now learn to keep their little chests covered). Prostitutes were concealed behind screens with only their shoes visible to the customers, who made choices based on shoe size. Concubines were selected at "tiny foot festivals" that were similar to our modern beauty contests. Beauty was culturally compressed into this one body part, which acquired such power that it could confirm or negate a woman's total attractiveness.

Well-bound feet were essential in the economics of nuptial exchange: the smaller the foot, the greater its value. A tiny foot could compensate for an ugly face, but nothing could make up for an unpruned "goosefoot." As one woman recounts:

> My mother did not feel bad about the pain suffered when my feet were bound. . . . If a girl was plain looking but had small feet, she might still be considered a beauty. If she had large feet . . . no matter how good looking she might be, no one would marry her.[23]

It is hard for us to appreciate how foot size could acquire that much social power. However, once a particular beauty symbol is worshiped as the essence of femininity, nothing can compensate for its absence. Today, a hairy lip or a heavy hip can likewise cancel a woman's erotic appeal. In its current form, the beauty myth still requires women to display their feet in dainty slippers— with spiked heels or open toes. Sensible shoes repudiate the female foot as an erotic object and thereby signal an unerotic woman.

Our modern high heel is a descendant of the platform sandals worn by Venetian whores in the sixteenth century. Today, a well-heeled woman declares her interest in being provocative. Why do high heels work as erotic bait? They lengthen the leg, reshape its contours, thrust out the bosom and the backside. Walking takes on the bump and grind of a chorus girl (which is why beauty contestants parade in the incongruous combination

of swimsuits and high heels). In animals the extended leg is a
sign of sexual availability. High heels create an analogous "courtship strut" that carries the eye toward the pelvis.[24]

High heels enhance hedonic power at the same time that they
render women partially powerless. Here again a cosmetic adornment increases one form of power while decreasing another. The
higher the heel, the greater its power to attract. The higher the
heel, the greater the hell of bunions, corns, twisted ankles, spinal
deformities, and shortened calf muscles. Glamourous shoes cause
pain, and someone in pain is distracted, distempered, and dis-
abled. Half the women in one survey admitted that they wore
painful shoes because the styles look good. The shoes with the
most erotic power are often the most incapacitating. They cause
debilitating side effects such as missing trains and taxis because
running is impossible, carrying extra shoes along for "walking,"
or being left behind when the going gets too rough.

Glamourized feet transform a woman into what she is already
expected to be: a pretty, graceful, passive, dependent, vulnerable
person. Chinese foot binding supported an undisguised ideology
of subjugation. The acknowledged purpose was to prevent women
from freely wandering around. Next to his foot-bound wife, a
man stood firm and felt powerful. One husband commented:

> My memory is not strong. . . . I cut a poor figure. I am timid
> and my voice is not strong among men. But to my footbound wife,
> confined for life to her house except when I bear her in my arms,
> my stride is heroic, my voice is that of a roaring lion, my wisdom
> is of the sages. To her I am the world: I am life itself.[25]

Fashions do change, yet we remain hostage to the tradition of
female subordination. A newly divorced woman admitted, "All
my life I've held back and let my husband take the lead. I felt
safe with him up front and it seemed like my proper place to
follow a few steps behind. Now I have no one to follow and I'm
terrified."

The mutilations of history are meaningful when they shed light
on the present. A traditional Chinese bride spent months em-
broidering dozens of shoes for her trousseau. Elizabeth, whose
beauty obsession was described in the last chapter, owns fifty-
seven pairs of shoes—pumps, boots, sandals, clogs, wedges, and

platforms—in a rainbow of colors. "When it comes to shoes, I have no control," she admits. "It's the one indulgence I feel absolutely no guilt over. Besides, my husband loves me in sexy shoes." Does she need fifty-seven varieties because of his obsession or because of her own? In fact, clinicians report that most fetishists are men, and the commonest fetish is a woman's shoe.

A thousand years of Chinese tradition ended in the early twentieth century, when foot binding was forbidden by decree. How far has western culture come in liberating the female foot? Shoes of the 1980s, with their spiked heels and pointed fronts, are reminiscent of the 1950s, when the little toe was being lopped off to enable women to fit into such styles. Women continue to alter the flesh when the shoe misfits. By binding feet, by molding posture and gait in the contours of fashion, women trade one form of power for another. They relinquish the right and ability to function at full capacity; they learn to move with style rather than with speed or security; and they give away direct power to men, on whom they must then lean for support, thereby legitimizing men's role as protector. In exchange, women gain the masochistic satisfaction of suffering to please others. They enjoy the narcissistic pleasure of looking at their own lovely limbs, silky smooth and seductively shod in satin pumps.

Mobility distinguishes a toddler from an infant; stability and agility are acquired with time. Glamourized feet are clearly regressive. They confound signals of power with those of gender. The power to act is exchanged for the power to attract. With feet bound in crystal beads, females step into a partly sequestered world.

To sequester means to segregate or seclude, as in a menstrual taboo. Oriental wives sometimes sat behind screens, where they could see without being seen. In effect, they were also sequestered by the bindings on their tiny feet, which entwined beauty with forced isolation. In the Middle East, gender and power were similarly interwoven in the fabric of the veil, a fashion that likewise curtained females off.

Moslem women must cover their mouths, like an improper private part. Veiling, like foot binding, began as a status symbol. In time it was "democratically" extended to all women and served to seclude them from public life. A veil that muzzles the mouth

also muffles its sounds. There has been virtually no female influence in hundreds of years of Islamic culture. The feminine
voice has effectively been screened out.

American women still shroud themselves in the white veils of
weddings and the black veils of funerals. Though worn fleetingly,
these ritual remnants symbolize feminine traits that are assumed
to exist continuously: delicacy, modesty, purity, emotionality.
Veils add the power of intrigue, the allure of the hidden and the
forbidden. A face that is blurred behind a veil can be refocused
through a lens of fantasy or magnified through the magic of imagination. Who can forget the Kennedy women, their sorrow tucked
behind their veils, their unseen eyes commanding our own to look
back again and again? Veils are a form of disguise that enhances
a woman's beauty while sequestering her in privacy.

A veil conceals the inner person. It blocks eye contact, encouraging the downcast look of a subordinate. Veils are like myths
that distort vision and foreshorten perspective. Whether veiled
beneath a layer of bridal lace or a layer of cosmetics, females are
psychologically set apart. By distorting a sharp image, the veil of
beauty leads to self-effacement. Woolf observed that the pseu-
donym "Anonymous" was used as a verbal veil by countless female writers for their unsigned work. Others, like George Eliot
and George Sand, used men's names as their mask of anonymity.
"They did homage to the convention that . . . publicity in a
woman is detestable. Anonymity runs in their blood. The desire
to be veiled still possesses them," wrote Woolf.[26] The myth of
female beauty is part of the psychological veil that blocks women
from recognizing their full potential. It diverts them from assertive
action; it camouflages their ambition in artifice; it deflects their
energies into the hedonic mode of power.

Balancing Power

Both agonic and hedonic forms of power are useful. There is
a time and a place for each. When we assign them separately to
the masculine or the feminine role, gender inequality is perpet-
uated. As long as attraction belongs primarily to women and
action primarily to men, strong women will be viewed with sus-

picion, and homely women (along with weak men) will be judged
with contempt. As long as women remain the fair sex, they also
remain the weaker sex.

There is a tendency for people to rationalize existing power
structures as equitable. Dominants convince themselves and others that their status derives from some natural superiority or was
personally merited; subordinates accept inequalities which they
feel helpless to change. But power is, after all, conferred through
human interaction. Just as men serve as a well-primed audience
for female beauty, so women serve to amplify male potency.
Signals of subordination, dressed in fascinating femininity, reassure men of their superior place.

The beauty myth conveniently justifies the prevailing social
order. It encourages females to use attractiveness as a major source
of influence. It encourages males to see and judge women as
aesthetic but passive objects. Clearly, the gestures of gender mimic
the gestures of power. We have seen how feminine beauty transformations simultaneously yield a gain and a loss of strength: the
elegant foot elevates as it anchors; the veiled face seduces as it
sequesters; the glamourized image aggrandizes as it immobilizes.

The power of beauty is real and valuable, but such power
corrupts when it requires physical constraint. It corrupts when
it signals subordination. It corrupts when it creates dependency,
leaving a person vulnerable and insecure. We need to question a
system that so readily rewards women for their long hair and
dainty feet but denies them access to money and authority.

Elizabeth Janeway begins her book, *The Powers of the Weak*,
with the following quote from Karl Marx: "Anyone who knows
anything of history knows that great social changes are impossible
without the feminine ferment. Social progress can be measured
exactly by the social position of the fair sex (the ugly ones included)."[27] Janeway interprets the final parenthetical phrase as
more than a whimsical joke. She sees it as a warning that women
should not depend on the status acquired through their bonds
with important men. Females cannot count on male preference
for pretty women to grant security to women as a group, nor can
they allow male contempt for ugly women to block their ambitions, cautions Janeway. For ultimately the status of women is
not an individual affair. Because privilege is offered so generously

to those with beauty, women have been quick to identify themselves with the pretty ones. Yet the power that good looks bestow
on some cannot compensate for the problems thereby generated
for females as a class, she concludes.[28]

Janeway identifies several factors that maintain powerlessness
among the weak: first, a trivialization of their lives, which con-
vinces the weak that nothing they do or feel is very important;
second, a deep sense of isolation; and finally, a basic lack of
confidence and self-respect. These three "disorders of vision"
combine to form a psychological barrier that keeps the weak in
their place and prevents them from challenging their own subordination, she writes.

The myth of female beauty relates to each of these three factors,
thereby sustaining women in weakness. First, the pursuit of beauty
diverts women's energy into the trivial rituals of body display,
creating feelings of insignificance. Second, it confines women in
a cosmetic world, producing a sense of isolation. Finally, it al-
ienates women from their own bodies, breeding insecurity and
self-rejection.

Achieving a better balance between agonic and hedonic forms
of power would mean a gain in well-being for both sexes. Beauty
is inherently pleasing, ego enhancing, and potentially available
in equal measure to men and women. Males can enjoy the pleasure
of hedonic power as they have in times past—adorning with paint,
decorating with ornaments, displaying themselves in dance as well
as in daring. Women can reduce their heavy reliance on exhibi-
tionism while legitimizing direct power as appropriately feminine—earning degrees, making money, demanding to be heard,
and refusing to comply. Acquiring and using agonic power will
in turn give women a sense of psychological security that tran-
scends appearance.

As females expand their power base beyond the powder room,
one of their greatest challenges will be to resist the masculine goal
of one-upmanship, a goal that can feel as ill-fitting to a woman
as a man-tailored suit. Power need not be used primarily to dominate others but can be used to empower oneself to act assertively.
Integrating beauty with strength, balancing agonic with hedonic
power, will require novel forms of each. As an example, aerobic
dance combines both modes of power through synchronized

movement. It is not a true sport in the traditional masculine sense. There is no score, and there are no winners or losers. Still, as women have popularized this activity to gain physical power and to move harmoniously with others, some men have begun to join in.

In recent years, formal and informal networks of women have identified as their goal not just the personal empowerment of the individual, but also the reciprocal empowerment of others. Gloria Steinem observes that many of us had beautiful mothers, but few of us had mothers who were allowed to act powerfully in the world. Therefore, our mothers could not serve as adequate role models. And so, she suggests, we must now mother each other by mutually creating and conferring the power our mothers could not give us. [29] If we act collectively to shake off the beauty myth as a feminine obligation, and if we stop sanctioning agonic power as a masculine prerogative, then we may have a more solid legacy to pass on to our own children.

Marx suggested that cultural progress can be measured by the social position of plain looking women. If so, there is reason for cautious optimism. The presence of strong women empowered beyond mere beauty has become a catalyst for change. Consequently, men are being challenged to reconsider their position in the power structure and to examine things they formerly took for granted as natural—for instance, choosing the driver's seat or renaming their wives. Neither agonic nor hedonic power is a limited resource. Both are continually generated in limitless quantities through human interaction. As gender myths change and as beauty takes new forms, power constantly shifts. But a shift in power need not mean a loss for one sex and a gain for the other. If power is used to fulfill one's own potential and to empower others to do the same, then everyone stands to benefit as the weak grow stronger—the ugly ones included.

5

Is Anatomy Destiny?

A man may keep his nose to the grindstone, but a woman
had better stop now and again to powder hers.

— Susan Brownmiller[1]

WOMEN'S efforts to reshape their image are entangled with
their efforts to reshape the world. Feminine beauty is so
readily rewarded that it becomes enmeshed with other motives—
for mastery, for security, for self-esteem. Adornment and
achievement are two ends of a seesaw that females ride as they
seek to balance their need for love with their need for work.
Pushing high toward one end, they are too often judged for the
other. Swinging down again, they collide with their own ambitions as well as with their own ambivalence.

Aristotle wrote that "beauty is a greater recommendation than
any letter of introduction." Empirical evidence concerning the
role of attractiveness in the work force is not so clear, however.
Sometimes the power of good looks paves the way for career
success; other times it stands as a roadblock. We know that what
is beautiful is also thought to be good. But the conflict between
beauty and brains in the world of work is still very much alive.

A number of studies do confirm that attractive people are considered more competent and better qualified for certain jobs, and
thus more likely candidates. When pictures were attached to resumés, a woman's projected income rose by as much as 12 percent
if a personnel interviewer was shown a picture after she had
undergone cosmetic make-over, rather than before.[2] Women are

aware that looks are important in the work force, and they try to alter their appearance accordingly. Candidates applying for a research job wore more makeup and jewelry and dressed in more feminine ways when they were told beforehand that the interviewer was a male chauvinist.[3]

Physically attractive people are generally selected over less attractive ones, particularly for jobs considered appropriate for the sex of the candidate. But good looks are less of an asset for someone seeking a job considered inappropriate for her sex. Therefore, a woman who aspires to a high-level executive job may find beauty a liability. Her attractiveness is seen as incompatible with authority, strength, decisiveness—the so-called masculine traits which these kinds of jobs demand. In contrast, pretty women have an advantage when applying for "pink collar jobs" (librarian, secretary), where more "feminine" traits are required.[4] Further studies indicate that attractive women are more likely to be hired for low-level jobs than their less attractive sisters but less likely to be chosen for managerial jobs.[5]

Beauty can be a professional hindrance if it is interpreted as a sexual sign. When voters know nothing about political candidates except what they look like, the more attractive male candidates tend to win votes, whereas the more attractive female candidates tend to lose votes. Good looks in women are equated with sex appeal, whereas good looks in men are associated with kindness.[6] Rarely does a handsome man complain that people ignore his talents because of his looks or that he is tired of being viewed only as a sex object. Such complaints are universal among attractive, aspiring women.

Even when a woman achieves an extremely high position of eminence, one frequently hears "She's so brilliant, capable, talented . . . and beautiful too." Soon after Sandra Day O'Connor was sworn in to the Supreme Court, Chief Justice Warren Burger remarked to waiting photographers, "You've never seen me with a better-looking justice, have you?" The *Washington Post* described the new justice as "an achieving woman without an edge. She is good-looking without being alienatingly beautiful and bright without being alarmingly intellectual."[7] Another paper reported: "Dressed in a tailored violet suit and soft feminine blouse, Mrs. O'Connor struck an even balance of professionalism and femininity." Similar descriptions of a male Supreme Court justice would seem ludicrous. This type of commentary conveys how hard it is to straddle the line between adornment and achievement, between beauty and brains.

Women are judged not only for what they do but especially for how they look while doing it. Historians in past centuries argued that Queen Elizabeth I must have been either a man in disguise or a hermaphrodite, thus explaining her "masculine features" as well as her "masculine mind." Here we have an extreme example of how a powerful woman can literally be "unsexed" by her success. In a similar vein, working mothers were judged in a 1976 study to be "unfeminine and frigid."[8] Moreover, such bias works in both directions. A professional reference for a colleague once described her as "a fine teacher, who has a good rapport with students—who find this attractive rather feminine person an excellent model to emulate." Would she have had less satisfactory rapport with students and been a less desirable role model if she were less attractive or less feminine?

Many writers have described the tormenting conflict felt by talented artists who try to set free their creative powers but are entrapped in the ornamental undertow of the feminine role. For example, Tillie Olsen, who struggled so long to lift the veil of silence from her voice, speaks of:

> The self-doubt . . . questioned by the hours agonizing over appearance; concentration shredded into attracting, being attractive; the absorbing real need and love for working with words felt as a hypocritical self-delusion (I'm not truly dedicated) for what seems (and is) esteemed as being attractive to men.[9]

Erica Jong warns that women artists will continue to feel a deep sense of conflict about their femaleness "as long as femininity is associated with ruffles and flourishes and a lack of directness and honesty . . . for they are never praised without being patronized. Their jacket photographs are reviewed instead of their books." She adds that there are lots of handsome male poets, but no one says, " 'Isn't W. S. Merwin a cutie?' . . . With women they always talk about it. And if a woman's ugly, they harp on that too."[10]

Success remains problematic for a woman when it is experienced as a mixed blessing. How can she comfortably wear its image while still looking and acting attractively feminine? A specialist in career counseling reports that whenever she lectures to women's groups, the question session invariably begins with "What should I wear?" Because the signals of feminine gender and agonic power are incompatible, it is harder for women than it is for men to find clothes that imply serious intent. Rules for women's clothing are more complex than for men's clothing. Candidates groomed in less feminine styles were selected in photos as having a better chance of reaching top management positions.[11] The running shoes commonly worn by female executives as they commute to work imply their desire to win rather than to woo.

Articles in business magazines warn executive women to "avoid frills like the plague and never wear dresses that make nipples apparent through clothing." "The more your clothes wipe out, the better, so tailor your suits to cover any bumps or curves." In essence, conceal evidence of the sexual body beneath. Tailored suits declare, "I'm a V.P. first, a woman second" (much like T-shirts that read, "I'm a lady first, an athlete second"). As women try to dress for success, their suits seem like carbon copies of men's designs. In the 1980s these suits are always skirted, however, perhaps to indicate who still wears the pants. Women are encouraged to imitate but not to take over; to mimic but at the same time to retain certain distinctive signals of feminine rank.

Is it beauty or brains, or the combination of both, that makes women suspect? Marina Verola, a twenty-nine-year-old successful stockbroker, agreed in 1983 to pose for *Playboy* magazine stripped of her pinstripe suit. Her motive, she claimed, was to demonstrate that beauty and brains are indeed compatible. But her employer was not convinced that a woman who is stacked can also sell stocks. By going bare Marina also went bust, for she was promptly fired.

Are beauty and brains still viewed as incompatible? Do people still believe the old sayings that "Women have long hair and short wits" and that "No dress or garment is less becoming to a woman than a show of intelligence?" Do mothers still unconsciously teach their daughters, as Mary Montagu did in 1753, to hide their learning as they would a "physical defect"?[12] In fact, the majority of adolescent girls report in 1983 that they frequently play dumb in order to remain popular. They say they would rather be liked than be best.[13] When women were asked what factors were important to their happiness, twice as many checked "losing weight" as checked "success at work."

In the past, gifted girls have rarely grown up to fulfill their potential as gifted women. Of the truly brilliant females with IQs over 150 who were observed in the famous Terman lifetime study, two-thirds wound up as homemakers or office workers.[14] Certain doors were chivalrously held wide open for these women, but the doors that might have unlocked their genius to themselves and to others remained closed. A study of highly achieving women with six-figure incomes showed that most of them had felt embarrassed about being unattractive as children. Achievement was used as their compensation.

Although more and more women have entered the work force a survey of the number of females pictured on the cover of *Time* magazine over the past thirty years shows little change. In 1953, for instance, there were nine women featured there, including Queen Elizabeth II, Queen Fredrika, Grandma Moses, and Mamie Eisenhower, along with several glamourous actresses. Yet in 1982, after a decade of feminist reform, only two women were depicted (compared to twenty-two men). One of them was a pregnant actress whose photo was on the cover because of a story on the baby boom (i.e., woman as mother); the other was an unidentified female in a leotard for a story on fitness as the new beauty ideal (i.e., woman as sex object). Not a single woman of accomplishment was featured on the cover of *Time* in all of 1982!

The conflict between adornment and achievement, between beauty and brains, places a woman back in the familiar double bind when she tries to be both a healthy female and a healthy person. Here again she winds up in a no-win situation. If she succeeds in achieving the beauty ideal and uses its power to attract attention (by displaying herself as a low-cut, long-haired, high-heeled, gorgeous woman), then she threatens her credibility as a competent person. The flashy symbols of femininity are incompatible with simultaneous signals of brilliance. On the other hand, if she ignores her role as beauty object and concentrates on business only, her achievements may go unnoticed. Moreover, lacking beauty, her credibility as a woman diminishes, and she may be less likely to succeed in the personal realm.

Being a woman means taking seriously the work of maintaining relationships. Females have long been socialized to be "givers" and to derive a sense of identity and satisfaction in "being there for others." Psychiatrist Jean Baker Miller observes that women are constantly asking themselves whether they are giving enough, constantly feeling guilty about "selfish" decisions. Men are more concerned with doing than with giving, concludes Miller. Their self-doubts center on "Am I a doer?" not "Am I a giver?"[15] Even in nursery school, there is a high correlation between the efforts girls make to accomplish something and the efforts they make to gain love and approval. In boys these two kinds of activities are more independent.[16] Males seek mastery mainly for its own sake, whereas females often regard mastery as a way of developing relations and gaining approval.

One way that females effectively nurture relationships is by sacrificing personal ambitions and becoming attractive, enthusiastic cheerleaders for males who are doing the "more important" stuff of life. Most high school and college cheering squads are made up of females, chosen mainly for their good looks and costumed to show off their charms. Cheerleaders provide an entertaining foreground for the serious business taking place on the playing field beyond. Even with today's greater emphasis on female sports, the cheering squad is still more likely to be found at the football game than at the women's field hockey playoff. Cheerleaders are a colorful and anonymous chorus line, working to show the team that people care. They convey the underlying message that women have a useful decorative place just outside of center court, cheering males on to victory. As we can see in the photograph of the long-legged, short-skirted Dallas Cowgirls, this message is projected into millions of living rooms every week during football season. And it is unconsciously absorbed.

A patient once explained that he had strayed into an affair with a much younger woman because his wife of twenty-five years had stopped being a good enough cheerleader. He felt that her enthusiastic support had waned of late, along with her good looks. Women sense that it is not what they achieve but how well they cheer that keeps men contentedly bonded to them. An important part of the cheerleader's value, of course, is her hedonic power to attract and stimulate others by dancing about and entertaining them visually.

In fact, evidence suggests that a man gains the most social status not from his wife's economic or professional level but from her degree of attractiveness and sexual desirability. The rub-off effect gives him the most points for having scored with a pretty mate.[17] Even in the rare cases where a wife's career has a much higher status and earns more money, the husband's occupation is still considered twice as important in determining the couple's social standing. Studies show that in many marriages both spouses covertly conspire to hide the wife's underlying power (as in the "I Love Lucy" type of situation comedy). They pretend to each other and to the world that the husband securely "wears the pants," while concealing the wife's real dominance behind public gestures of submission.

Increasingly, women are pushing open the doors that lead to the masculine world of direct agonic power. When women succeed at doing men's work, however, the masculine sphere is denigrated and diminished. For this reason men feel understandably threatened by women who turn from the pursuit of beauty to the pursuit of power. And they are likely to reject such women, both personally and professionally, overtly and covertly.

There is a widespread belief that if women can succeed at something, it can't be very hard to do. Research shows a persistent stereotype that females are not as talented as males and that women's work is considered less difficult and less important.[18] Success at jobs that are stereotypically feminine is attributed more often to easiness of the job rather than to hard work or talent. Even when women and men perform the same task, they are not viewed as equally competent (nor are they equally compensated). When an increasing number of women enter a formerly "masculine field" (like bank telling in the 1960s or medicine in the 1980s), the status and relative economic rank of the field begin to drop.[19]

Consequently, many women retain a belief that what they do does not matter as much as what men do. They suffer from a built-in problem of achievement denigration. If they manage to meet difficult challenges, their very success reduces the value of the accomplishment both to themselves and to others. Even when they do exhibit competence, many women attribute it less to internal factors like intelligence or ability and more to external factors like good luck or good looks. These attributions further perpetuate feelings of powerlessness, even in the face of high achievement.

Modesty precludes women from triumphantly flaunting their victories. Perhaps they are also fearful that success will prompt a backlash against them. As Susan Brownmiller points out, the open exaltation over one's achievements is as unfeminine as the display of direct anger by women.

> Arms raised in a winner's salute . . . is unladylike, to say the least. . . . More appropriate to femininity are the predictable tears of the new Miss America as she accepts her crown and scepter. Trembling lip and brimming eyes suggest a Cinderella who has stumbled upon good fortune through unbelievable, undeserved luck.[20]

Here then is another destructive by-product of beauty contests: pageant winners model the appropriate feminine look of success by acting incredulous, tearful, and humbly grateful.

Forty years ago, sociologist Talcott Parsons identified beauty as a compensation for women's exclusion from the occupational world. He noted that beauty provides one of the few chances women have to strive for success in a way that does not compete *with* men, but rather *for* them. "To the woman who is excluded from the struggle for power and prestige in the occupational sphere, it is the most direct path to a sense of superiority and importance," he wrote.[21]

Economics are of course a basic source of personal and marital power. Someone who is beautiful but financially dependent is generally at a power disadvantage. All cultures divide labor by sex, and all cultures need and value women's work to a greater or lesser extent. But nineteenth-century capitalism came to regard "the leisured woman" as an embodiment of social progress. One of its implicit goals was to emancipate women from the work force. A wife's "nonworking" status served as proof of her husband's success and of a generally high standard of living. Supported by a productive husband, a leisured woman was encouraged to busy herself with family concerns and with self-adornment. Her job was to make a good showing, to enjoy the pleasure of being seen, and to remain happily occupied maintaining a state of well-groomed idleness.

In his *Theory of the Leisure Class,* written at the turn of the century, Thorstein Veblen notes that prosperity conferred on women "a vicarious life." Brains and productivity were taken over by men, while beauty and leisure fell to women. The sexual division of labor and leisure separated the modes of power available to each sex: hedonic power to women, agonic power to men. Veblen also noted that conspicuous leisure is often signaled by constrictive clothing, tight skirts, high heels, and fragile fabrics— all of which announce that the wearer cannot or does not do work and that she requires someone else to dress and comb her.[22] As a therapist, I have seen a number of "affluent" women facing divorce with virtually no assets in their own name except for the jewelry, furs, and clothes they have amassed as part of their "leisured" life. Despite a high standard of living, their only tangible assets are those associated with personal adornment.

Love and work have been identified as two essential ingredients of mental health. When life is stressful in one area, the other can become a useful compensation. According to psychoanalytic theory, healthy men redirect part of their sexual tension into productive work. A man's libido fuels his efforts to remodel the universe. A woman, on the other hand (if she is truly feminine) is expected to redirect sexual energy into remaking her appearance.

Bent Reflections

CASSIUS. Tell me, good Brutus, can you see your face?
BRUTUS. No Cassius; for the eye sees not itself
But by reflection, by some other things.
CASSIUS. . . . it is very much lamented, Brutus,
That you have no such mirrors as will turn
Your hidden worthiness into your eye . . .
— Shakespeare, *Julius Caesar*[23]

A sixteenth-century Italian anatomist once wrote that nature has arranged things so that every time a woman thinks of herself she will feel humbled and ashamed. His words are reminiscent of the twentieth-century Viennese analyst who believed that nature had fashioned women for a lifetime of longing. In Freud's view, healthy feminine adjustment required "heightened narcissism and excessive vanity" as a defense against feelings of shame and inferiority. His analysis of women as the fair sex parallels the argument here presented; namely, that the identification of beauty with femininity is a useful compensation for a belief in female deficency. In psychoanalytic theory, however, genital anatomy rather than social mythology dictates the destiny of women as beauty objects.

Freud's phallocentric model of the personality was erected on the tip of the penis. Gender differences were explained in terms of the presence or absence of masculine traits. A woman's deficient anatomy determined her destiny as a misbegotten person; she needed to be "made over" to make up for her defects. Hence, the well-known Freudian dictum that man is born (that is, arrives in an intact form) whereas woman is made (that is, needs reconstruction to compensate for her missing elements). Analytic theory assumed that when a little girl discovered her body had been "castrated," the painful sense of loss generated a feeling of inferiority which undermined her self-love. Penis envy was construed as a permanent wound to woman's self-esteem. Freud wrote:

> The castration complex of girls is started by the sight of the genitals of the other sex. . . . They feel seriously wronged, often declare that they want to "have something like it, too," and fall victim to envy for the penis, which will leave ineradicable traces on their development.[24]

A tone of compassion pervades his descriptions of this traumatic discovery that destines females to a life of envy, shame, and compensatory behavior. His writings convey not only that a girl sees her genitals as inadequate, but that they *are* in fact inadequate. The clitoris is referred to as an "atrophied penis" and girls must conceal "the *fact* [italics mine] of their genital deficiency."

Theodor Reik further exposed female genitals as unsightly as well as inferior. He described the vulva as aesthetically deficient and concluded that women search for beauty partly to cover up their genital ugliness.

> I assume that the little girl who compares her genitals to those of the little boy finds her own ugly. Not only the greater modesty of women but their never ceasing striving toward beautifying and adorning their bodies is to be understood as displacement and extension of their effort to overcompensate for the original impression that their genitals are ugly.[25]

Reik noted that women are aware of the "foul odors coming from their unclean bodies" and that they become obsessed therefore with cleanliness as well as with beauty. (Recall that preoccupation with neatness as well as with appearance was considered characteristic of healthy females in the Broverman study).

And so the vulva (as symbolic of woman) is described as castrated, atrophied, unaesthetic, malodorous, and a primary cause of female shame and inferiority. If the genitals are deficient, so is the whole person. Psychoanalytic theory explained that girls generalize feelings of physical inadequacy to their overall self-concept. Contempt for the self is projected onto the mother, who is viewed as similarly castrated, and eventually contempt is extended to women in general. In the words of Freud:

> After a woman has become aware of the wound to her narcissism, she develops, like a scar, a sense of inferiority. When she has passed beyond her first attempt to explain her lack of a penis as being a punishment personal to herself and has realized that the sexual character is a universal one, she begins to share the contempt felt by men for a sex which is the lesser in so important a respect.[26]

Analytic theory further assumed that daughters would blame their mothers for giving them a defective body. Anger at Mother eventually turns into disdain as both sons and daughters begin to see her as a deficient adult, helpless and dependent like themselves. Resolution of the Oedipal conflict in boys is expected to result in "a normal male contempt for women." And so woman as mother, woman as the possessor of a castrated body, woman as the bearer of castrated daughters, woman as childishly dependent, is demeaned by both her sons and her daughters. Since girls identify with the mother, contempt for her means continued contempt for the self. In shorthand this is the Freudian scenario that leads females from anatomy to destiny; from penis envy to a lifetime of longing; from self-rejection to attempts at self-restoration.

How can a woman resolve her inferiority complex? The analytic script offers narcissistic self-adornment and excessive vanity as a solution. While there is no way to actually correct for "defective" genitals, beauty provides a partial answer. Heightened preoccupation with appearance was considered an effective defense against feelings of inferiority. Shame could be overcome through physical attractiveness; beauty could serve as a compensation for phallic loss.

"The effect of penis envy has a share, further, in the physical vanity of women, since they are bound to value their charms more highly as a late compensation for their original sexual inferiority," wrote Freud. "Long before the age at which a man can earn a position in society, nature has determined woman's destiny through beauty, charm and sweetness. . . ."[27] Narcissism and vanity bolstered the damaged female ego and were considered essential to the making of a well-adjusted woman. Beauty, like a penis, could be exhibited as a prize possession. (There is little evidence that women's fantasies are filled with longing for a lost phallus, yet studies do show that women daydream more often about appearance than men do. Adolescent girls especially report constant thoughts about being "pretty and feminine.")[28] In short, Freud counseled the daughters of Eve to cultivate vanity as a means of correcting the castrated body that destiny had dealt to them.

Of course, penis envy has been interpreted symbolically rather than literally. The phallus is explained as a symbol of force—a tool to get what one wants. A woman's feelings of having been cut off can be understood not just as an irrational response to genital anatomy but as a rational response to social reality. She is in fact denied part of her destiny; severed from the masculine world of money, politics, and direct power; sequestered in the feminine world of family and fashion. As Elizabeth Janeway writes, "Women are evident social castrates, and the mutilation of their potentiality as achieving human creatures" is analogous to the supposed physical wound to their anatomy that has so often been described.[29] When Freud asks "What do women want?" and then concludes that what they want is the penis they can never have, female deviance becomes irremedial. A castrated woman can never make herself whole and lovable. Nor can she love herself in a healthy way. At best the narcissistic pursuit of beauty can only be a poor substitute. Analogously, females accept and enact their role as the fair sex to defend against social castration. While beauty can enhance status and is a powerful tool, it never fully normalizes females and only confirms that they need remodeling.

Although psychoanalytic theory is deeply rooted in the phallus, Freud acknowledged that social factors foster narcissism and vanity in women. He even warned that idealization of feminine charms creates an enormous temptation for females to indulge in excessive preoccupation with their bodies. Through idealization, beauty becomes exalted and used to defend against underlying anxiety.

Just as heightened narcissism was linked to genital shame, idealized female beauty grows from cultural castration. Belief in female deficiency still permeates our social system as well as our psychological processes. The analytic interpretation of female vanity as a defense against penis envy parallels the premise that the myth of female beauty balances the myth of female deviance. Beauty is assigned to the feminine role to compensate for woman's presumed defects. Females turn to their bodies not in search of a lost phallus but in pursuit of a sense of normalcy, which is so difficult for them to achieve in a culture that devalues them in so many ways.

Narcissism: Healthy and Unhealthy

Narcissism, passivity, and masochism became key elements in the analytic interpretation of female adjustment. These three traits were identified as the feminine core of the personality. Narcissism means choosing and valuing oneself as a love object. It originates in infancy, when babies experience the world strictly in terms of their own needs. Narcissism can foster self-awareness and enhance feelings of worth, but it can also hinder psychological growth by locking behavior into egocentric and infantile patterns.

When narcissism is healthy, it helps one gain a sense of identity.

It promotes sensual pleasure, for instance, through decorating the body, through observing, displaying, and caressing it. Love of self can be shared and thereby can unite people through friendship and sexual intimacy. A woman who likes her body can say "look at me so we both can take pleasure," not "Look at me because I need confirmation of my worth." A healthy sense of narcissism fosters positive body images that are generated from within rather than dictated from without.

In contrast, excessive narcissism can lead to an idealized self-perception that is based on fantasy. The unattainable images that result can be tormenting. Narcissism is unhealthy when it demands perpetual youthfulness or when it concentrates self-worth into the limited arena of looks alone.

The evils of infantile narcissism are portrayed in the story *Snow White*, in which a mother is driven to murder by her obsession to remain forever fairest of them all. In that fairy tale, it is Snow White's own narcissism that tempts her to taste the poisoned apple. Although forewarned, she is enticed by the promise of rosier cheeks and a lovelier face. With one bite, she is cast back into the endless sleep of an infantile state. Anesthetized, Snow White is all beauty and facade. Moreover, she cannot restore herself but must wait in the coffin to be kissed back into life.

Analyzing this fairy tale, Madonna Kolbenschlag notes that women are driven by narcissism to transform themselves into the "formula female," a fictional heroine whose tranquil exterior masks an inner life fraught with anxiety, envy, and anger. Conflicted, women vacillate between the extremes of vanity and self-rejection, explains Kolbenschlag. Adornment substitutes for assertive action, as beauty is used to fill a void in identity.[30]

When a woman plugs into a formula for feminine beauty, her inner life is disguised. Like the sleeping Snow White, she displays a pretty but passive exterior. Beauty isolates her within and from herself. In time she unconsciously identifies with the formula female she has been impersonating—a flashy blonde, a cute pixie, a *Vogue* vision, a natural sweetheart—someone as unreal as a fairy-tale figure. Her body becomes a major source of gratification, as it was in infancy. Excessive narcissism traps her at a primitive level of psychological development.

The association of femininity with narcissism in analytic theory did not imply a healthy self-love but just the opposite: an uncertainty about whether one is lovable, which increases the need to feel loved. This powerful drive turns inward, and love of self interferes with love of others. Psychoanalytic parlance uses the term "object relations" to refer to interpersonal bonds. Paradoxically, as a woman transforms into a beauty object in order to secure love, her objectification isolates the inner being. Displayed as an erotic object, she is overlooked as a total person. Human relations are distorted literally into object relations rather than interpersonal encounters.

Self-love is surely essential to psychological well-being. But finding a balance between healthy and unhealthy narcissism is not easy. It becomes even harder when idealized beauty is mandated as essential to femininity. The beauty myth offers women a convenient resolution to inner conflict. To love oneself within the feminine role seems simpler when self-love can be channeled into self-adornment. In the end, however, excessive narcissism is destructive if a woman must submerge her ego while searching for self-love; if she must drown like Narcissus while trying to embrace her own image; if she ends up obsessed with beauty but still depressed about her body and about herself.

Masochism

> Survival forces a people to learn to perform. They act so well
> that they convince themselves of the fiction. Thus an irreparable damage was done to their souls.
>
> — Susan Griffin[31]

The Broverman study showed that a healthy woman (but not a healthy person) is expected to be highly invested in looks. Once adornment is internalized as a gender requirement, a woman cannot ignore it, for fear of feeling unfeminine. The greater her investment and the greater her sacrifice in personal make-over, the greater the proof of her commitment to the feminine role.

It is not mere coincidence that pain is part of many beauty rituals, so that feeling bad becomes a prerequisite to looking good. Curling, bleaching, piercing, waxing, binding, teasing, plucking, girdling, all hurt. As Montaigne once observed, there is no torture a woman will not endure to enhance her beauty ("Il faut soufrir pour être belle").

Why do women willingly endure painful and mutilating cosmetic transformations? After all, such rituals involve living flesh. We read of the tortures of foot binding and tight lacing. We hear of the torments of anorexia and chronic dieting. Yet women continue to suffer largely in silence. What anesthetic numbs the senses in the pursuit of beauty? Are females really as masochistic as Freud suggested?

Masochism is the desire to seek physical and psychological pain or to submit oneself to the will of another. It has been called sadism turned inward, for one part of the person damages another part. Helene Deutsch, one of the early psychoanalysts, called it "the most elemental power in female mental life." She thought that masochism derived not from penis envy but from the biological experiences of womanhood. Pain is an inevitable part of female reproductive destiny, inherent to menstruation, defloration, intercourse, childbirth. Deutsch described women's willingness to suffer in the "service of the species" as necessary and psychologically healthy. From her perspective, the masochistic pursuit of beauty would be part of the natural burden of being female.

Karen Horney rejected Deutsch's biological analysis, and explained feminine masochism as an adaptation to oppressive social forces. She asserted, furthermore, that a masochistic need to please at any price was inevitable in a society that encouraged female dependency. Among the conditions that predispose women to masochism, Horney lists sexual repression, economic dependency, blockage of achievement aspirations, and the generally low evaluation of women as a group. "Women adopt the social behavior that makes them acceptable and these feminine characteristics become internalized."[32] Once certain beliefs (myths) are fixed in a culture (for instance, that females are innately narcissistic, masochistic, or beautiful), these ideologies serve to reconcile people to their role as natural and unalterable. Once a woman accepts the idea that masochistic behavior is commendable, she will eagerly act out her "true nature" even when it entails pain. Masochistic behavior, explains Horney, is a way of minimizing the self. By cringing into a painful corner, a person confirms the unconscious belief that she is "insignificant and worthless." This description certainly fits the image of an anorectic, tormented by hunger pangs but pleased to disappear into a shadow of herself.

A driving need for acceptance can transform even the most oppressive beauty ritual into a pleasurable act. Self-sacrifice feels good to someone highly committed to serving others. Indeed, most of us enjoy our beauty routines; we love to shop, decorate, and display, even when pain is part of the process. Suffering feels satisfying when it confirms one's commitment to the feminine role. Pretty pleases at any price. As a woman of the eighteenth century once wrote, "I shall not think three hours business I usually devote to my toilet below the dignity of a rational soul. I am content to suffer great torment from my stays, that my shape may be graceful in the eyes of others."[33] Elizabeth explained in a similar voice, "I have dozens of pairs of excruciating high heels that really kill my feet. But I buy whatever looks good, regardless of how they feel. Joe loves me in sexy shoes and I try to make him happy." Like the pain portrayed in pornographic violence, the pain of masochistic beauty rituals conveys an underlying message: "Ask anything of me . . . do anything to me . . . because everything feels good if it pleases you."

Behavior which on the surface seems neurotically masochistic may at a deeper level represent an adaptive attempt to adjust to stress. Suffering to squeeze into a glass slipper can be understood as a rational defense against the more painful consequence of feeling rejected. If some form of pain seems inevitable, then the wisest decision may be to choose freely to suffer. When Elizabeth buys whatever shoes look good regardless of the pain, she sees little choice, since there seems to be no other way of being feminine and lovable. By freely choosing to victimize herself, she protects against the humiliation of being victimized. In this way she preserves a sense of personal control. However, the pretense that she truly likes the pain may gradually become unconscious. The masochism inherent in many beauty transformations is not a component of healthy female adjustment, as Deutsch's model might imply. Rather it reveals a victim struggling to adapt to a sadistic system.

Psychologist Paula Caplan points out that the pain women suffer through self-denial is labeled masochistic, but theorists forget that "women have been frightened by the threat of being judged unfeminine, ugly, and so on if they do not behave selflessly." Society conditions women to want to please at any price. Then a term like *inherent masochism* is coined to explain the conditioned need and eventually it is viewed as an innate feminine trait, observes Caplan.[34]

Faced with sex discrimination in employment, socialized to be dependent, unprepared to compete aggressively, women require financial support. They have little chance of economic security if they are uneducated, are solely responsible for the care of young children, are middle-aged without paid work experience, or have been conditioned to desire a "leisured life." Having beauty is like having an American Express card. It is good almost anywhere. It can secure a meal, a job promotion, an invitation to the prom or to the altar. Without it, and without the relationships it brings, a woman's life may be literally impoverished; hence her "willingness" to suffer in its pursuit. In an essay on cultural pressures and the psychology of women written several decades ago, psychoanalyst Clara Thompson observed the following:

> In the past [a woman] could feel safe after she had married and could then risk neglecting her charms, but today with the ease of divorce, the woman who depends on a man for her means of support and social position must continue to devote a great deal of her time to what may be called narcissistic pursuits, that is, body culture, and concern about clothes. One sees that woman's alleged narcissism and greater need to be loved may be entirely the result of economic necessity.[35]

It is tempting to blame victims for their self-oppression when they have no other viable choice. Some painful beauty rituals are forced on little girls. Foot binding and clitoridectomy are extreme examples of cosmetic mutilations inflicted on children because tradition demands them. However, most women willingly choose to pay the beauty price. Quite simply, they cannot afford not to: the economics of social exchange require it.

People are driven by basic physical, emotional, and economic forces. We all need food and shelter. We all need to love and be loved. We all need to feel that our work is valued. Women also need reliable husbands and caring fathers for their children. These needs combine, producing a powerful drive to maintain relations with men. After all, men have been the primary guardians of society's resources. Women share these assets mainly by bonding with men. In order to attract a suitable partner or to keep the one she has, a woman must look young enough, sophisticated enough, wholesome, seductive, glamourous, modest, thin, buxom, innocent, punk, or whatever she believes he wants. As we saw earlier, research on dating and mating shows that beauty buys attention and affection; it yields rewards for the sacrifices it demands. When beauty is assigned to the feminine role it becomes a primary asset, a basic commodity of gender exchange, and a key to economic survival.

Women would be less willing to transform themselves masochistically into the fair sex if they were treated more fairly. Too many women spend too many hours in therapy trying to overcome their failure to adjust to the feminine role when it is not the masochist within but the sadist without that needs reform. Too many women spend too many hours remaking their faces, when the mirror of society is so badly in need of refacing. As long as they continue to gaze at the myth in society's mirror, women will be ashamed of what they see in their own and will feel compelled to straighten a bent reflection.

6

Myth America Grows Up

My mother was pregnant,
She grew enormously large,
And then I was born—
A perfectly normal baby,
Attached to the fingers of my right hand
Was a typewriter,
And attached to the fingers of my left hand
Was a Brillo pad.
On my body was a bra,
And my cute baby blue eyes
Had a pair of false eyelashes attached to them.
The doctor said
"Congratulations, it's a girl!"

— Sandi Shepard[1]

I COMBED the beaches last summer counting topless toddlers. Few could be found. On the Riviera, women freely bare their breasts to the Mediterranean sun. Here at home, the uncomplicated chests of little girls are discreetly covered. In this way young bodies are draped in gender, poured into the female mold, to be shaped, reshaped, and misshapen by it. Three-year-olds veiled behind bikini tops learn a small lesson in body awareness, one that often leads to heightened self-consciousness and sometimes to tormenting obsessions.

In every society, certain behaviors are considered more appropriate for one sex than for the other. Gender divergence includes occupational, recreational, and legal distinctions, as well as decorative and ornamental ones. How do children acquire this complex set of gender rules? A five-year-old confidently tells me that "girls play at being pretty, but boys play cars. . . ." How did she learn these components of masculinity and femininity so soon?

The socialization of gender begins in infancy, continues through adolescence, and involves almost every aspect of experience, including toys, clothes, media images, and, of course, parental expectations and behavior. Although studies of infants reveal few sex-based differences in emotional and cognitive functions, parents believe that their sons and daughters are quite different right from birth. Girls and boys do grow up in different "climates of expectation."

During pregnancy, parents prepare not just for a new baby but for a strong masculine son or a beautiful feminine daughter. Consequently, these are the qualities that they project onto their newborns. As noted in an earlier chapter, when parents rated firstborn infants, they saw their daughters as beautiful, soft, pretty, cute, and delicate, whereas they viewed their sons as strong, better coordinated, and hardier, even though the male and female infants had been carefully matched for equivalent physical characteristics.[2] People who played with a three-month-old dressed in yellow more often judged it a boy because of "the strength of his grasp and his lack of hair." Those who thought the baby was a girl remarked on her "roundness, softness, and fragility."[3] The cuter the baby, the more likely it is to be judged a girl.

Long before birth, babies are imagined through fantasies that devalue girls even while idealizing their appearance. In a song from the show *Carousel*, Bill ponders his unborn child. First a son "with head held high, feet planted firm"; a boy who, in his father's daydream, "grows tall and tough as a tree." Then, in the softer tones of an afterthought, Bill considers a daughter, "pink, and white as peaches and cream"; a girl with "ribbons in her hair, brighter than girls are meant to be," yet still needing to be "sheltered and dressed in the best that money can buy."

Old autograph books sometimes "wish you hope, wish you joy, wish you first a baby boy." A widespread preference for male offspring persists. In a recent American sample, over 90 percent of the couples wanted a firstborn son. Nearly all the men and three-fourths of the women said they would want a boy if they were to have only one child.[4] A frequent reason given by those few women who did prefer a girl was that "it would be fun to dress her and fuss with her hair."[5] When asked what kind of a person they want their child to become, parents mentioned "being attractive" far more often for daughters than for sons.

Imagine a growing girl who represents the collective experiences of many youngsters whose lives were studied for this chapter. The composite experiences of Linda typify the socialization process which teaches girls their role as members of the fair sex. Linda is initiated into the beautified female world through the subtle lessons of daily life. Her few strands of baby hair are swept into a curl in the hospital nursery. Her ears are pierced before her first birthday, her nails polished for her second. She is securely wrapped in a strawberry-shortcake universe: roses on her walls, ribbons in her hair, ruffles on her shirts. "Early in life, the pink world starts to process the girls to value it."[6]

Intuitively, children sense when and how they are touched or avoided, admired or ignored, complimented or criticized. Girls are initially sturdier than boys and developmentally ahead of them, but are perceived as more fragile. Handled more delicately, they receive less physical stimulation and less encouragement for energetic or exploratory behavior. Parents show greater anxiety about a girl's safety even while she is still in diapers. Fathers begin by engaging in more rough-and-tumble play with sons and by spending nearly twice as much time with sons as with daughters.[7] As Bill concludes in his song, "You can have fun with a son, but you gotta be a father to a girl."

Interestingly, fathers seem to sex-type youngsters even more consciously than mothers do, for example by giving children toys that are more gender-stereotyped. Men show greater anxiety over effeminate behavior in sons, while actively encouraging it in daughters. Fathers seem to want their little girls to fit their own personal image of an attractive female, within the bounds of what is appropriate for a child. Wives report that husbands urge them to keep their daughters' hair long and to "doll them up" even when the mothers themselves don't feel that these things are very important. Linda's father echoes the voices of many dads who describe their preschool daughters as "a bit of a flirt": "she cuddles and flatters in subtle ways"; "she's coy and sexy."[8]

Whether such descriptions of "daddy's little girl" are accurate, fathers enjoy and encourage seductive appearance in their daughters, which in turn enhances these Oedipal flirtations. In this way, Linda is more or less explicitly directed toward a kind of "predatory coquetry." Her enactment of the beauty role is therefore shaped by the way her father reinforces Linda's appearance, independently of how her mother may model feminine beauty.

According to Piaget's theory of intellectual growth, children strive to adapt to life by trying to understand their experiences. We are biologically programmed, says Piaget, to mentally reconstruct the world by forming concepts about ourselves and our surroundings. Mental file cards are written and rewritten to conform ever more closely to social "reality." Concepts of masculinity and femininity are learned as part of this general process of intellectual growth.

In acquiring her sense of gender, Linda first develops a rudimentary idea that people come in two separate forms. Her mental file cards are scribbled with vague notions of mommy/daddy, boy/girl, man/woman, along with perceptions about clothing, hair styles, and other gender markers. By her third birthday, she is well aware that girls and boys look and act differently, apart from any underlying genital structure. An anecdote describes two toddlers looking at a statue of Adam and Eve. "Which is which?" asks one. "I could tell if only they had their clothes on," replies the other.

Though she does not yet understand gender constancy (once a girl, always a girl), Linda knows her own gender membership. Confidently she asserts, "I'm a girl," because she has written "me" on the file card that is filled with "feminine" concepts. Once gender has been established internally, Linda begins to strive for consistency between what she knows about herself and what she knows about girls in general. The dialogue in her head runs something like this: "Since I'm a girl, and since girls look and act in certain ways, then I, too, should look and act the way they do." And so she begins to enact her feminine role. The need to establish consistency between oneself and one's gender role is the same for the toddler as for the adult. The problem for Linda (as for all women) is how to bring together her self-perception as a female with an understanding of gender role.

Femininity soon becomes associated with beauty, and to the internal dialogue a subtheme is added. "Since I'm a girl," Linda thinks intuitively, "and since girls are pretty, then I, too, should be (will be, must be) pretty, just like Mommy." In this way, beauty becomes part of her self-perception as a female. When she confirms the belief that she is a girl by enacting some part of the beauty role (such as putting ribbons in her hair), she achieves a sense of cognitive consistency that in turn feels satisfying. Hence, the inner dialogue concludes with the sentiment "I enjoy being a girl!" By maintaining harmony between two concepts (self-image and feminine image), Linda keeps her mental file cards in order, and in this way makes the world more comfortable and predictable.

Piaget explains that knowledge of one's gender role is partly imposed from within, that is, self-motivated through the basic drive to create intellectual order out of chaotic experiences. But gender role is also externally imposed. It is culturally conditioned through the direct experience of hearing Cinderella tales, dressing Barbie dolls, watching Miss America, Miss Teen, Miss Hemisphere. It is also overtly reinforced. Throughout the elementary school years, girls receive more compliments than boys on their appearance. They are given a bigger wardrobe to choose from and are admired especially when they wear dresses.[9] Linda repeatedly hears others say "You look so pretty," and eventually greets her own reflection with "I'm so pretty" or "Am I pretty? . . . . as pretty as other girls? . . . as pretty as others expect me to be?" Finally she begins to wonder, "How can I be prettier?" *Pretty* becomes a framework within which she paints her feminine self-image.

Although parents are beginning to treat sons and daughters more similarly, they still give their children sex-typed clothing, toys, and books. These act as powerful conditioning agents that socialize the importance of female beauty. Emphasis on feminine attractiveness is obvious in fairy tales and in picture books for preschoolers, in which female animals are depicted with long curly eyelashes and ribbons on their tails. A study of school texts, found that these books traditionally portrayed women as mothers who wear aprons and who "seem to want and do nothing personally for themselves." The notable exception was cited of a mother who "treated herself to some earrings on a shopping trip."[10]

Before 1970, textbooks rarely showed females engaged in independent activities. When the occupational world of women was presented, it consisted of either service jobs (nurse, teacher) or "glamour" jobs (model, dancer, actress), in which body display is an important component. A popular children's book of the 1970s shows a small boy and girl fantasizing about their future: when the boy becomes a jungle explorer and captures a lion, the girl "curls the lion's mane in her beauty shop for animals"; when he dreams of being a deep-sea diver, she becomes "a mermaid who serves him tea and ice cream."[11]

Books are somewhat less stereotyped today, although children's toys remain highly gender-typed. While boys are given action dolls equipped to capture the enemies of outer space, girls are given fashion dolls equipped with exotic outfits for capturing attention. Over 250 million Barbies have been sold in the past twenty-five years, a doll population that equals the number of living Americans. Over 20 million outfits a year are bought for Barbie and her friends, as the seeds of clothing addiction are sown. One collector concludes that Barbie remains the most popular fashion doll simply because she is the prettiest. (Barbie is both thinner and "sexier looking" than when first created in 1959.) Fashions for Barbie in 1984 featured her in elegant gowns because "glamour is back." Toy stores also sell makeup for dolls. With "Fashion Face," Linda can "put on Barbie's face, wash it off, change her look again and again." A single tube costs several dollars, and remember, this is makeup for a doll!

On Christmas morning, Linda eagerly unwraps her very own superdeluxe makeup set, "just like Mommy's." Here, packaged innocently with fun titles like "Fresh and Fancy" and "Pretty Party" are the sugar and spice that feed the beauty myth. These high-priced glamour rehearsal kits contain the essential tools of the trade. For Linda's hair there are rollers, styling combs, curling irons, "falls," wash-in color, and sparkles. For her face there are

paints, gloss, frosting, liners, blush, shadow, and mascara. For
her hands there are lotions, polish, nail crayons, and decals. Also
included is gold foil for "beauty accents" and glitter for "today's
metallic look." The tubes smell like candy and taste like soda pop.
They come complete with magnifying mirror in a convenient
carrying case so that she can take it anywhere and check her looks
perpetually. Here is the making of a mirror junkie. The box covers
of cosmetic kits carry reassuring messages to parents. "These toys
are suitable for children as young as three"; they will help your
child "personalize her own pretty face"; help her "create dozens
of fashion looks and become a beauty consultant for her friends";
teach her the "fun way to learn beauty secrets."

What else do they teach Linda about herself and her role in
society? That feminine beauty requires many faces and she can
cultivate them all; that the easy way to impersonate a real grown-
up lady is to put on the same disguise that Mommy wears; that
playtime means narcissistic preening; that fantasy fun means enacting Cinderella; that spending time and money on beautifying
oneself is approved by parents; that others like her to look fresh,
fancy, and seductive; that her own face, though pretty, is somehow inadequate and needs to be made even lovelier—a double
message that fosters negative body image and self-doubt.

For some girls, "glamouring up" is not just child's play. There
has been a phenomenal growth in children's beauty contests since
those protestors picketed the Miss America Pageant in 1968. Paradoxically, during the very years when the women's movement
became a pervasive social force, beauty pageants for children,
shown in the illustration, also gained in popularity. The Miss
Hemisphere Pageant, with numerous divisions for girls ages three
to twenty-seven, has mushroomed in size from a few hundred
contestants in 1963 to hundreds of thousands of participants today. It is billed as the largest single beauty pageant in the world.
Toddlers barely out of diapers (sometimes wearing false eyelashes
and tasseled bikinis) are paraded before judges who scrutinize
their "beauty, charm, poise and personality." The separate "masters" division for boys up to age nine attracts far fewer contestants.

Why do parents pay sizable entrance fees, invest in elaborate
outfits, and drive hundreds of miles to these contests? Besides
seeking prizes and modeling opportunities, many sincerely believe

that they are helping girls to develop into "ambitious but feminine women, like Bess Myerson." Some experience a strong element of vicarious achievement. They describe the thrill of seeing their daughters on display. One father remarked, "Taking my girls around to pageants is my activity, like a hobby. The contests are flashier than Little League and the children don't get hurt."[12]

But perhaps they do get hurt, in ways less obvious yet more odious than a sprained ankle in a ballgame. Pediatrician Lee Salk warns that children's beauty contests do more harm than good. He describes them as perfect setups for failure, as girls experience tremendous pressure to accept and identify with exaggerated physical stereotypes. Realizing that they lack the winning look, many suffer deep feelings of inadequacy.

"Girls Like Rainbows, Boys Don't"

Although children start with only rudimentary concepts of masculinity and femininity, they soon fill in the details. Awareness of gender dualism expands and crystallizes with age, as cognitive file cards are refined. Each day, children learn from their books and toys, from parental reaction to their behavior, and from models that constantly surround them, that beauty is a critical part of femininity. When asked how boys and girls are different from each other, children's compositions show a clear understanding that beauty belongs to females. Although genital and reproductive differences are rarely mentioned, youngsters universally say that girls wear makeup, have pretty hair, "don't get as dirty and aren't as tough" as boys. It is tempting to think that times have changed, that the next generation is already liberated from gender stereotypes and is no longer bound by beauty myths. But consider this response written in 1982 by a fifth-grader:

> Because I am a girl I am different in many ways. Girls put on eye shoudo and boys ware nothing like eye shoudo. And girls ware gowns and shoes and take a pocket book around. Boys don't do that. Alls they have to do is put on a tie and shine shoes. Girls put lipstick on their lips and girls put on earings, then they put on stockings and put thier hair in a bun or fix up the hair. Girls

do housework and take care of a baby if they have one. Boys just sit around and watch football games and other sports.

The following comments from seven- and eight-year-olds are cited because they particularly reflect an awareness that beauty is central to the female role.[13]

"How are boys and girls different?"
— Girls play at being pretty but boys play cars. Boys' voices are louder. Girls wear more jewelry.
— Girls like pink, boys like blue. Boys take their shirts off when it's hot but girls don't.
— Girls are prettier and boys are bossy. Boys stay outside as long as they want, but girls can't.
— Boys don't clean house and girls don't get dirty. Most girls do not get hit by their mothers because girls are more beautiful.
— Girls are cute and harmless, don't get as muddy as boys. Girls like rainbows, but boys don't.
— Boys don't dance, or play hopscotch. Girls don't play rough or get sweaty (but they have the same rights as us).

More articulate ten- and eleven-year-olds made the following observations:

— Girls are very sensitive and delicate. They like perfume and like looking good and sweet. Boys are rough, tough, and insensitive.
— Girls can wear anything they like, but boys can only wear pants. Girls have more clothes. They are more into pink rooms and looking pretty.
— Girls put on makeup and boys don't because they don't want to look pretty. Girls like to stay clean and neat. Some boys say they don't want to take a bath and they want to stay smelly and dirty.
— Girls don't have a mustache, boys don't have a baby. Boys have short hair and drive better than girls. Girls can cook better but boys are stronger.
— Girls are soft like cotton but boys are rough like a truck. But we are nice to each other—that's what counts.

Clearly, these children believe that the male body is to be

strengthened and developed, while the female body is to be protected and beautified. In fact, young children evaluate physical attractiveness in much the same way as adults do.[14] In nursery school, they can reliably judge the attractiveness of classmates and prefer to play with those who are better-looking.[15] Preschoolers also connect sex-related personality traits to appearance. They rate unattractive boys as more "scary and aggressive" but rate unattractive girls as more "fearful of things." (Good looks may inhibit assertive behavior in pretty girls who feel out of character when behaving more actively or aggressively than others expect.)

Children sex-typed a pretty face as feminine and a strong muscular physique as masculine. These stereotypes in turn influence the self-concepts of boys and girls in different directions. In a survey of eight- to fifteen-year-olds, girls at each age level worried more about their appearance than boys. Over half the fifth-grade girls in another sample ranked themselves as the least attractive person in their class. Follow-up interviews showed they were not simply motivated by modesty but were truly troubled by their "poor appearance."[16] The older the girl, the greater the influence of attractiveness on her popularity, as if children's understanding of the disproportionate social value of beauty to females gradually increases.

Linda grows up dressing and undressing Barbie, playing with her "Pretty Party" glamour kit, watching the selection of Miss Universe each year. She believes that beauty is something that happens at adolescence. Patiently she awaits it. While marking time, Linda may try on the role of the tomboy. Why do so many tomboys appear only to disappear? What can they teach us about the growing of little Myth America?

Tomboyism is a temporary detour on the road to female development, a last adventure before the final commitment to womanhood. Tomboys are familiar figures. Bred in every neighborhood, they roam like tomcats over the noisy, competitive, outdoor masculine turf. High on energy, they use their bodies freely to explore the world of people and things. The term *tomboy* traces back to the 1600s, when it was first directed at boys to

censure them for "rude, boisterous or forward behavior." Soon
the label was transferred to "girls who behave like unruly boys,"
and girls have worn it ever since.[17]

Tomboys not only act the part, they look it as well. We recognize them by their smudged faces and ragged clothes. The frills
of Miss Muffet are not for them. Patched, scruffy, and unkempt,
they need shoes they can run in, pants they can climb in. A
tomboy's appearance enables the very behavior it proclaims. For
packaging can create both the image *and* the limits of a person.
A female is what she looks like as much as what she does.

One of the most striking aspects of tomboyism is its current
popularity. A majority of female college students describe themselves as former tomboys. With bright eyes and a tinge of nos-
talgia, they recount their tomboy adventures without shame or
embarrassment. Tomboyism is the rule rather than the exception.
More than half the adult women surveyed recall having been
tomboys. Among growing girls, nearly three out of four currently
place themselves in the tomboy category.[18]

Although tomboyism is almost universal in western cultures,
it has no counterpart among males. Parents, especially fathers,
react strongly against effeminate appearance in sons. A young
boy in mommy's high heels, pearls, and nail polish, makes parents
fidgety, to say the least. Such adornments remain a gender distinction reserved for the other sex. The term *sissy* is sometimes
suggested as a parallel to *tomboy*, although the two are not really
equivalent. Any child, whether boy or girl, who is noncombative,
fearful, prim, and proper can be dubbed a sissy and ridiculed for
possessing such "effeminate" qualities. Whereas *sissy* is clearly
perjorative for both sexes, the term *tomboy* confers little stigma
before puberty; it is never directed at boys and is often considered
a tacit compliment for girls. Differences between the two terms
clearly reflect the bias that male attributes are normative.

Why does our culture produce so many tomboys? Why do we
first dichotomize gender roles and then permit and even encourage
girls to "cross over" temporarily? Why do we set them apart with
a distinct label?

Answers to these questions lead back to the belief in female deviance. Recall that one strategy women use to normalize their social position is to become one of the boys. Tomboyism has survived for centuries because it serves a purpose: to defer the full impact of being just another girl. As a tomboy, Linda straddles two gender roles and thereby expands the territory of the self into the valued male domain.

Both boys and girls internalize the cultural devaluation of females. Even preschoolers are aware that masculine traits are accorded higher value and yield greater rewards. In tests where children can express a preference for being one sex or the other, only one boy in ten chooses to be female, whereas one girl in three chooses to be male.[19] Similar results are found in age groups ranging from toddlers to adults. Fewer boys than girls believe it would be better to have been born the opposite sex. As one boy remarked, "If I'd been born a girl, I would have to be pretty and no one would be interested in my brains." Nearly a quarter of adult women surveyed recall a conscious desire to be a boy during childhood, but fewer than 5 percent of adult men remember ever wanting to be female.[20] At twelve Linda writes:

> I am a female. I play football and baseball with a lot of boys. They sometimes beg me to play with them. I don't think it is fair that boys can do everything and girls can't. Boys have a baseball league but girls can't. . . . Nobody knows if girls could do more than boys or if boys could do more than girls. . . . Girls have to wash the dishes and suffer by doing everything while the boys have all the fun. One day, I want it to be fair.

Tomboys gain temporary access to the valued masculine world. As "one of the boys," they shake off the girlish stigma and enjoy membership in a privileged club. In fact, rejection of personal adornment and adoption of a boyish look accomplishes for the prepubertal girl very much what beauty rituals accomplish for the adult woman. Both facilitate access to male company; both influence body image and self-esteem; and both defend against an underlying feeling of inferiority. Adopting tomboyism, like cultivating beauty, brings similar tangible rewards: visibility, attention, adventure.

Some young girls (like their mothers) maintain a dual repertoire of tomboy togs along with more coquettish drag, using one or the other as events require. In fact, such role diversity and flexibility may epitomize the best of an androgynous gender model. However, a time comes during adolescence when tomboyism evokes more anxiety than satisfaction, and its rewards no longer balance its costs. Though tolerated before puberty, tomboyism becomes increasingly threatening and is usually abandoned as gender file cards are updated. By the late teens, few girls continue to wear the title. When asked why they gave it up, college students replied:

> I just outgrew it. It was more or less a natural process that happened over a long period of time. . . . I started wearing more dresses because I like them and because Mom decided I should look nice. . . . When dating, it was difficult to be myself, so I had to change my image in dressing and mannerisms.

Their responses convey an underlying feeling of loss. Some young women are searching for new labels that can link them to their former selves. At age nineteen Linda says, "If a tomboy is a woman who is very assertive or aggressive, I guess I'm still a tomboy. . . . I don't use the term *tomboy* because that connotes being very young, but I'm still very active, though less athletic, and still consider myself androgynous." The effects of tomboyism reach into adulthood. A survey showed that women who had been overtly tomboyish as children preferred a more tailored style of dress, wore more muted colors, and decorated their homes with a nonfrilly, functional design. Women who had never been tomboys preferred more ruffly clothes, were more marriage-oriented and less career-minded.

Attracting an Identity

"A boy expands into a man; a girl contracts into a woman." So goes an old saying. With each contraction Linda sheds a piece of her comfortable old skin to emerge naked and pink into the pastel shades of womanhood. Transforming into the fair sex, she delivers a new self. Yet labor is painful. Adolescence marks a major crisis in gender acquisition. Puberty rings out, sounding the death knell for a tomboy. Gentle curves on breast and hip expose her. In poetry, Anne Sexton assures her daughter: "There is nothing in your body that lies / All that is new is telling the truth."[21] Revealed as woman, Linda can no longer masquerade as an impostor in a tomboy's costume. Contracting, she abandons the ballfield for the prince's ball, trades in her old uniform, learns to play new games and to compete in new arenas. Contracting, she must outfit herself with the eleven traits that professionals in the Broverman study judged as feminine and must gradually abandon the long list of thirty-eight attributes they rated as masculine.

Puberty arrives uninvited—sometimes prematurely, other times long overdue. Many girls experience it as a turning point in their self-image. At age eleven, Linda was asked to describe herself by making a series of statements starting with "I am a . . ." She began: "I am a human being, I am a girl, I am a truthful person, I am not pretty. . . ." One of the striking sex differences to emerge at adolescence is a greater self-consciousness in females. Girls find it harder than boys do to measure up against the idealized norms for their own sex. In a study of fourth- through tenth-graders, the oldest girls had the poorest self-image of any group in the sample.[22] Nearly half the girls in a survey of twenty thousand teenagers reported they frequently felt ugly.[23] To the extent that adolescent girls dislike their bodies, they also dislike themselves.

Twice as many high school girls as boys want to change their looks. Girls are dissatisfied with a greater number of body parts than boys. They generally see themselves as less attractive than other girls, whereas boys tend to rate themselves as better-looking than their peers.[24] A correlation exists between intelligence and body satisfaction in boys, that is, the brighter the boy, the more satisfied he is with his appearance. No such relationship is found in girls, possibly because bright girls are all too aware that they can never attain the beauty ideal.[25]

By college age, 75 percent of males report they feel good about their overall looks and facial features, as compared with only 45 percent of females.[26] Adolescent girls are tormented by poor body image, partly because they have learned during childhood to overvalue, display, and mistrust their appearance. They enter puberty with a strong need to feel attractive, and therefore suffer greater insecurity than boys do when their developing bodies feel awkward and out of control. Moreover, girls are socialized to search for self-identity through male attention. To transform from tomboy to Tom's girl, Linda must depend in large part on being pretty.

Since good looks are stereotypically associated with desirable personality traits, an "unattractive" changing body threatens self-esteem. The connection between appearance and worthiness for females can become so deeply ingrained during puberty that it remains throughout a woman's life, making her continuously insecure about her appearance and, consequently, about herself. Looking back, women describe their teens as a time filled with awkwardness, embarrassment, feelings of inadequacy, fear of sexuality and of separation. Some become frozen into the negative body images that develop during this transitional stage and are never able to accept themselves as attractive women.

Even those girls who are naturally well endowed with beauty (or who manage to achieve it) report that good looks can be a mixed blessing. Pretty is nice but not always better. Nubile beauties become vulnerable to sexual exploitation, sometimes at a very young age. They may be shown off by parents or "used" by peers who seek social prestige through contacts with them. Many begin to resent attention that is based solely on looks and that disregards who they are as people. Good-looking boys rarely suffer from these special hazards.

Adolescents face the major task of achieving psychological separation from parents. Because girls are allowed more passive, dependent behavior than boys throughout childhood, they have greater conflicts over parental separation. Identified with her mother, Linda wants to grow into that familiar model of womanhood. Yet she realizes that the limitations of her mother's life are linked with being female. Mother as a model must be transcended. She must again withdraw from the safe maternal body, must cast off the mother as an alter ego. Separation conflicts first experienced in infancy now resurface. The adolescent struggle for independence often refocuses on the body issues of early childhood: food, sleep, safety, sexuality. The anorectic, for example, transforms her need for self-identity into a destructive feeding contest. She refuses nourishment in much the same way as a baby who spits out food.

While trying to create her own image, Linda may concentrate on how *not* to look like or be like her mother. Since beauty standards constantly change, they provide an easy focus for separation conflict. Recall the case of Barbara, who was denied permission by her mother to pierce a second hole in her ears and who then defiantly took a needle and pierced them herself. Using a beauty issue, she proclaimed both her power to cast off maternal control and her right to display her body as she wished. By rejecting her mother's values for personal appearance, she rejected her mother as well. The peer group can provide a critical support system in this struggle toward separation. Unfortunately, peer groups tend to glorify dating and popularity, pressuring girls to conform to a rigid fashion code.

Perched on a teeter-totter of rebellion, Linda swings first up into freedom, then back down into constraint. Her mother's ambivalence further intensifies the conflict. Linda's struggle for separation from her mother, who prods her forward into womanhood and then pulls her back into girlish dependency is reminiscent of the dilemmas faced by daughters in fairy tales: how to escape from the stepmother who confines Cinderella to the hearth; from the sorceress-mother who isolates Rapunzel in virgin loneliness; from the jealous mother who threatens Snow White with the endless sleep of infancy.

Bettelheim explains that fairy tales often depict rites of passage. They portray the metaphoric death of an old inadequate self, followed by rebirth on a higher plane of existence. Snow White's fairest face evokes maternal jealousy but later attracts the kiss of salvation. Rapunzel's splendid hair is cut off but only after she pulls in a prince and climbs away from mother, out into life. In such tales it is the girl's changing, pubescent body that initially triggers maternal conflict but that ultimately provides the key to maternal separation.

Fairy-tale mothers respond to their daughters' emerging sexual beauty by isolating, rejecting, or confining them. Real mothers likewise feel threatened by a daughter who is blooming into adolescence just at the time of life when their own looks are fading. In a "Snow White syndrome" of envy and jealousy, mothers send ambivalent double messages: pride mixed with hostility, encouragement mixed with anxiety, overt acceptance mixed with unconscious rejection. Mothers buy the clothes and model the makeup, but they also impose curfews or refuse permission. "Package yourself for consumption, but don't let yourself be consumed. Don't disgrace me by indulging yourself; don't replace me by becoming yourself." The godmother tells Cinderella that she will transform her into an irresistible vision, but that Cinderella must break away before it is "too late." Both the good and the bad fairy-tale mothers may be anxious to market daughters as brides yet fear their unbridled sexuality.

Where are the fathers? For Cinderella, Snow White, and Rapunzel, Father is passive or nonexistent. Fairy-tale fathers seem to abandon their daughters to cruel mothers, while the girls appear to accept paternal rejection without complaint. In reality, men often feel threatened by a lovely, nubile daughter. Oedipal problems resurface when girls reach puberty. The father who once delighted in his toddler's coquetry, who for years enjoyed her company and encouraged her accomplishments, may suddenly recoil from her womanly body. One day he sees his own child as sexually seductive, feels anxious and guilty over his incestuous attraction, and fears possible loss of control. He may withdraw suddenly or subtly, consciously or unconsciously. Sometimes his rejection is cruel and overt (as in Elizabeth's case when her father called her a clown and a tramp whenever he saw her wearing makeup). Fathers, like mothers, send double messages: "Become a sexy lady but remain my little girl." A number of women report that they first began to dislike their bodies during puberty, when their fathers' teasing led to feelings of disgust. As Linda struggles with problems of maternal envy and maternal separation, the added pain of paternal rejection can leave her especially lonely and insecure. These forces combine, creating a powerful drive to find another love object, to transfer affection from parent to prince. The cultivation of beauty is, of course, a crucial aspect of that search.

In fairy tales, body parts are imaginatively enhanced through fantasy—the foot as tiny as a doll's, the hair as long as a ladder, the lips as red as blood. These exaggerations serve as a catalyst for emancipation. They propel a girl away from childish dependency toward sexual maturity. Notice that it is not a strong and competent body but rather a beautiful or special one that serves as the liberating force in such tales. Like the storybook heroines worshiped in childhood, Linda turns to her body for help. After all, notes Bettelheim, when we are needy, what more reliable source of recovery do we have than our own flesh? How can she enhance and exaggerate her maturing body to help her achieve independence and self-esteem? How can she attain, without a fairy godmother's magic wand, the superbeauty that will deliver a prince?

In their quest for a separate identity, adolescent girls become especially vulnerable to beauty problems that threaten their health and well-being. For example, sophisticated medical techniques now lure girls into cosmetic surgery even before they are fully grown. Nose jobs, chin implants, and breast reductions are being performed on minors as modern medicine perpetuates the myth of female beauty. The vast majority of teenage aesthetic surgery patients are girls, not boys. Before they can adjust to their own changing profiles, growing girls are considered suitable candidates for cosmetic overhaul. Parents are paying for it; professionals are providing it.

Girls as young as age fourteen are now undergoing breast alterations. This is a good example of how beauty stereotypes interact with the maturational process, producing adjustment problems that in turn prompt cosmetic surgery. Because breasts are so symbolic of feminine beauty (in western cultures), many physically normal girls experience an almost paralyzing self-consciousness during breast development. Advertisements for bust "improvement" products abound in teen magazines. Breast development begins early in puberty, often by age ten. Girls start to mature before boys, and can be several years ahead of boys in the same grade. Full-breasted girls must carry the burden of their early maturation "up front." They suffer embarrassment, ostracism, and overt ridicule. (In fact, large-breasted females of any age are stereotyped as unintelligent, incompetent, immoral, and immodest.)[27] To these young girls, surgical correction of their breast problem seems to be a wonderful solution. In rare cases such a solution may be justifiable; usually it is premature.

Until recently, breast reduction surgery was not performed on minors. Now it is being offered to girls barely beyond puberty. One plastic surgeon notes that parents often initiate the surgical request. He cautions doctors to be certain that the girl herself really wants the operation and also understands the pain and potential consequences. Complications in reduction mammoplasty are common, including unsightly scarring and loss of nipple sensitivity. Is it possible for a fourteen-year-old with a poor body image who is being ridiculed and who is emotionally immature to make a wise decision about cosmetic breast surgery? Research suggests that college-age women feel much more postively about their breasts than they did during early puberty. Searching for a quick solution, some girls are being tempted into an irreversible procedure that they may later regret.

The use of cosmetics is another beauty transformation that poses a special health hazard for adolescents. Makeup serves as a critical initiation rite into womanhood. It is an essential fashion prop that helps to exaggerate gender differences. An estimated one-third of the girls who regularly use cosmetics will develop a condition dermatologists are now calling acne cosmetica. Genetic in origin, acne is triggered by increasing hormone production during puberty. The potent ingredients used in cosmetics can induce serious skin problems even in girls who are not genetically prone. Since it takes several months for cosmetic acne to develop, the cause may go unsuspected. Once the acne has developed, a vicious cycle ensues: as it becomes worse, more makeup is used to cover it, which only further escalates the condition.[28]

Another skin problem, called excoriated acne is caused by compulsive picking at trivial blemishes. Teens who suffer from this condition begin with a poor image of themselves. To confirm their feelings of ugliness and worthlessness, they punish themselves by gouging their faces. Excoriated acne is found almost exclusively in adolescent girls. Acne reportedly has a greater psychological impact on girls than on boys because appearance is more critical to female identity. Although boys with acne also suffer embarrassment, they can more easily find social acceptance through sports or academic achievements.

Pursuit of mythical beauty turns the adolescent girl into an active consumer. Giant industries create, define, and cater to her special beauty "needs" and siphon her babysitting money into the purchase of bust developers and Ultralash. A *New York Times* editorial asked, "Why does a fourteen-year-old Brooklyn girl need to spend $40 on a manicure and $700 on pants, sweaters, head-bands and makeup to complete her back-to-school wardrobe?"[29] The very next day this newspaper carried a full back-page ad directed at potential advertisers for *Seventeen* magazine: "*Seventeen* readers don't love you and leave you. As adults 34% still rinse with the same mouthwash and 33% use the same nail polish. Talk to them in their teens and they'll be customers for life."

After analyzing magazine ads aimed at female adolescents, a researcher concludes that girls are bombarded with one essential message about their purpose in life: "learning the art of body adornment through clothing, cosmetics, jewelry, hair products, perfumes."[30] In these ads cosmetic transformations are made to seem a natural accentuation of what already exists. "I look myself, only better," says the young model, confiding the secret formula that brought out the highlights of her hair. Narcissism is fostered by ads that focus again and again on appearance as the primary source of female identity. Cosmetic advertisements have been shown to affect the "conception of social reality" of teenage girls. A single fifteen-minute exposure to a series of beauty commercials increased the degree to which they perceived beauty as being "important to their own personality and important to being pop-ular with boys."[31]

Ads attempt to convince Linda that she must make up and make over in order to make it in life. She is directed to her mirror to discover herself. In effect, the question "Who am I?" is trans-lated into "What should I look like?" Her natural adolescent drive to attain a personal identity is distorted into a need to package herself as a product. In the end, costly and painful beauty rituals do not produce a sense of individuality. Just the opposite occurs: girls wind up all looking the same and are thus more easily ste-reotyped. "They look alike, think alike, and even worse . . . believe they are not alike."[32]

Marking Time in Moratorium

You wait, little girl, on an empty stage
for fate to turn the light on;
your life, little girl, is an empty page
that men will want to write on.
(From *The Sound of Music*,
"Sixteen Going On Seventeen")[33]

According to the developmental theory of Erik Erikson, the early stages of psychological growth are quite similar for boys and girls. He describes a somewhat different adjustment pattern at adolescence, however, for each sex. Erikson's account of gender divergence during adolescence illustrates how female deviance and beauty are explained and sustained by an influential psychological model.

Adolescents are struggling above all for psychological independence. In their search for self, they use new levels of adult reasoning to test various lifestyles. For a boy, Erikson explains, the quest for identity is a dynamic one in which alternatives are actively tried on and cast off. In contrast, the adolescent girl must place herself in a "psychological moratorium," where she waits, "ready and willing to fuse with a male" who will provide the framework within which she can discover herself. Her task, says Erikson, is to remain flexible and fluid, to hold her "inner space ready for the man who will one day rescue her from emptiness and loneliness by filling it." Womanhood arrives when "*attractiveness* [italics mine] and experience have succeeded in selecting what is to be admitted to the welcome of the inner space for keeps." Adolescent girls are therefore expected to use their bodies as a basis for "incorporating others."[34]

Erikson's description brings to mind the image of Snow White suspended in "moratorium." The happy tomboy who once played and worked with the dwarves lies passively on display in a forest of hunters. She is shrouded in beauty, her lips and her inner space held out as bait. By contracting into a coma she prepares for rebirth. But it is not nature alone that lulls the adolescent girl into the slumber of a beautified image; culture also dictates her destiny. For Linda must adjust not only to the maturational changes of puberty but also to society's response to them. Just when nature invites her to waltz into womanhood, culture cautions her to hold back: Restrain yourself, guard your body, keep close to home, set modest goals, look lovely, act ladylike. While nature prompts growth, culture imposes constraint. Society writes rules to regulate Linda's activities, to restrict her sexuality, reduce her options, redirect her fantasies.

Just when sexual expression becomes crucial to self-identity, culture cautions against direct pursuit. "Nice" girls are still warned against making the first move. Even in the liberated 1980s, "experts" like Ann Landers and Joyce Brothers advise that "a girl who knows how to use her femininity and her charm has a better chance than a girl who acts directly." In essence, they advise Linda not to call him up but to dial the hairdresser instead.

The challenge facing Linda is how to become attractive enough to be courted and rescued from the insecurity of an identity moratorium. To walk beside Mr. Right she must put her best face forward. Research presented in an earlier chapter confirms that the prettier the girl, the more frequently she will date. When asked what characteristics they sought in a girlfriend, teenage boys placed "good looks first, good body second." In contrast, girls listed "intelligence" as the most important characteristic sought in a boyfriend. Girls choose boyfriends for a variety of qualities, including academic, athletic, and leadership abilities. Boys still choose girlfriends primarily for their appearance.

Erikson observes that "much of a young woman's identity is already defined in her kind of attractiveness and in the selectivity of her search for the man by whom she wishes to be sought."[35] While boys pursue an identity by developing their talents, girls pour time and energy into fashioning an external image. Hours of combing, washing, dieting, shopping, dressing, and making up are invested in the all-important cosmetic exterior. These obsessive beauty rituals have been called the "put on a happy face phenomenon." They are in direct contrast to girls' behavior during the tomboy phase. Yet the end result is similar: girls get to spend time with the boys. Instead of competing with and against them, they now compete with each other for boys' attention. Anaïs Nin once wrote, "Every girl of fifteen has put the same question to a mirror: Am I beautiful? . . . The mirror is not going to answer. She will have to look for the answer in the eyes and faces of the boys who dance with her."[36]

In his comprehensive survey of American high schools during the 1950s, James Coleman concluded that one of the crucial lessons taught in the underground school curriculum was the importance of physical attractiveness for girls.

> . . . in none of these areas of adult life are physical beauty, an enticing manner, and nice clothes as important for performing successfully as they are in high school. . . . If the adult society wants high schools to inculcate the attributes that make girls objects to attract men's attention, then these values of good looks and nice clothes . . . are just right. If not, then the values are quite inappropriate.[37]

While schools have changed since then, the emphasis on female beauty continues to influence adolescent adjustment. In a textbook published in 1981 on the psychology of women, Bernice Lott concluded that the fundamental task facing today's young woman remains unchanged: to enhance her attractiveness and find a boyfriend. Girls therefore learn to "smile a lot, be pleasant, nonassertive, well groomed, friendly and available." These generalities are considered by Lott to be as relevant to contemporary girls of all social and ethnic groups as they were twenty years ago.[38] As a sophomore, Linda comments,

> Most of the girls started wearing makeup to school in the seventh grade . . . usually lipstick, blush, and eye shadow. Some of the mothers objected but they couldn't do much about it. We would just wait till we got to school to put it on. Now I never go off in the morning without it. We don't wear anything different for parties. School is the most important place because that's where we really get seen.

According to Erikson's theory, Linda must try out a variety of identifications with males while she practices being their "counterpart and principal attraction." But can she really achieve selfhood in the role of an attractive counterpart? Can someone resolve an identity crisis by regressing into a dependent state?

Inevitably, psychological theories based on the masculine as normative generate a perspective from which females appear either deficient or peculiar in their growth. Despite feminist criticism, Erikson's *Eight Stages of Man* are still included in nearly every psychology text as a valid interpretation of female experience. In recent articles Erikson continues to retreat to woman's "inner space" for a biological explanation of gender role divergence, while elsewhere he recognizes that social factors are crucial to personality development.

Culture does count. It is not the anchor of her inner space that grounds Linda and prevents her from sailing actively toward the adult horizon. The mainstream simply does not flow in her direction. By depicting a psychological moratorium as normal and desirable, Erikson places the stamp of professional approval on it. His model equates what seems to be with what must and should be, thereby condoning and encouraging adolescent gender divergence. It is easy to conclude from his model that it is normal for the inner space of a young girl's purse to be cluttered with lipstick and mascara and for the inner space of her mind to be overflowing with fantasies of glamour and romance. Is it really healthy for a growing person to place herself on hold? Part of the self atrophies, leaving only a skeleton that must be fleshed out by another person's ego.

Surely if Linda's identity becomes synonymous with being loved as an attractive counterpart, she will have trouble loving herself until and unless another finds her worthy of adoration. To sustain self-acceptance, she will need continuous affirmation that she remains "adorable." She must perpetually peer into the eyes of others for reflected self-worth. Perhaps, as Kolbenschlag eloquently puts it, "the kiss that Sleeping Beauty waits for is not that of any Prince, but the embrace of her own being."[39]

Beauty as Achievement

What happens if Linda rouses herself from the mirror and steps beyond the boundaries of moratorium? What if she races off at top speed to find herself, forgetting the "make up" required to maintain an attractive feminine image?

When psychologist Matina Horner asked female college students to write brief stories about "Ann, who is at the top of her medical school class," they did not respond with fairy tales but with accounts that ended unhappily. "Ann doesn't really want to

be a doctor," they wrote. "Ann drops out of medical school. . . .
Ann is beaten up by jealous classmates. . . . She is a social
outcast, an acne-faced bookworm . . . who ends up a bitter spin-
ster."[40] Horner concluded that these negative outcomes reflect an
unconscious fear of success. Females are afraid that high achievement will lead to social rejection, and their fear of success, in
turn, inhibits achievement motivation and performance, she wrote.

Intrigued but skeptical when first reading Horner's work, I
asked my eleven-year-old to write a story about "Jill, who was
elected president of her fifth-grade class." Here is what my own
daughter wrote in 1971:

> All the girls are cheering Jill and the boys are booing. The girls
> wanted Jill to win and had promised her a soda if she did. The
> boys thought she would not win. The girls are feeling great but
> soon lose interest. The boys are full of revenge. They go to the
> princebel (*sic*) and convince him Jill is not fit for the job. So the
> job is taken away and given to someone else.*

Doubts about Horner's theory dissolved in a flood of maternal
concern. Here was a classic fear-of-success story. Boys had taken
revenge against a successful girl by stripping her of her status,
while other girls had withdrawn their support. Horner must be
right. But how had my child developed this insidious fear when
I had tried so hard to provide a healthy model of female achievement? And how would fear of success influence her adolescent
growth?

Studying a group of high school seniors, I found that girls
performed quite well on certain tasks. But their achievement expectations were much lower than boys' and also lower than their
actual performance. Furthermore, their achievement stories contained fear of failure as well as fear of success. As Horner had
predicted, they seemed as afraid of failing in the interpersonal

---

* The following classical myth from St. Augustine bears a striking resemblance to that
story: "Cecrops called an assembly to decide which of the two Gods the citizens wished
to have name their city. The men voted for Neptune, the women for Minerva, and
since there was one more woman, Minerva won. Neptune was angry and caused a
great flood. To appease him, the women were punished threefold: They would lose
their right of suffrage; their children would no longer take the names of their mothers;
and women would no longer be called Athenians."[41]

arena as they were of succeeding in the achievement arena.[42] Girls report that peer and adult acceptance are the main factors that make them feel important. They are less likely than boys to name competitive achievement as a source of personal esteem.[43] Their fantasies are dominated by themes of beauty and popularity.

Excellence can make girls feel socially unattractive. Consider the following: Seventh-graders were given a so-called intelligence test against an opposite-sex classmate. Then each student was told privately that he or she had won. The girls' scores dropped on the next part of the test, whereas the boys' scores went up. Girls later explained that they didn't like to beat boys in a competitive game; they would "rather be popular than have good grades or win against a boy."[44] Sensing that winning is a threat to social status, they reduced their performance (perhaps unconsciously) in order to preserve their popularity. In effect, they put their brains on hold while striving for social acceptance. The desire for achievement and for affiliation are, of course, equally legitimate and should not have to conflict with each other in the mind of a twelve-year-old.

In a 1983 study on attitudes toward mathematics, nearly half the high school girls surveyed reported feeling embarrassment because they were smart. The majority admitted to playing dumb at times and believed that doing so is common among girls but not readily admitted to. One conclusion of this study was that conflicts between intellectual excellence and the feminine sex role are still very much alive.[45]

Fear of success has been found to increase through junior and senior high school, indicating that achievement becomes more and more threatening. While underachieving boys usually have a history of low grades starting in elementary school, underachievement in girls tends to begin at puberty. Gifted girls are viewed by their peers more negatively than girls of average ability, and more negatively than equally gifted boys. Students describe gifted girls as "bossy, conceited, snobbish, show-off, dull, self-centered." Underachievement can thus be understood as a useful strategy for preserving self-esteem.[46]

Caught between her desires for achievement and for affiliation, Linda is drawn toward both but realizes that she cannot divide herself. At this fork in the developmental path, beauty beckons to her. As she tries to redirect achievement motives toward less threatening, more feminine goals, the pursuit of physical attractiveness provides a convenient solution. Working to become pretty, thin, and chic can yield many of the same returns as other achievement efforts, as can be seen in the photograph of the lovely debutantes. It offers a challenge, fills time, enhances status, raises self-esteem, brings social and financial rewards. It does not threaten the feminine identity that Linda has been taught to value throughout childhood. Beauty will not undermine her popularity or attractiveness. She need not fear being "unsexed by success" if she becomes fairest of them all.

In patriarchal cultures, achievement has generally been defined by "the things men do" and the traits men value. Yet in these same cultures, many females are strongly motivated toward more feminine goals, such as "interpersonal bonding, maternal satisfaction, and maintaining an attractive appearance."[47] Moreover, the pursuit of beauty has instrinsic appeal to a narcissistic teenager.

Heightened narcissism is normal at puberty and is sometimes referred to as the hallmark of adolescence. While teenagers of both sexes may be equally narcissistic, they learn to express it in different ways. Boys show off through status and power, thus displaying their potency. Girls "flash beauty," thus seeking admiration as they signal their sexual availability.[48] Freud interpreted increased narcissism in adolescent girls as resulting from a new awareness of their deficiencies and a greater sense of inferiority. Narcissistic concern over appearance in teenage girls does not have to be interpreted as a developmental failure, but can be viewed as a new way of responding to and nurturing the self. If fear of success is part of the larger anxiety of stepping outside the female role, then cosmetic rituals can help pull an adolescent girl firmly back into the familiar feminine ground. The narcissistic pursuit of beauty thereby provides achievement satisfaction while reducing both fear of success and fear of failure.

To complicate matters further, evaluation of female performance is often confounded by appearance. Analysis of college recommendations written by high school guidance counselors reveals frequent comments about girls' grooming, neatness, charm, and attractiveness, whereas such factors are rarely mentioned in recommendations for boys. Girls do not always know whether they are being judged for their ability or for their looks. Sometimes the bias is in the positive direction, other times in the negative. For example, male college students rated essays more favorably when the essays were presented along with a picture of an attractive rather than an unattractive female author. But female students rated the same combination less favorably. In contrast, essays written by males were judged by both sexes without regard to the author's appearance.[49]

Some attitudes toward female achievement are changing. Contrary to the stereotype of the ugly, brainy bookworm, a 1981 study found that girls who took traditionally masculine courses—such as physics and calculus—were not perceived as physically unattractive by their classmates.[50] Adolescent girls need support in handling their conflicted feelings about achievement, affiliation, and attractiveness, and they can be reassured that commitment to a traditionally masculine field does not automatically brand them as ugly or unfeminine.

More than a decade has passed since my fifth-grade daughter wrote a classic fear-of-success story. For her they were years of confusion about appearance and achievement. They were also years of cultural ferment over feminist issues of equality and reform. Her class was the first in the high school's history to march into graduation in a single line, unsegregated by sex. However, her classmates at Columbia University deprecatingly referred to courses at Barnard as "tit courses." What is female is still subject to devaluation.

Gender myths resurface in different ways as the members of each generation learn their roles all too well. We may wonder what lies ahead for the toddlers just beginning to program their pink and blue mental file cards? Powerful media networks are cabling a feast of strawberry-shortcake images into their eager eyes. More and more applications for the Little Miss Hemisphere Pageant are received each year. Toy models of Brooke Shields, packaged with makeup and rollers, pile up at the local toy store (next to the Barbella dolls), ready for the Christmas rush. The belief in female deviance, from which the need for female beauty derives, continues to cast its shadow on our children.

There is some cause for optimism, however. Counterpressures

are recasting gender roles in a new light. Feminism encourages diversity of appearance, acceptance of personal differences, and cultivation of competent bodies instead of merely decorative ones. New textbooks portray greater interdependence between boys and girls while de-emphasizing women in glamour and service roles. Title IX has brought millions of girls out of the powder room into the locker room and onto the playing field.

Children develop from the first stage of gender confusion in early childhood into the second stage of gender conformity during adolescence. The third and final stage is called gender transcendence. It is reached when the highly polarized sex roles, typical in adolescence, are replaced by androgynous ones that are more flexible. Few people attain this highest level, yet many parents are striving to transcend gender constraints and to achieve greater role equality within the family. As the next generation of children grow up with less polarized adult models, they may be less likely to equate femininity with beauty and better able to accept their own changing bodies. The words of a fourth-grader are encouraging. "Do you feel that boys and girls are different?" he was asked.

> No. I don't think they are different, because we can both accomplish the same thing. We might not have been brought up the same way but we are all very, very, very, very, very much the same kind of people.

7

Shaping Down and Shaping Up

The sense of fullness and swelling, of curves and softness, of
the awareness of plenitude and abundance which filled me
with disgust and alarm, were actually the qualities of a woman's body.

— Kim Chernin[1]

CONSIDER for a moment the most ancient human images
known: the intriguing Venus figures that date back twenty-
five thousand years to Paleolithic times. Found in regions stretching from Spain to Eurasia, these relics depict a full-bodied female,
her large pendulous breasts spilling over a swollen abdomen, her
mammoth thighs supporting a rotund rump. Some archaeologists
interpret them as goddesses who embodied man's awe of woman's
reproductive power and who were worshiped at a time when
famine was constant and fertility was a mystery.

But perhaps, as others suggest, the Venus figures were not
fertility symbols at all, but rather served as a kind of pornographic
amulet—an ancient precursor of the pinup centerfold. Imagine a
hominid hunter, far from home and lonely, fingering the curvaceous belly and breasts of a Venus figure for comfort and erotic
pleasure. A fanciful picture, perhaps; but if true these relics represent the ideal of paleolithic pulchritude: not an image of a real
woman but one built out of lust and longing.

We might also fantasize a young female hominid struggling to
transform herself into the prevailing beauty image, much as her

modern counterpart does. Just as obsessed with weight, just as depressed over a flat chest, she binged on bananas while envying her plump sisters. Of course, if somehow she did attain the ideal size, her mammoth body would make her vulnerable and dependent. The effects of a distorted beauty image were probably just as debilitating then as now. Today's fat female, alas, cannot pass for an erotic fertility figure. Today she is weighed and rejected by a myth that has scaled feminine beauty down to a smaller size.

Being thin as a prerequisite for being pretty is a tormenting dimension of the current beauty ideal. The past few decades have witnessed a dramatic thinning of the American woman. One out of every two women is on a diet "most of the time." Three out of four feel they are naturally prone to being overweight.[2] Women consider thinness the most basic element of physical attractiveness. Weight obsession, now one of the most common clinical disorders among females, is a problem shared alike by obese, bulimic, anorectic, and especially normal-weight women.

Revised standards adopted by insurance companies in the 1950s defined the majority of us as overweight and led to an epidemic of self-rejection. In one recent year, more than two hundred diet books were published. A dozen of them became best-sellers. Billions are spent each year on reducing programs, none of which have been proven effective over the long run. A casual survey at my twenty-fifth high school reunion showed that a collective female weight loss of several hundred pounds occurred before the event. These former classmates trimmed down for the ball, even without the promise of a princely payoff.

Estrogen pads the female body with more fat than the male body. Women therefore deviate from the popular lean and muscular masculine norm. Hence females of normal weight are misjudged and also misjudge themselves as overweight. Men are more accurate than women in assessing their proper weight; women feel overweight when they are not. The number of women who consider themselves too fat has doubled in the past decade. When *Glamour* magazine surveyed its readers in 1984, 75 percent felt too heavy and only 15 percent felt just right. Nearly half of those who were actually underweight reported feeling too fat and wanting to diet.[3] Among a sample of college women, 40 percent felt overweight when only 12 percent actually were too heavy.[4] Nine out of ten participants in diet programs are female, many of whom are already close to their proper weight. As compared to men, women weigh themselves more frequently and seek medical help for weight problems more often.

While females experience even a few extra pounds as a profound dimension in their lives, males who are as much as one hundred pounds too heavy say that being fat does not matter very much to them. Men are far less introspective about weight and are less embarrassed by it. They are allowed a much greater margin of variance than women are before being defined by others as too heavy.[5] Many fat men were athletes when young and still think of themselves as "big men." They neither recognize their obesity as a problem nor seek help. In men, fat is sometimes viewed as a symbol of virility or treated with good humor (as in Pavarotti's case). In women, obesity nearly always signals inferiority because it nullifies beauty. The double standard for weight is applied professionally as well as socially. For example, it took Carole Gerdom a decade in court to challenge the weight restrictions that Continental Airlines used to fire hundreds of stewardesses but never applied to male flight attendants.

In a study of male and female perceptions of ideal body shape, women more often overestimated their relative weight and rated their bodies as heavier than they thought men preferred as an ideal. In contrast, men judged their relative weight more accurately, and generally felt that their current body shape was very close to what women wanted in an ideal man. Thus man's perceptions help to keep them satisfied with their bodies, whereas women's perceptions motivate them toward weight obsession and dieting. The authors of this study conclude that women exaggerate the degree of thinness that men actually desire, due to idealized media images and to advertisements fostered by diet industries.[6]

Weight fads come and go. The Greeks envied the Cretans for a mysterious drug that kept them thin, while the Romans, who hated obesity but also loved to feast, used regurgitation to keep the scale figures down. In western cultures, female beauty has been equated with slimness for only sixty of the past six hundred years. Between 1400 and 1700, the maternal role was idealized, and fat was considered both fashionable and erotic. Womanhood

was equated with motherhood. Wives were desired for their pro-
creative value and spent much of their lives either pregnant or
nursing. Beauty images portrayed matronly plumpness, full nur-
turant breasts, and the earthy, fruitful look of a Botticelli nymph.
Again in the late nineteenth century, the ideal feminine shape
was big and heavy. Bottoms were broadened with bustles. Doctors encouraged plumpness as a sign of good health (much as
doctors are pushing diets one hundred years later). Mammoth
sculptures, like the Statue of Liberty depicted big-boned, solid,
but sensually rounded figures.[7]

Starting with the flappers, Americans began to give up their
fetish for curves, and the thinning of the modern woman was
under way. Maternity lost much of its value in a world striving
for Zero Population Growth. Even pregnancy was no excuse for
an abundant maternal look. In the 1960s, obstetricians routinely
placed expectant mothers on strict diets that permitted a maximum gain of twenty pounds (a procedure they later rejected because it threatened fetal growth). Maternal images were replaced
by sexual ones as women devoted a smaller portion of their lives
to motherhood. Slimness became a sign of emancipation, a symbol
of nonreproductive sexuality and independence. The accent shifted
to looking like a playgirl rather than an earth mother. In fact, the
Playboy centerfold models have grown slimmer every year since
the magazine's inception.[8] Between 1954 and 1978, the average
winner of the Miss America Pageant grew one inch taller and five
pounds thinner. At the height of her modeling career, five-foot-
seven-inch Twiggy weighed in at ninety-seven pounds. The trend
toward a slimmer ideal is contradicted by an actual weight increase
in women under thirty due to better nutrition. The result of this
contradiction is a greater discrepancy between real weight and
ideal weight: our current beauty ideal is at the lowest 5 percent
of the actual weight curve.[9] The female body represents fertility
and mortality. The flapper or the Twiggy look strips it of its
fleshy, fruitful dimensions, and hides woman's reproductive power
behind a neutered image. When fashioned as a boyish imp, or
most recently as an angular jock, the fearful mother figure is
deflated and safely disguised.

Commercial images both reflect and influence the prevailing
weight trend. For example, the familiar White Rock girl has

undergone several revisions, each time becoming longer and lea-
ner. In 1894, a five-feet-four-inch, 140-pound model with a thirty-
seven inch bust and thirty-eight-inch hips represented the ideal
form to our great-grandmothers. She was slimmed down first in
1947 to 125 pounds, then again in 1975, when she was reduced
to a mere 118 pounds despite having grown to five feet, eight
inches.[10]

Analysis of media images confirms that a very thin body-type
predominates and that positive social attributes are related to
thinness, whereas negative ones are related to fatness. Women are
told that they can be loved only when they are svelte. Virtually
every woman's magazine runs a regular diet column. These pub-
lications increase concern over excess pounds and then sell ques-
tionable products as cures. One fashion model reports that it took
a crew of people to get her into a pair of size three designer jeans
and to carry her into position to be photographed. She could
neither walk nor bend. "To look like I looked in that ad, you
would have to fast for two months and hold your breath for twenty
minutes," she quipped. A major department store ran the following copy for a new fashion line: "Bean lean, slender as the night,
narrow as an arrow, pencil thin, get the point? . . ." Through
such commercial imagery, thinness in women has become equated
not only with beauty and sexuality but also with status.

Weight and wealth have long been associated with each other.
The Duchess of Windsor reportedly was first to declare, "You
can't be too rich or too thin." Fads tend to filter down from the
"haves" and to end once they become attainable by the "have
nots." In the ancient Oriental view, a well-fed woman brought
honor to her husband. Her abundance confirmed his affluence
(much as a wife's designer clothes do today). Powerful chieftains
sometimes force-fed their women as a testimony to their own
wealth. Sociologist Thorstein Veblen noted a century ago that
body shape reflected conspicuous consumption and curves sig-
nified luxury. When resources are scarce, weight is associated
with prosperity and plump women are admired. However, when
resources are plentiful, the weight caste system reverses. As the
rich become thin, the body becomes a form of "inconspicuous
consumption" that distinguishes the upper classes from the lower.[11]
Although social class differences in weight are minimal among

American men, obesity occurs seven times more frequently in American women of the lowest socioeconomic levels than in those of the highest. Conversely, anorexia has increased among upper-class women but is rare in lower-class families.

Beauty standards are thus linked to larger political and economic factors. The lean image conforms to our American value system, which admires hard work and self-denial. Slimness takes on virtuous connotations that are linked with economic success, while overweight is viewed as shameful and lower-class. Today, fat is considered unsightly because it represents low social status as well as lack of self-control. The belief that the happiest females are both rich and thin is tormenting for average-weight middle-class women who, as a result of it spend much of their lives on a diet. By the end of high school, the majority of girls have already begun a lifelong battle with the scale.

Dieting entails narcissistic self-preoccupation and masochistic self-denial. It is a painful and exhausting process. Results are frustrating. Nearly every pound that is lost is eventually regained. Even when overweight, the chronic dieter may suffer from malnutrition, gastric problems, irritability, anxiety, lethargy, fatigue, tension, insomnia, and depression—all tormenting side effects of the latest food fad promoted from Scarsdale or Beverly Hills. The dieter never connects her symptoms with the quest for beauty. Instead, she is referred to a doctor, who often prescribes anti-depressants, tranquilizers, or psychotherapy, further reducing her sense of self-control.

Like other beauty obsessions, chronic dieting often stems from a desire to normalize an unacceptable body. Dieting requires denial of hunger, denial of fullness, denial of natural sensations. One woman comments, "What I resent about dieting is that it makes one so terribly self-centered, so preoccupied with things that apply to oneself only, that there is no energy left to be spontaneous, relaxed and outgoing."[12] Another describes the quest for thinness as a "kind of caricature, a self-mockery of the experience of being a woman, since it demonstrates the physical discomfort and self-sacrifice required in the female role."[13]

A major obstacle to maintaining normal weight seems to be a "fat head," that is, the belief that one is too heavy even when one's weight is within normal range. Dieting regimes themselves are implicated as a major cause of eating disorders. Severe dieting, especially during adolescence, leads to a lowering of the metabolic rate, which in turn makes weight maintenance more difficult. Self-starvation leads to binges, and a vicious cycle ensues: dieting, starving, binging, vomiting, guilt, and self-disgust.

Weighty Dialogues

Bodies make social statements. Eating disorders can therefore be used as a form of communication. Such disorders now afflict females three to ten times more often than males. Why do so many women use their bodies to express their feelings? What are they trying to say by either starving or binging?

In her analysis of fat as a feminist issue, Susie Orbach explains that fat is sometimes a symbolic way of saying "Fuck you." Each heavy woman "creates a crack in the popular culture's ability to make us mere products," she writes.[14] Obesity can provide a confrontation with a constricting feminine image, a way of protesting against society's unreasonable demand for superslimness.

Obesity refutes the fragile, dependent, and childlike aspects of the feminine mystique. Greater weight conveys greater strength, countering the stereotype of a delicate, dependent creature who needs help through doorways or into chairs. For a woman with big ideas who wants to become a substantial person, gaining weight may appear to be a good way of gaining recognition. Big people are hard to ignore; their movements have impact, and by throwing their weight around they can make a dent in the world. One thinks of Bella Abzug, Sarah Caldwell, Barbara Jordan, Gertrude Stein. For someone who wants to become significant, dieting may seem like a trivial waste of time. "The littleness of it, so picayune. . . . I hate the small chattering magpie kind of woman. . . . Being big is my real aspiration. . . . That means not to be a woman but to be somewhat more. . . ." says one.[15] Fat confers the masculine qualities of strength and dominance on a woman and creates a more substantial self-image, in the same way that fitness does. In fact, the current vogue of thinness has been attributed to an underlying fear of female power.

Some heavy women report a recurrent desire from childhood

onward to become someone special, something more than just another pretty face. They conceal their femininity behind layers of flesh. By making the package too large to unwrap, they are saved from exposure as merely another ordinary chick. Being overweight can then serve as a convenient explanation for all kinds of problems. The "true self" is spared the test of public scrutiny; failures are attributed to being overweight and unattractive. Although the fat outer self may be rejected, the thin inner self remains protected. As mind and body are dissociated and contrary feelings experienced from each, it is hard to maintain a unified sense of self. Women with eating disorders frequently speak of the body as if it were under someone else's control, which prompts still further weight manipulation to achieve a more secure self-identity. Analogously, when women are disguised behind a false beauty mask, a similar mind-body dissociation occurs as the true self, the unmade-up self, becomes inaccessible.

Thinness equals beauty equals sexual desirability. Conversely, fat equals ugly equals nonerotic. Obesity is sometimes used to control frightening sexual impulses by creating a barrier between the sexual and the nonsexual self. Once "neutered by fat," an overweight woman loses part of the power of beauty.

But she may acquire power of a different kind. People are less likely to respond to her with the stereotypical attitudes and behavior they direct toward thinner, sexier women. Men are more likely to deal with her for what she is saying or doing rather than because they enjoy looking at her or anticipate some sexual favor. She is rarely accused of sleeping her way to the top. Like the eunuch who roams freely through the harem without threatening the sheik's property, an overweight "asexual" woman can sometimes enjoy opportunities not available to her thinner sisters. The anxiety experienced by some heavy women when they do begin to lose weight stems partly from a fear of being trivialized or sexualized as they become thinner and more attractive. Loss of weight reveals their womanhood and consequently may cancel out part of their personhood.[16] Fat can also be used as a test of love. The loyalty of a lover, in spite of a woman's fat, proves she is valued for herself, not merely for her sexual beauty.

Psychoanalytic literature traditionally describes females as suffering from weak psychological boundaries. This means they have trouble knowing where they begin and end, or how much "psychological room" they take up in the world.[17] As a form of body communication, obesity can help define woman's space. We all need room of our own, a private place to retreat for sustenance and recovery. Fat can become an indirect form of self-protection. Pumping up the bulk of her body, an overweight woman reclaims more personal space. She creates a buffer zone against the demands of others. She veils herself in flesh, just as the anorectic shrouds herself in thinness, or as most women conceal themselves in cosmetics, and all women are veiled by the beauty mystique. The effect of these strategies is the same; a dialogue where body language leads to distortion and disguise.

Psychological Body Binding

Karen spent her childhood in what is described as a happy and unusually tight-knit family. Her parents set high achievement standards, and exerted a strong influence on her, well into her adult years. A vibrant and energetic teenager, Karen stood five feet, four inches tall, with a full, curvaceous body. One friend recalls, "She had a classic pear-shaped figure—was chubby and very self-conscious about it." By the time she was 20, Karen had developed a "psychotic obsession" about food and weight.

Talented and ambitious, she began making pop recordings with her brother. They won three Grammy awards and entertained at the White House, where President Nixon described them as "Young America at its best." Yet even while pushing herself to live up to this image, Karen was engaged in a desperate struggle against food. Her records were selling in the millions as her weight slipped to 90 pounds. Hospitalized for "exhaustion," her illness was kept a secret. Finally, she moved out of the family and married an older businessman, but was divorced two years later. "I tried to help," he said, "but she wouldn't admit she had an eating problem."

Dangerously thin at 85 pounds and addicted to laxative purging, Karen contacted a specialist for a quick cure. He advised that long-term treatment was the only useful approach, and she flew to New York determined to get well. The following year was spent in intensive hospital treatment. Her weight gradually climbed to a near normal 108 pounds. Filled with

new hope she returned home for Christmas, got a new hairdo
and announced to friends: "I have a lot of living left to do."
Two weeks later, her heart suddenly succumbed to the long
12-year battle with anorexia nervosa. Karen Carpenter died
on February 4, 1983, at the age of 32.[18]

The demands of a myth can be cruel, driving people even to
the extreme of death. Humans are unique among animals; we
alone can willfully starve the flesh to satiate the psyche. Thousands of Karen Carpenters who succumb to anorexia nervosa each
year provide a tragic example of self-sacrifice on the altar of beauty.

Victorian women painfully laced themselves in whalebone and
steel to fashion an hour-glass figure. Today the anorectic is equally
constrained by her corset of self-control. Seeking the same goals
as her foremothers—beauty, love, and self-acceptance—she re-
models herself through psychological body binding. Like the
tightly laced women of former times, she too is convinced that
her natural flesh is unacceptable if left uncontrolled. As pounds
are shed, signs of sexual maturation disappear, as does menstruation. Eventually, the anorectic's emaciated state and distorted
appearance lead to social rejection, family crises, and serious medical problems. She relentlessly pursues an ultrafeminine beauty
image but becomes, paradoxically, an infertile person.

Anorexia nervosa has the highest mortality rate of any psy-
chiatric illness. Nearly all those who die from it are women. It
affects about 1 percent of females between the ages of twelve and
twenty-five, and the incidence is believed to have increased significantly in recent years. So-called subclinical anorexia, consist-
ing of weight obsession and uncontrolled dieting and binging
without serious weight loss, is described as virtually epidemic
among college coeds. Fear of obesity is even widely reported now
among prepubertal girls.[19] Anorexia is a complex disorder in which
many causative factors are implicated. The following discussion
is not intended as a full analysis of its etiology. Rather, it considers
how the demands for feminine beauty contribute to this illness.

David Garner, a specialist in eating disorders at the Toronto
General Hospital, concludes that social factors are largely responsible for the rising incidence of eating disorders suffered
almost exclusively by young women. These factors include the
pressure to be thin, the glorification of childlike qualities as part

of femininity, a rejection of the maternal look, and an emphasis on glamour and independence.[20]

According to traditional psychoanalytic theory, anorexia is triggered when Oedipal urges resurface at adolescence. Self-starvation is interpreted as a defense against incestuous desire for the father, or anxiety over oral aggression. Rejection of food is interpreted as rejection of womanhood, and the one psychodynamic issue most consistently stressed is "unconscious fear of oral impregnation." A contrasting view explains anorexia not as a rejection of womanhood at all, but just the opposite: a dramatic attempt to achieve ultrafemininity. Psychologist Marlene Boskind-Lodahl explains:

> Their obsessive pursuit of thinness constitutes an acceptance of the feminine ideal, and an exaggerated striving to achieve it. Their attempts to control their physical appearance demonstrate a disproportionate concern with pleasing others, particularly men—a reliance on others to validate their sense of worth. They devote their lives to fulfilling the feminine role, rather than the individual person.[21]

Anorectics are seeking beauty through body transformation (just as most "healthy" women do). The goal is not to reject womanliness but to enact it by becoming thinner and lovelier than anyone else. They respond to the adolescent challenge of taking control of their lives by an obsessive effort to control their looks. Like other women, they use the body as a source of power. Like Cinderella's stepsisters, they cut themselves down to the desired size. Theirs is a familiar fairy-tale attempt to win love through magical make-over, an attempt that in this case gets dangerously out of hand.

Girls normally experience a rapid increase in fat during puberty. Higher estrogen levels bind fat, particularly on the breasts, thighs, and hips, "filling out" the female form. Fat comprises about 30 percent of female body weight, in contrast to only 15 percent in males. Boys do not experience the same dramatic increase in body fat, nor are they exposed to emaciated masculine models. Several theorists conclude that anorexia is rare among males because of these two factors.

Girls and boys attribute fat to different causes. Heavy boys often believe they have "excess bone and muscle" and see their extra weight as desirable. Girls, however, attribute their fat to overeating and respond by dieting.[22] Among high school students, half the girls were concerned with being overweight, as compared with only 13 percent of the boys. At any given time, one-third of high school girls but only one-twentieth of the boys are trying to lose weight. Analysis of admission practices at prestigious colleges in the 1960s showed a rejection rate three times higher for overweight girls than for overweight boys with similar academic records.[23]

The lean, lithe look now worshiped as the ideal is in fact the look of a prepubertal girl. Fashion ads depict drawings of models with the superlong legs that are characteristic of a late-maturing fourteen-year-old who is in the early phases of puberty. Those girls whose bodies approximate this image tend to have more positive self-concepts.[24]

In a sense, puberty betrays the growing girl by making her both more and less attractive at the same time. Hormones round out her breasts, but they also layer her thighs with "unsightly" fat and cover her legs with "unwanted, superfluous" hair. Long before adolescence, girls have learned that looking pretty means being delicate, graceful, willowy—a princess with the smallest foot in the land or the palest skin. "As soft and as pink as a nursery . . . a doll he can carry . . . she'll purr like a kitten. . . . the girl that he marries" must have odorless genitals, hairless underarms, and the silky smooth legs of a cherub. When a street-corner survey asked people to describe "the key to being sexy," one cheerleader astutely answered: "Just keep a kind of little-girl air about yourself, while still having grown-up features."

In advertisements teenage girls are portrayed in two extremes: either as extroverted free spirits packaged in artifice or as introverted dolls cloaked in innocence. The girls in these ads sport a variety of childish features—apple-pink cheeks, wide eyes that gaze unfocused, bodies draped in gentle pastels. They are shown napping or curled in fetal position, hugging bunnies, stroking their own bodies, sucking on something.[25] A little-girl look is sexually alluring, but also conveys neediness. It is designed to attract a man who can protect and "father" this kittenish vamp. The contours, smells, and texture of a real woman contradict the childish dimensions of female beauty. To remain a pretty little girl while portraying a beautiful woman, the pubescent girl must simultaneously reveal and conceal her newly developed body.

Like Hamlet wrestling with whether "to be or not to be," an anorectic struggles to be and not be at once. In fulfilling the feminine role, women are often required to disappear because of their difference as females but to conveniently reappear because of their beauty. Think of the Moslem wife, who is present but veiled; the Chinese mistress who patiently waits behind a screen; Mrs. John Smith, who is there but nameless; the good girl who should be seen but not heard—attractive and available but not offensive. Similarly, the anorectic shrinks away while preserving an inner delusion of loveliness. This is her solution to the dilemma of being both childlike and womanly. Yet a person cannot be and not be at once—a truth never learned by thousands like Karen Carpenter who die in their attempt to achieve a childlike beauty ideal.

Victims of anorexia often suffer a delusional disturbance of body image. They actually see a kind of phantom body around them, like the phantom limb felt by an amputee. They will argue when weighing only 80 pounds that they still look too heavy. Karen's husband observed, "I tried to help but she wouldn't admit she had an eating problem." A dissociation occurs between the mind's eye and the mirror's image. This is another instance of mind-body split fostered by the search for idealized beauty. The body is psychologically distanced, distorted, then remodeled through a perceptual delusion. Separating mind from body makes the hunger pangs more tolerable because the pain seems to occur outside the self.

Karen's case illustrates the typical anorectic; a model child who is sweet, obedient, and hardworking, like any storybook heroine. These good girls have never learned how to act autonomously in their own interest. Instead they behave in response to other people's demands. "I thought I was happy if I made everyone else happy," one remarked. The desire for independence during adolescence creates conflicts in "good girls" who have never achieved a sense of self-determination. Boys have typically separated more completely from parents during early childhood. Therefore, they can detach themselves more successfully at adolescence and rarely use eating disorders to prove their independence.[26]

Karen was talented, ambitious, and successful, yet she never felt satisfied with herself. Anorectics are typically hardworking perfectionists during childhood. However, at adolescence, as noted in the last chapter, a girl's reward system shifts from the achievement arena to the social arena. She is now praised as much for what she looks like and whom she dates as for what she does. The script changes just when her body feels out of control. Steven Levenkron, an authority on the treatment of anorexia, suggests that the illness does not usually start as a bid for attention or as a rejection of sexuality but as a desire for the highest level of achievement.[27]

These girls get the same feeling of accomplishment that boys typically get on the ball field. As is true of many beauty rituals, the process becomes obsessive and addictive. The aim of reaching a certain weight is distorted into losing weight in and of itself.

> You have one great fear, namely that of being ordinary or average or common—just not good enough. You want to prove that you have control, that you can do it. The peculiar part of it is that it makes you feel "I can accomplish something" . . . better than all those people who are sloppy and piggish and don't have the discipline to control themselves.[28]

Recall that the pursuit of beauty provides a safe achievement goal for girls who experience fear of success. Rather than risk social rejection for competitive behavior, they concentrate on perfecting their appearance. Self-denial and hard work, which brought rewards in childhood, become focused on weight control. The anorectic clings to her disease, concludes Levenkron, because she needs it as an arena for achievement.

Anorectics frequently come from performance-oriented families in which mothers have been preoccupied with dieting and fathers are demanding of a perfect appearance. Enormous energy can be invested in dieting without threatening one's femininity. Parents take pride in having beautifully thin daughters and initially encourage weight loss as an extension of their own success. One study showed that half the friends and relatives of anorectics actually "admired" their appearance and envied their self-control.[29]

Moreover, the media have sensationalized and glorified the illness, creating a kind of social contagion. Articles headline anorexia as "The Golden Girl Disease," making it seem like an enviable condition characteristic of princesses like Diana or actresses like Jane Fonda. Karen Carpenter was featured as an anorectic not once but several times on the cover of *People* magazine.

Similar dynamics are found in other eating disorders as well. Bulimics are described as hardworking perfectionists, trapped by the need for achievement and the desire to remain attractive. Bulimia, the regular use of vomiting and purging to control weight, is an ancient custom recently rediscovered by an estimated 20 to 30 percent of the female college population.[30] A bulimic may binge on thousands of calories at one sitting but then suffers severe guilt. Vomiting and purging become her way of regaining self-control and overcoming self-hatred. Bulimia grants her the power to do what no one else can do: binge freely and not gain weight. Like anorectics, bulimics often do not realize or admit they have a problem. Vomiting and purging are done behind closed doors (like many other beauty rituals), and bulimics sometimes go undetected for years. No one suspects the price they pay to retain a "naturally" slim appearance. Both bulimics and anorectics are caught in a poignant search for a feminine identity that paradoxically ends in psychological castration. They become locked in a battle against their own bodies. But throwing up cannot substitute for growing up, nor can a woman really normalize herself as a person by disappearing into a beauty image.

Levenkron notes that "anorectic girls are hungry. They are starving to death. They want to eat, but their fear of eating is greater than their fear of dying. There is a tendency for people to see them as culprits, but they are all victims. . . . That's why they die."[31] They are victims of a social system that makes it hard to grow up both female and healthy.

The hard-driving, achievement-oriented young girl must now

contend with a new definition of beauty that incorporates a fitness cult within a thinness cult. Shaping down has become only the first step on the road toward shaping up.

Weights and Measures

Sixty years after Margaret Gorman was crowned the original Miss America, Rachel McLish won the title of Miss Olympia at the first professional bodybuilding competition for women. Spectators gathered to watch a bevy of muscular beauties flex their deltoids and pop out their pectorals, as shown in the photograph. Critics questioned whether contests like this were sporting events or beauty pageants. Such competitions would have been unthinkable during the ladylike fifties. Not until the end of the liberated seventies, when a well-entrenched feminist movement coincided with a worldwide fitness mania, could a new link between bodybuilding and beauty be fashioned. One of the early champions, Lisa Lyons, who also appeared in *Playboy*, describes bodybuilding in this way:

> [It's] a natural evolution of the concept of femininity. Muscularity is something that's very animal, but it's in no way a contradiction with femininity. Why should muscles be considered masculine? It's redefining the whole idea of femininity. You don't have to be soft, you don't have to be weak. You can be strong, muscular—you can make that visual statement and at the same time be feminine.[32]

Until recently, few people agreed with her perspective. Muscular females were labeled unsightly and masculine by traditional standards. Adolescents who judged silhouettes of slender, muscular, and heavy body types in 1969 chose the muscular type as ideal for boys and the slender type for girls.[33] While self-esteem was related to fitness and strength in boys, self-esteem in girls was a function of attractiveness rather than fitness. An athletic body build helps boys attain social prestige and proves their "toughness," whereas muscularity in girls is generally not a social advantage.

Athleticism has long been associated with tomboyism. When college women explained why they had given up being tomboys, they frequently mentioned the conflict between athletics and the feminine role. "I began to realize that I was losing my femininity while I was trying to prove my athletic ability. . . . Now I'm still active but less competitive," one said. Despite the new emphasis on fitness as beautiful, stigmatization of female athletes continues, especially in sports that involve body contact or are less "aesthetically pleasing." Those who play rougher sports are still considered either less feminine to begin with or masculinized through their participation. In a high school sample, over half of the female basketball players and one-third of the swimmers and gymnasts felt they were negatively judged because they were athletes.[34] High school coaches complain that girls show up at track meets with jewelry dangling from their wrists and ears. Some professional athletes make a special effort to signal femininity. Pro golfer Jan Stephenson, for instance, underwent a complete cosmetic overhaul to project a more glamourous image.

By the end of puberty, females have not only more fat but less muscle mass than males. Extra fat is rarely an athletic advantage, except in very long distance events in which fat can be burned as an energy reserve. The incidence of anorexia and bulimia is especially high among gymnasts, skaters, and ballerinas, for whom the aesthetic dimension of slimness gives a competitive edge. Young ballet dancers were found on the average to be 13 percent below normal weight, and over one-third had serious eating disorders.[35] Some large-bosomed women are now surgically removing the floppy breast tissue that obstructs their backhand or keeps them from bouncing comfortably around the track. They are, in a way, like a new breed of Amazons who sacrifice their breasts in order to succeed in combat.

Gender differences in size, strength, and muscle mass are socially as well as biologically determined. The socialization of body build begins in infancy, when male babies are handled more roughly than female babies. It continues at school, when gym teachers hand softballs to girls and footballs to boys. Doing can change the shape of things. Female body builders, with their small breasts, sinewy thighs, and articulated stomach muscles, demonstrate the maleability of the female form. A body that is developed to compete athletically acquires a different look, one that may or may not be considered aesthetically pleasing. As women shape up, they also reshape the boundaries of the beauty myth.

Times do change and bodies change as well. Athleticism has been superimposed onto a superthin beauty ideal that requires dieting to trim down plus exercise to firm up. Fitness manuals have replaced diet books on the best-seller lists. No sooner had Justice Sandra Day O'Connor taken her seat on the Supreme Court bench when she claimed a spot on the previously all-male gym floor and started a workout class for female staff members. Exercise is tauted as nature's best makeup. The woman who used to avoid sports because she hated ugly muscles today complains, "I'm ugly because I have no muscles."

Time magazine periodically runs a feature article to update readers on the latest version of the beauty mystique. In 1958 the cover story, titled "The Pink Jungle," focused on the giant cosmetic industries that were turning out royal honeybee jellies at fifteen dollars per ounce to help the American woman hunt her man. That article ended with a brief paragraph on exercise as a healthy alternative to cosmetic addiction.[36] A quarter of a century later, in August 1982, the cover of *Time* featured a curvaceous figure in a leotard. The new beauty ideal, we are told, is "taut, toned, and coming on strong." It is not enough merely to be thin and graceful. Contemporary beauty is "the vibrancy of someone who's got blood rushing through her body" and who sports the "powerful shoulders of a swimmer, the thunder thighs of a marathoner or the huge forearms of a tennis pro."[37] A New York modeling executive reports that she now gets girls *(sic)* who have legs like Muhammad Ali's. "It's part of the eighties look, a firm body . . . and a look of serene determination in the eye."

Beauty and athleticism have been paired on and off since the days of ancient Sparta. Across the pages of history march some marvelous archetypes whose beauty is embodied in powerful physiques. Two examples from the Hellenistic Greek period, the Venus de Medici and the Venus de Milo, portray full-bodied, broad-shouldered, muscular bodies, Sicilian mosaics, as illustrated, date back to the third century, and show amazingly modern-looking gymnasts in skimpy bikinis, swinging barbells over their heads. Now the archetype is embodied by the wonder women who partner James Bond in and out of bed. Germaine Greer describes these modern Amazons, with their "swirling clouds of hair who prowl through thriller comics . . . the musculature of their shoulders and thighs is incredible, their breasts like grenades, their waists encircled with steel belts."[38] Even Barbie must now compete with a rival Barbella doll, a barbarian babe in a peek-a-boo blouse that reveals her rippling body.

The fashion pendulum swings back and forth between times when muscles are demanded as essential and times when they are demeaned as unnatural. In the early nineteenth century, Americans worshiped soft, round curves as the epitome of femininity and considered muscles an abomination. The Women's Christian Temperance Union warned women not to indulge in unladylike sports that would threaten their proper appearance. Feminists literally climbed onto their bicycles and took to the roads to prove that females could be athletic and still remain as attractive as their sedentary sisters.

Health reformers of the nineteenth century argued that activity, not cosmetics, was the natural key to beauty. "Live right, eat right; exercise and beauty will be yours," they promised. Today's heavy emphasis on fitness is motivated by a desire for beauty as well as for health. In fact, the two goals have frequently been fused. Lydia Pynkham's famous vegetable compound, for example, was first introduced to cure "female complaints" but was later sold for cosmetic purposes. The *New York Times* now runs a combined health-and-beauty column, addressing both issues as one.

Susan B. Anthony advised that women need strong bodies as well as quick minds in their battle for equality. A vigorous body refutes the stereotype of the passive, sleeping princess that lingers on as part of the feminine ideal. Physical development does enhance feelings of power. Running fast, jumping high, and breaking records are psychologically important because they prove that weakness can be overcome. They confirm one's capacity to do and to win. Female athletes tend to view their bodies not merely as decorative sexual objects but as sources of achievement and pleasure.[39]

Through the discipline of exercise, women are forging a new unity between mind and body. Powerful and beautiful role models like Lisa Lyons testify not only to the pleasure derived from physical development but also to the positive feelings that can grow along with one's lateral dorceps. One contender for Miss Olympia observed that "the changes I've felt from body building make me a firm believer in the maxim 'physical strength leads to inner strength'. . . . I've learned to be a stronger person, with a more powerful will and more constructive mind."[40]

Exercise is being successfully incorporated into a program designed to improve self-image. A thirty-minute run was used as part of a series of group therapy sessions to generate questions about physical awareness: How does it feel to be sweaty, messy, unfeminine in the traditional sense? How do heavy women deal with the self-consciousness of exercising in public? How does clothing influence activity? As participants became more physically fit and more psychologically aware of their bodies, their self-images changed along with their conceptions of beauty and femininity.[41]

Strong women are carrying their newfound strength out of the weight room and into the bedroom. More in touch with their bodies, they are also more in touch with their sexuality. Someone who knows how to make her body work to its best advantage is free to be more sexually assertive. She can enjoy the benefits of looking and feeling sexually desirable later into life if she is firm, flexible, and energetic.

Women certainly benefit when beauty norms are consistent with mental and physical health. However, not all the effects of the new fitness craze are positive. As the beauty ideal shifts from fat to fit, as the old fat farms are revamped into exotic health spas, fat profits are still being reaped from female insecurity about appearance.

Recall that beauty standards constantly shift and typically filter down from upper to lower classes. Aristocratic women were for-

merly fat and well fed, then thin and delicate. Now they strive
to be firm and fit. It is still mainly upper-middle-class women
who have the time and money needed to pursue the "jock chic"
look. Just as fat has been considered an indication of impropriety
and of lower-class status, fitness has taken on its own moral dimensions. Those who have it look down on those who don't:

> In her best-selling exercise book, for example, Jane Fonda com-
> plains at great length about "male-defined" standards of beauty,
> but she is as firm as any male fashion designer in her insistence
> that a lean, well-muscled body is something every woman should
> strive for—even if it means spending several hours a day working
> at it. What is worse, Fonda equates physical fitness with moral
> soundness and political purity.[42]

The rash of new fitness magazines for women preach a kind
of enlightened narcissism based on health. But their pages are
filled with fashion tips, weight-loss testimonials, an emphasis on
vanity, and a demand for self-sacrifice. On the whole, the message
is not so very different from the one found in traditional fashion
magazines. It is a familiar appeal for masochistic make-over in
the name of beauty, this time cloaked in a mesomorphic cover-
up.

Fitness is being sold as the foolproof antidote to becoming an
unattractive misfit. Peddled as an imperative, it is simply another
insidious beauty oppression. If the drive to stay in shape derives
mainly from insecurity about attractiveness, then the goal of looking good can undermine the goal of feeling good. Therapists are
reporting an increasing number of women obsessed with exercising. Such patients are terrified of losing control of their bodies.
They feel instantly loathsome and flabby if they gain a pound or
miss a single workout. This phobic syndrome relates directly to
the changing standards of beauty.

In Elaine's case, weight obsession combined with fitness com-
pulsion to produce increased stress and a recurrence of psychosomatic symptoms. Elaine was referred for therapy by a physician
who had been unsuccessful in curing her tension headaches. She
had been a chronic dieter ever since high school, when she first
labeled herself overweight. At age twenty-eight, after her son's

birth, she felt especially unsightly and joined a postpartum exercise class:

> For the first time in my adult life I really lost weight and kept it off. My friends told me I looked terrific. My husband was thrilled and bought me a whole new wardrobe. I enjoyed getting out of the house and found the class a challenge. Thanks to that class I felt better about myself than ever before. For several months my headaches totally disappeared. It was great, but it didn't last long.

Elaine began to jog with a local club and soon was spending several hours each day either running, working out, or taking aerobic classes. As her exercise routine increased, her tension headaches returned, along with occasional panic attacks:

> Even though I'm thin and pretty now, I still feel so insecure. I'm scared that if I ever stop exercising, even for a few days, I'll blow up like a balloon. I can actually see it happen if I slack off. You see, I have no control over food. Exercise is the only thing that keeps me looking decent. Now I feel trapped by my fear of gaining weight. I push harder and harder to stay fit, but my headaches only get worse.

Whereas Elaine used to judge herself by the scale, she now "measures up" by adding an extra leg lift or another mile to her daily workout. She is driven by a need to take over a body that threatens to go out of control, and she feels anxious and depressed whenever she fails to reach her goal. Like other addictions, exercise provides Elaine with a way of avoiding a painful confrontation with the larger problem of self-acceptance. Like dieting, exercising may begin as a protective defense against anxiety but can escalate into an obsessive-compulsive disorder.

Compulsive exercising and chronic dieting have been called a twin obsession. In fact, hyperactivity is a common symptom of anorexia. Anorectics and "compulsive runners" share similar personality traits. Both exhibit a single-mindedness and perfectionism; both use compulsive behavior to gain self-esteem; both must prove themselves over and over again because they cannot maintain an enduring sense of self-worth. On the surface, both take pride in their accomplishments (either being thin or running far), but underneath they suffer from repressed anger and a painful insecurity.

The beauty ideal has shifted from thin and frail to thin and strong. As the fashion image changes, so do the symptoms. The equation of beauty with brawn can be just as coercive as the equation of beauty with emaciation, or with an hour-glass figure. Whether the myth demands broad shoulders, a broad smile, or a broad behind, females are equally objectified as broads. Fitness defines the newest shape within which women are expected to normalize themselves. It has a special appeal, for it seems intrinsically healthy. However, Jane Fonda's beauty formula is a high hurdle to sweat over. It can generate as much anxiety as the formula it replaced. In the pursuit of beauty, novelty is part of the sport but never a final answer.

Climbing Off the Scale

I am not real to my civilization. I am not real to the culture that has spawned me and made use of me. I am only a collection of myths. I am an existential stand-in.

— Vivian Gornick[43]

The current epidemic of dieting, binging, vomiting, pumping of iron, has spread within a climate of feminist reform. Unwittingly, feminism may have contributed to these disorders. Today a young girl grows up surrounded by role models who assertively seek power and actively demand their rights. She is socialized to believe that she can and should take control of her life. She has seen Sandra Day O'Connor enter the highest court and Sally Ride enter outer space. Yet she also gets conflicting messages about woman's body and woman's place from a culture in the throes of gender upheaval. Double messages bounce her back and forth between traditional expectations and future promises. As one former anorectic describes the dilemma:

Personally, I feel that my illness was a product of the conflicts all women have to deal with being a female in our society today. There is such a gross contradiction in the emphasis on being a powerful, full-bodied, strong-willed female and on being skinny, tiny, angular, fragile and young-looking. How ironic that feminism is running side by side with a school of thought that haunts our every waking hour with visual and mental images of frailty, denial and unimportance.[44]

In one sense, eating disorders can be interpreted as a form of rebellion. A refusal to eat is an infantile protest. By choosing to starve rather than to accommodate, the anorectic challenges her role as a good girl who should please others. (One writer notes that anorectics and feminists use analogous gestures of protest. Feminist demonstrators cast off their bras as a sign of liberation, while anorectics literally shed their breasts.)

In another sense the anorectic remains obedient to the stereotype that women should influence others through body transformation. Self-starvation is consistent with the expectation that females should use their looks to solve their problems. While eating disorders may represent an unconscious attempt to break free of gender constraint, transforming the body to make the break remains a conventional feminine mode of protest. It is the same mode that has always been offered to women. Turn to your face; control, adorn, or display your body when feeling needy or angry. Eating disorders and fitness obsession require the same misdirection of energy as other beauty rituals do, the same distortion of sensations, the same denial of feelings. Ultimately they produce the same confirmation of woman as a deviant person. The anorectic seals her lips like a baby; the bulimic spits out her guilt; the binger fills her angry cries with food. They are telling the world off by how they look instead of what they say.

Many women are legitimately angry because their work is undervalued; because their attempts to act independently are thwarted; because their appearance is constantly scrutinized and criticized. But the expression of anger has long been denied to females, as it is denied to other subordinate groups. Good girls learn to act like Cinderella, to accept their lot, to ask little in return, to cry rather than fight, to smile when furious, to look good when feeling bad. Consequently, their anger goes unrecognized, even to themselves. When it does surface out of control, anger exposes them as unattractive. An angry face is neither pretty nor pleasing. Hence women try to repress and conceal anger. "Lots of women are pretty until they open their mouths," observed one man. Closemouthed silence preserves attractiveness and protects women from being labeled ballbusters or castrating shrews. Eating can serve as a safe outlet for anger. The mouth aggressively attacks food, biting, tearing, and finally destroying it. Unconscious rage can be expressed at each meal through binging *or* starving.

Eating disorders exemplify the destructive use of power over the body to produce a generalized feeling of potency. Anorexia seems to confer the power to transcend nature and survive without food. Bulimia seems to empower one to binge freely but also to remain slim. One woman explains that she started dieting in response to feeling worthless and ineffective. As the pounds dropped away, she felt in charge of herself for the first time. "Anorexia provided me with the illusion that I was in control, not only of my body and my own status within the community, but of the community itself. I became convinced of my own omnipotence."[45] Mastery of flesh can thus become confused with mastery of life.

Few women choose to risk open conflict with the dominant culture. Many turn instead to the silent rebellion of an eating disorder to express their rage, their sorrow, their frustration. These private protests typically go unnoticed as symptoms of social problems. Individual cries are easily dismissed as personal problems, while their social dimensions go unrecognized. The anorectic is diagnosed as suffering from a phobic anxiety over oral impregnation. It is she that is labeled neurotic, not the culture that worships an emaciated beauty ideal. Her private rebellion isolates her even further.

Eating disorders do not develop in a vacuum. Personal experience takes place in a political context, as feminists have always stressed. Only when a great many mental file cards are simultaneously rewritten can a stereotype be successfully challenged. Attempts to alter myths must therefore be collective to be effective.

How can the constricting equation of beauty with thinness be challenged? First, by closing our mouths—not to food but to incessant discussion of weight control. We can stop complimenting others for weight loss; stop suggesting yet another diet scheme; stop announcing the numbers on the scale as an index of personal achievement. Looking thin has not always been equivalent to looking good. Second, by opening our mouths—to admit the binges and purges, the hunger pangs, the obsessive thoughts of food, the disgust over fat thighs, the compulsive daily weigh-ins. When people finally began to speak out about incest, rape, and wife battering, these phenomena were transformed from private agonies into public issues. Eating disorders can be brought out of the pantry closet. As a constructive example, drama groups have been performing on campuses, carrying the message that such illnesses are common problems.

"A mystique does not compel its own acceptance," wrote Betty Friedan. Set free to seek its own proportions, the body can speak for itself. Tuning out the static of a mystique and tuning in to inner sensation, women will hear clearer messages of hunger and satiation. Recent research suggests that weight may not be easily controllable. Constitutional factors seem to be the major determinant of body weight. A new set-point theory suggests that each body has a genetically determined metabolic balance that it strives to maintain, regardless of food intake. Dieters have long suspected this fact. If most people have only limited influence over weight, then the equation of beauty with superslimness is all the more oppressive.

Challenging the formula that beauty equals thinness equals happiness means looking with new eyes at the emaciated *or* muscular models portrayed by the media and rejecting them as exploitative rather than enviable. If women look from a different perspective, they will be able to conceptualize beauty norms that are more flexible, norms that can expand to embrace women whose shapes are rounded by natural fat and by their maternal function.

Just as the health and the very life of the anorectic are threatened by her disturbed self-perception, the mental health of all women is undermined by gender myths that distort women's image, whether in the direction of deviance or in the direction of beauty. Treatment of anorectics always involves correction of inaccurate body perception. They have to be taught to really see their emaciated flesh, their protruding bones and sunken cheeks. Likewise, the healthy development of all women requires a realistic beauty image. As long as women are stereotyped both as deficient human beings and as mythical beauties, they will remain psychologically hungry. Their energy will be drained by the effort to normalize their appearance instead of used to nourish their growth as people.

Recall those full-bodied Venus figures that have survived from Paleolithic time. Whether they were worshiped as goddesses or enjoyed for erotic pleasure, they were certainly valued. And they have survived all these centuries partly because they were so substantial. Beauty can take many forms. Some women are destined to be gloriously curvaceous; a few will be mighty and mesomorphic; still others will be singularly svelte. Yet all women can feel equally feminine, equally accepting of the shape their female bodies ultimately take.

8

Attraction and Selection

In case you haven't noticed it yet, genes are back in style.
Designer genes. You can hardly open a publication these days
without being confronted by the latest recycled fashion. Once
again we are being told that "The Designer of Us All created
men and women out of entirely different patterns."

— Ellen Goodman[1]

EVOLUTION casts us in an ancient mold. Stamped on our flesh
is a collective account of history. The great droughts, the
glaciers of the Pleistocene epoch, the sexual arrangements of our
early hominid ancestors are carved on the rounded contours of
each centerfold Playgirl. The relationship between beauty, body,
and behavior goes back beyond our own conception to the infancy
of the human race. For as Virginia Woolf observed, "we are all
partly our ancestors, partly man and partly woman."

A genetic approach attributes sex differences in beauty to natural forces. Attracting and selecting are, after all, basic elements
of the mating game. Visual cues prompt the sexual couplings that
keep the species going. Have females been endowed with an added
dose of good looks to whet the appetites of hungry males, who
are in turn programmed to see them as delectable? Has nature
groomed women for sexual competition, and is beauty therefore
woman's biological destiny? How does culture confuse the complex messages embroidered on the genetic template?

We begin with the case of Ann, who, despite a pretty face and
a set of adequate genes, is unwed and unhappy. Seeking a mate,
she placed a personal ad in a singles publication.

SWNMF [single, white, never married, female]:
age 31, very attractive, 5'5", curvaceous, green
eyes, long blonde hair, sensitive, intelligent, warm
and affectionate; likes all kinds of music, tennis,
camping; seeks mature, successful male, under 45,
who is kind-hearted, sincere, and looking for a
serious relationship.

Ann is a physical therapist living in the Midwest. Wanting children and feeling pressured to settle down, she has become increasingly anxious about her single status. One serious relationship in her twenties ended because her boyfriend was afraid to make a permanent commitment. Recently she has been involved with a divorced man who already has two children and does not want more. Ann feels "up against the clock" as her reproductive years tick by:

My thirtieth birthday was a real blow! Being single in my twenties felt OK. I enjoyed the fun and freedom, dated a lot, and was happy to be so independent. Then 30 just hit me. Like a friend once said, it's all downhill after that. I haven't even gotten started with the home and family I've always wanted. Many of the men I meet are already divorced and trying to support two households. Or else they're dating girls in their early twenties who have more time to play around. I've begun to worry a lot about my looks. I was always a few pounds overweight. But now I'm totally self-conscious about every little change I see. I know I'd be a good mother and feel I have a lot to offer some man. That's why I placed the ad.

Ann's motives for advertising herself have less to do with dating than with mating and matrimony. Though she is sexually attractive and sexually active, Ann is reproductively unfulfilled. Sex neither lures nor assures a committed partner in a world where culture and contraception alter nature's built-in mechanisms.

At some point in human evolution, the estrous cycle was replaced by the menstrual cycle. Females stopped going into heat. We are the only primates that show no sign of estrus. This change is considered a crucial landmark in human development. In most primates, the female is sexually receptive and fertile only during a brief estrous period marked by three special characteristics: first, attractivity—she becomes highly visible and sexually interesting to males; second, proceptivity—she actively solicits male attention through seductive behavior; and third, receptivity—she cooperatively maintains postures that allow copulation to occur.[2] As humans evolved beyond estrus, this automatic cycle of attractivity, proceptivity, and receptivity became inoperative. Sex was no longer dominated by hormones or confined to a brief seasonal period. Human sexuality was separated from its reproductive function, becoming less instinctive, more expressive, and subject to personal and cultural control. One writer observes that estrus is to animal behavior what a good wine is to a dinner party. It gets the juices flowing. Without estrus, human sexual affairs need other intoxicating stimulants.

Loss of estrus permitted both males and females to make sexual choices. Sex could be used for purposes other than reproduction; it could be traded for status or commitment; withheld, solicited, bought and sold. Ann became free to say yes on Monday and no on Tuesday, yes to one man and no to another.

Loss of the estrous cycle altered the signals of sexual attractivity. Ann cannot depend on her hormones periodically to heat up an array of eager suitors. Without estrus, sexual attractivity can be as much socially as biologically determined. New beauty signals can be imaginatively created; new body hot spots can be redefined by consensus or redesigned through cosmetic transformations.

During estrus the vulva becomes one of the hottest of all hot spots in mammals. It swells, it smells, it serves as an irresistible lure. When humans began to walk upright, swollen labia and pungent odors became hidden between upright legs. Eye contact and language replaced smell as a primary form of human communication. Boys began watching the girls stroll by, and streetwalking women learned to display themselves in new ways. Attractivity was brought more and more under conscious control. Ann can paint a picture of herself with words, appealing to fantasy and imagination as much as to sexual instinct.

Why did human females stop going into heat? The Greek term or estrus means gadfly. Some theorists believe that estrus eventually became nonadaptive because irresistible gadabout women in heat were disruptive to the important business of civilization. Others argue that the development of hunting-gathering societies required women to be continuously receptive when men returned home after long hunts. Still other theorists stress that infants survive better when fathers are committed to them, and that the indiscriminate mating associated with estrus makes paternity uncertain. Loss of estrus made possible continuous and monogamous sexual receptivity, which provided the glue that held couples together and kept fathers attached to the mother-child family unit. Estrus loss is thus explained as a special human adaptation that strengthened the pair bond, permitted paternal commitment, kept women at home with their babies, and solidified group relations.[3]

Sarah Blaffer Hrdy, a specialist in primate behavior, rejects these explanations as inadequate. She argues that anthropologists have mistakenly equated freedom from estrus with reduced sexual drive in females. The nonestrous female is incorrectly described as "permanently receptive to one male." In fact, she remained potentially receptive to many males and capable of choosing whether and when she wished to have sex, explains Hrdy.

Freedom from estrus did not confine Ann's sexual drive to one man alone or to one man continuously, but flexibly expanded her sexual control. Though males may wish it, neither Ann nor Eve was made exclusively for Adam's pleasure. Nor is the nonestrus human female continuously in heat. An ethologist once quipped that "any male who believes that women are 'constantly receptive' must be a very old man with a short memory or a very young man due for a bitter disappointment."[4] One of the most commonly reported male sexual fantasies is that of the "omni-available female," a woman who is continuously eager, attractive, proceptive, and receptive: on call twenty-four hours a day, so to speak.

The myth of female beauty fuels the fantasy that women are or could be sexually ever ready, like a battery needing only to be plugged in. Cultured beauty surrounds men with women who look, smell, and feel as if they are "turned on." Whereas estrus signals are brief and periodic, bottled beauty can be endlessly reapplied and perpetually flashed.

Through cosmetic magic, Ann plays sexual tricks. Her rosy Revlon mouth mimics the swollen vulva of a chimp in heat or the succulent kissable lips of a nursing infant. Her rounded Playtex breasts and hips flow in high-heeled waves ("Moving like twin waterfalls," in the lyrics of Jacques Brel). Her golden Clairol locks are cherubic and angelic. Some beauty signals do mimic the natural signs of attractivity associated with estrus. However, they are not genetically controlled but culturally contrived.

Continuous sexual signals lead to miscommunication and confusion. When a female exhibits attractivity, then proceptivity and receptivity are supposed to follow. (In fact, one stereotype about very pretty women is that they engage in sex more often and enjoy it more than less attractive women.)[5] But unlike animals in heat, beautified women are often sending mixed messages. They flirt and tease, signaling attractivity while withholding receptivity. Men may misread such beauty signals as a sexual invitation. People still commonly believe that a rape victim was "asking for it" because she was dressed in a miniskirt, wore makeup, or advertised some such lure. In one case, a Utah judge overturned a verdict against a rapist because in his view the victim's flimsy dress was too provocative. Women are rewarded for looking sexy but blamed for their seductive behavior if they are attacked.

Freedom from estrus certainly has produced new sexual challenges. Without it, Ann can tune up her natural assets and advertise her availability on her body or in personal ads. Perhaps estrus was initially lost because people liked making sexual choices and were reproductively more successful. But sexual freedom also invites cultural constraint. Failure becomes more common when culture defines the "shoulds" of proper behavior; virginity should be guarded, men should be on top, orgasms should be vaginal, marriages should be monogamous. Males become more vulnerable to performance anxiety and impotence; females suffer sexual intimidation and repression. Precisely because the loss of estrus gave women freedom of choice along with a strong sex drive, societies have gone to great lengths to control female sexual behavior in order to keep wives safely at home, concealed behind a veil, locked in a chastity belt, sequestered by the bindings of their tiny feet, or bound by their economic dependency.

After comparing the social systems of many primates, Hrdy concludes that no other species so systematically oppresses female sexual behavior as do humans. The myth of female beauty adds to that oppression by socializing women to cultivate perpetual signals of attractivity that are not genetically determined but cul-turally dictated. It is not genes but the gender system that requires women to use their looks in ways that nature never intended.

Alas for Ann, marriages are not made in heaven but arranged for earthly reasons—economic, social, and personal. Gone are the estrous signals that attracted potential mates. Gone also are the wise elders who united compatible families. Gone are the matchmakers who picked perfect pairs. A cult of love and open courtship now dominates the mating game in western culture. When romantic love is revered as sacred, feminine beauty be-comes holy. Research shows that physical attractiveness plays a more important role in mate selection when marriages are self-arranged.[6] Beauty is a basic prerequisite at times when social mobility is high and when there is more transient sex based on early first impressions.

Ann must now compete for a mate directly on the open market. The odds are not in her favor. Suitable men are in short supply, due to higher rates of male mortality, mental retardation, ad-diction, incarceration, and homosexuality. Margaret Mead re-ported that the combination of monogamy and male scarcity triggers competition between females, which heightens their need for beauty signals.[7] Since female fertility ends at mid-life, the current trend toward early career development and delayed mar-riage puts enormous pressure on young women, who are truly racing against time. Finding a husband is easier in polygamous cultures. But Ann is not likely to consider the harem a good solution to her problem (although elderly women are increasingly reported to be "sharing a man").

Anthropologists are beginning to recognize female primates as strategizing creatures whose rivalry for limited resources is central to primate social systems. While male chimps compete overtly and aggressively, their female counterparts vie in more subtle ways for sex and for status. Human females are no exception.

Heightened competition to secure mates leads to a stepsister syndrome of cosmetic rivalry. As women like Ann emerge from the kitchen with greater independence and reproductive control, they can compete more intensely, not just *with* men in the office,

Marilyn Monroe appeared in this 1954 publicity shot with the
caption "Hey, Squeeze Me." Fashions sometimes require women
to reduce their proportions. A 3-inch foot, a 16-inch waist,
or a 100-pound body have all been admired as the essence
of femininity.

Karen Carpenter died at the age of 32, a victim of anorexia nervosa. Serious eating disorders are now described as virtually epidemic among college women. Victorian ladies laced themselves in whalebone corsets, whereas young women today are equally tortured in their corsets of self-control.

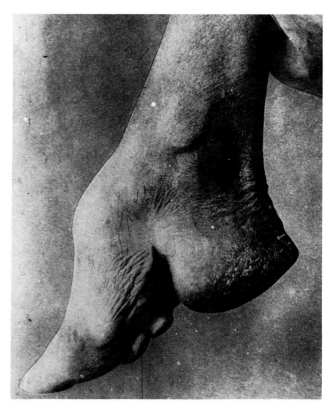

The Chinese tradition of footbinding, as shown here, literally fashioned a dainty-footed high-heeled woman out of living flesh. Glamorous feet are still an essential part of feminine adornment and they demonstrate how beauty, femininity, sexuality, and power become fused and then confused.

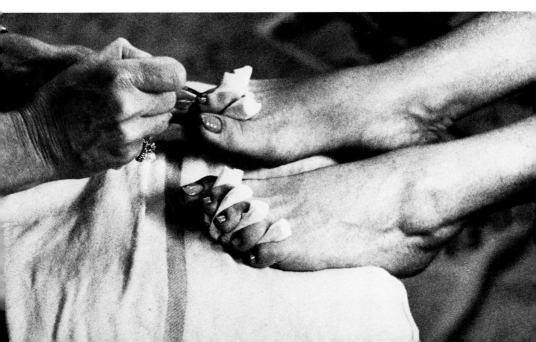

Abundant hair serves as a sexual lure, for free-flowing hair signals a free and easy woman. Rapunzel hung down her long locks to haul in a lover.

Glamorized hair blown out in billo waves swells the head of Far Fawcett with a halo of er power. Whether coile a crown of braids or jel into space-age spikes, h piled high adds stat and stat

Long-flowing hair suggests both girlish innocence and womanly sexuality. Cutting off long hair can be an act of rebellion that renounces the childish feminine role.

Fielding a ball, this athlete is hampered by the pretty hair that in effect veils her vision. Symbols of feminine beauty often increase the power to attract even while they decrease the power to act.

Women often trade youth and beauty for wealth and status in the so-called Jackie–Ari phenomenon. However, when an older or less attractive woman is coupled with a handsome younger man they look aesthetically mismatched.

The white veils of weddings and the black veils of funerals, although worn only briefly, symbolize feminine traits of modesty, purity, and emotionality. Veils create the fantasy of illusion while curtaining women off in privacy.

Renowned artist Georgia O'Keeffe at ages 33 and
with the look of serene determination that
has worn throughout her life. Although
created some of the world's most captivat
images, her own personal beauty requii
no formal compositi

Left: Sicilian mosaics from the third century show amazingly modern-looking gymnasts in skimpy bikinis. Beauty and athleticism have been paired since ancient Sparta, but the fashion pendulum swings back and forth. Muscles are sometimes demeaned as unfeminine, other times demanded as imperative.

Below left: Lorna Peterson working out at the Mid-City Body Building Gym in New York City.

Below: Rachel McLish, winner of the 1983 Miss Olympia contest, poses with some of the runners-up. Beauty images have recently been recast in a mesomorphic mold. Fitness is replacing fatness as the most tormenting beauty obsession.

Although they are nearly equal in height, the royal couple posed for their engagement photos with the Prince standing one step above, creating the illusion of a more dominant male figure. Princes are supposed to be taller (and darker) than the princesses who long for them. Imagine him standing a step below, his head nestled in her neck.

but *for* men in the social world. Suburban singles parties are top-heavy with glamourized gals on active display. Ann comments that "there are always twice as many women as men, all waiting to be looked over and picked over. The effort to get ready usually isn't worth it, but I feel I have no choice if I want to be socially active."

In most species, the sex that is wooed is the one that makes the greater reproductive investment. In species such as ours, in which females bear and care for offspring, nature usually decorates males so they can better compete for the female reproductive resource. However, in the rare cases where males play the more significant parental role, the situation is sometimes reversed. Females become the more competitive and more decorative sex, developing conspicuous displays and vying for mates as they would for any limited resource.[8] Such females are not competing for impregnation, since the cost of that is small to males; they are competing for paternal commitment to their offspring.

The basic primate family unit consists of a mother and her young. Human fathers are, in a sense, grafted on to that base. Paternity has been called a fragile, learned behavior, culturally imposed on males. Women compete for suitable fathers for their children; for fathers to attend Lamaze classes; for fathers to wipe noses and bottoms; for fathers to sign checks for braces and ballet lessons; for fathers to give emotional comfort and love. As divorce rates climb and the gender gap in wages continues, women must compete not once but over and over for potential fathers, stepfathers, substitute fathers, and even grandfathers for their offspring. Analysis of hundreds of personal ads shows that females are more likely to offer physical attractiveness while males offer financial security. Conversely, men seek beautiful women in their ads while women like Ann are looking for stable, successful men.[9]

Women continue to make by far the greater reproductive investment. Hence men should logically be competing for the best mothers for their offspring. But remember that there is a shortage of available males, owing in part to the pressures of monogamy. And remember the social factors that keep women economically and psychologically subordinate. Sociologist Jessie Bernard concludes that indeed women have become the pursuers instead of the pursued, despite their greater reproductive burden which in other species would ensure a reverse situation.

> Men do not have to compete very hard when the economic dependency of women makes their survival depend on marriage. It is certainly true that beauty in women became supremely important when there was little place for a woman outside her own home, and few opportunities for economic survival, much less comfort, unless provided by a husband. . . . Beauty matters. It may be that the competition among women for husbands is a temporary (historically speaking) aberration, a deviation from the Darwinian model, that as "being taken care of" by men in marriage becomes less and less essential for women, beauty will become a less urgent value in their world. They will increasingly be in a position to be the selecting rather than the selected ones.[10]

Who in fact is chasing whom? Who is the charmer and who the charmed? "What has happened to modern western man? Has the male really become the sought-after sex, the one that is in demand, the sex that can afford to be choosy?" asks one biologist.[11] Which sex does the displaying? which sex does the selecting? And what is being offered in exchange?

Selection—Natural and Unnatural

> [I]n human society nothing is natural, and the woman, like much else, is a product elaborated by civilization. . . . Woman is determined not by her hormones or by mysterious instincts but by the manner in which her body and her relations to the world are modified by the action of others.
>
> — Simone de Beauvoir[12]

As Darwin first explained the mating game, "the best man won," either by his power to conquer other males through *intra*-sexual selection (known as the He-Man Effect) or by his power to charm females through *inter*-sexual selection (the Peacock Effect). As a result of intra-sexual competition, males developed special conquering devices such as horns or sharp canine teeth to vanquish male foes. As a result of inter-sexual selection, males evolved special charming devices such as fancy feathers and bright colors to attract female attention. These two evolutionary trends equipped males to be the pursuers.

Eventually, Darwin amended his theory with respect to human sexual selection. In *The Descent of Man* he asserted that a reverse pattern had developed: women had become the wooers and men the wooed. Furthermore, he contended that sexual selection resulted in increased beauty traits in women:

> As women have long been selected for beauty it is not surprising that some of their variations should have been transmitted exclusively to the same sex; consequently that they should have transmitted beauty in a somewhat higher degree to their female than to their male offspring, and thus have become more beautiful, according to general opinion, than men. Women are everywhere conscious of the value of their own beauty; and when they have the means, they take more delight in decorating themselves with all sorts of ornaments than do men. They borrow the plummage of male birds, with which nature has decked this sex to charm the females. [13]

Even while labeled more beautiful, females were also described as inferior. Convinced of the natural superiority of the human male, Darwin considered it fortunate that males passed characteristics to all their children—"or man would have become as superior in mental endowment to woman as the peacock is in ornamental plummage to the peahen." Like all scientists, Darwin was first shaped by his times and then became a shaper of them. Evolutionary theory was quickly used to explain the existing social order as "natural, inevitable, and progressive." Evolutionists "logically" concluded that males had reached a higher stage of development than females, who were considered to be a kind of unfinished version of homo sapiens.

Women were compared to the "uncivilized" races, both being viewed as examples of evolutionary retardation. Furthermore, greater sexual differentiation was interpreted as proof of evolutionary progress. (Half a century later, Nazi anthropologists likewise concluded that sex differences were more highly developed in Aryans than in the "less evolved Negroid and Asians.")[14] Darwinists noted that muscular native women had not yet "acquired" the tiny feet, slim waists, and delicate features (or the modesty)

of the high-class Victorian Lady.[15] Civilized societies were identified by the decorative appearance of their women, and British
wives were advised to stay home and cultivate gentility in order
to develop a truly progressive nation.

Herbert Spencer concluded in *Psychology of the Sexes*, printed in
1873, that although women were an example of arrested development they must have acquired at least one highly evolved trait,
and that was the ability to attract and please males. Spencer
reasoned that those females who had managed to survive in a
primitive, savage world had done so by becoming "pleasing" to
the hostile males around them.[16] Like the loyal family dog, a
woman depended on the good will of her master for survival and
therefore must have acquired pleasing characteristics, Spencer
wrote. By wagging her lovely body, she could tame the brutes
and enhance her chances for survival. Women's subordination,
along with their beauty, was explained as the natural order of
things. Elaine Morgan wryly observed a century later in *The
Descent of Woman* that:

> It's just as hard for man to break the habit of thinking of himself
> as central to the species as it was to break the habit of thinking of
> himself as central to the universe. He sees himself quite uncon-
> sciously as the main line of evolution, with a female satellite re-
> volving around him as the moon revolves around the earth. . . .
> any modifications of her morphology are taken to be imitations of
> the Hunter's evolution or else designed solely for his delectation.[17]

Gender myths that are proven by so-called scientific fact tend
not to disappear with time but merely to reappear in more contemporary forms. Today, science no longer asserts that female
bodies are uncivilized and unevolved or that dimorphisms reflect
higher levels of evolution. However, the descendants of Darwin
still contend that women are "naturally" endowed with special
beauty—first because men are more easily aroused by visual stim-
uli, and second because men need "fresh features" to satisfy their
lusty sexual appetites. Let's look at this latest pair of "designer
genes" as determinants of the social order.

In *The Evolution of Human Sexuality*, published in 1979, Donald
Symons, an anthropologist, argues that males are endowed by
nature with a specially sensitive visual arousal system that primes

them to rapidly "fall in lust" with a pretty face.[18] "Criteria for evaluating sexual attractiveness probably developed in a more innate fashion in the male than the female," he writes. In simple terms, girl watching comes more naturally to males because, like window-shopping, it exposes them to the temptation of impulse buying. Symons explains that men's special sensitivity to visual arousal affords them a reproductive advantage. A man can sire many offspring; a female can bear relatively few, and she must make a greater physical investment in each one. Males can maximize their reproductive potential by being instantly responsive to every attractive female and having a variety of sexual partners, asserts Symons. In contrast, a more effective reproductive strategy for females is to be coy and less visually arousable.[19]

Now if men are naturally more tuned in to and turned on by visual cues, are women correspondingly endowed with more decorative bodies? Symons believes that the answer to this question is no. "There is no convincing evidence that the function of any human female anatomical characteristic is to stimulate males visually," he writes. Great cross-cultural variability in the components of beauty suggests little in the way of innate beauty characteristics. He disagrees, for instance, with theorists like Desmond Morris who argue that women's breasts and buttocks have evolved as sexual lures. The only part of the female body that males consistently and universally report to be visually arousing are genitals, yet no one believes that female genitals evolved to be visually stimulating to males.[20]

Most likely, female anatomy is visually arousing to males owing to evolution in male brains, not in female bodies, Symons contends. Females are not biologically designed more attractively, but men are primed to see them that way. In other words, feminine beauty is built in not to the body of the beheld but to the brain of the beholder, according to his theory.

What "facts" are offered to prove that males are supersensitive to visual seduction? First, some studies show that females prefer to make love in the dark, whereas men want to see what they are doing and with whom.[21] Does this mean that females are innately less interested in viewing male bodies, or merely more reluctant to expose their own? Though women are conditioned to display themselves as beauty objects, they are also socialized to be more modest. (Looking at their own genitals is highly embarrassing to some women.) Perhaps females prefer to make love with the lights out in order to shield themselves from constant scrutiny. Darkness veils their imperfections: the veins on their legs, the stretch marks on their bellies, the distorted faces of their passion. (Ben Franklin once advised young men to choose an older mistress since she would be less demanding and since "all mares look the same in the dark.")

A second "fact" that supposedly proves men are more visual than women is that many males but few females have vivid fantasies while masturbating.[22] Does this prove anything about the male brain, or does it reflect a lifetime of exposure to erotic female models in the media? The effect of experience on visual imagery is well documented. For instance, use of guided fantasy in therapy programs with nonorgasmic women shows that females can easily learn to produce erotic fantasy during sexual arousal, once self-censorship is overcome.

Finally, a sex difference in response to pornography is offered as further proof that males are more visually sensitive than females. Compared to the millions that men spend on pornography, there is virtually no female market for it. The majority of men find centerfold pinups highly arousing, but few women report a similar reaction to male centerfolds.[23] Moreover, when viewing pictures of nude males, women do not focus mainly on the genitals but explore the whole figure, especially the face, as if trying to find out about the person. In contrast, "men don't bother to look above the neck very much."[24]

Women who go to male strip shows enjoy them but report relatively little arousal. "It sure beats Tupperware parties," says one, but "I wasn't turned on by it." As Judith Brackley notes:

> There seems to be a fundamental difference between the way men view women stripteasers and the way women view their male counterparts. That difference may be power. Women seem uncomfortable in the role of voyeur. We were not teased, titillated and taunted by images of nude men as we were growing up. We aren't encouraged to pursue, conquer or score.[25]

Genes are not a necessary part of the explanation for why women are less oriented toward pornography. The pornographic image

has usually been created by and for men. It deliberately emphasizes transient, violent, or humiliating sex. Close-ups of genitals
offer little basis for fantasizing affectionate personal bonds, which
is what women have been taught to value. Pornography, like rape,
has to do less with sexual arousal than with power and conquest.
When violent elements are removed from pornography, it becomes erotica, and women do find many forms of erotic display
highly arousing.

The scientific facts that supposedly prove men's special visual
sensitivity to female beauty are not terribly convincing. As is true
of most human traits, males and females are probably quite similar
in terms of visual arousability. Females are certainly sensitive to
erotic imagery and do enjoy handsome men. If a sex difference
exists in response to physical beauty, it is no doubt influenced
by experience and expectation as much as by genetic predispo-
sition. The male brain is as well-primed by social perception as
by natural selection. In fact, research suggests that it is not males
but females who gaze more at human faces, remember them better, identify emotions more accurately, and respond more sen-
sitively to nonverbal cues than do men.[26]

A second version of designer genes emphasizes men's special
hunger for a varied sexual diet. When a male rat is placed with
a female in heat, he first mounts her repeatedly with gusto, gradually loses interest, and eventually ignores her altogether. If presented with a fresh partner, however, he immediately becomes
rearoused. Men with several wives report a similar boredom after
many consecutive nights with wife number one, but a revival of
desire with wife number two. Such facts are used as evidence
that men are innately more "partial to variety" than women, more
needy of fresh partners because of a naturally stronger sex drive.
Men's hearty appetites, we are told, require an ever-changing
menu, again because promiscuity is presumed to be reproductively advantageous to males but not to females.

According to this theory, every new woman looks somewhat
attractive simply because men are consciously or unconsciously
always "on the make" for a fresh partner. Symons argues that
"fresh features should be added to the list of innate criteria of
female physical attractiveness, but . . . fresh features are usually
unimportant in determining male attractiveness" to women.[27] He

adds that men's stronger need for variety dooms them to a "lifetime of longing," or drives them to break moral and religious
laws, often at great risk.

Both men and women do crave novelty as well as familiarity
in daily life. We all become satiated with the same old diet day
after day, yet our appetites revive when an old dish is served in
a new sauce. Sex can become habitual, boring, or obsessive without the periodicity imposed by the estrous cycle and/or without
the emotional spark called love.

Nudity, if treated as a rarity, helps rekindle desire. This is
why the ankle or neck takes on erotic value when it is concealed.
The fig leaf creates an erotic zone by covering it. However, "you
can't get nuder than nude," as Elaine Morgan observes, and "once
full frontal nakedness as a public spectacle has become another
déjà vu, there is no further for it to go except into the nightmare
of a cartoon, where the stripteaser gracefully pulls out her entrails
to the avid audience."[28]

What can a wife do when her husband is driven by an insatiable
longing for sex à la carte or a side dish of fresh features? Cosmetic
transformations are a handy antidote to sexual boredom. The
would-be Total Woman is advised:

> One of your husband's most basic needs is for you to be physically
> attractive to him. . . . He'll feel more alive coming home to you
> when your whole countenance . . . says "touch me, I'm yours."
> . . . You can be lots of different women to him. Costumes provide
> variety without him ever leaving the home. . . . Never let him
> know what to expect when he opens the front door; make it like
> opening a surprise package. . . . Be a sexpot, or an all-American
> fresh beauty. Be a pixie or a pirate—a cowgirl or a show girl.
> Keep him off guard. . . . Greet him at the door in pink baby
> doll pajamas and white boots.[29]

Exotic outfits, elegant hairdos, expensive smells, all create the
illusion of novelty. Through cosmetic magic a wife can impersonate the "other" woman or the younger woman, or a whole
harem. By attracting the interest of other men (within the bounds
of propriety), she can revive her husband's flagging desire as he
sees her anew through the eyes of his competitors.

Is the craving for fresh features really more natural for men, and is this why women are so busy beautifying themselves? Do males really benefit more than females do from promiscuity? Bees are expected to sample from many flower beds, while blossoms remain rooted at home. But which sex is the honeybee—and which supplies the nectar? A little logic demonstrates that heterosexual acts involving new lovers include one male and one female. So the number of fresh partners remains equal for both sexes. Perhaps women enjoy fresh-featured playmates as much as men do. Remember the gadfly in heat who buzzes around disrupting the work of civilization.

In other primates, sexuality is governed by the estrous cycle. No matter how insistent, dominant, or horny a male chimp may be, coitus occurs only when the hormones of the female incline her to say yes. A chimp in heat who actively attracts and eagerly receives one male after another is decidedly promiscuous. Human sexuality derives from this template. In *The Nature and Evolution of Female Sexuality*, Mary Jane Sherfey labels women's sexual drive "insatiable." It is a biological absurdity, says Sherfey, to assume that females have a relatively lower sexual capacity or that they are naturally less promiscuous.[30] Many women can and do experience dozens of orgasms in as many minutes and still want more. This certainly resembles a chimp in heat with a powerful drive to attract and enjoy an army of suitors.

Furthermore, the very mechanisms of intercourse refute the idea that seeking fresh partners is more natural to males. Men are transiently impotent after orgasm. Women can enjoy continuous sexual contact and multiple orgasms, which would logically promote promiscuity. That some women achieve orgasm only after long periods of stimulation could be interpreted as nature's way of encouraging females toward multiple mating.[31]

Hrdy concludes that promiscuity even has reproductive advantages for females. By attracting many males and inciting competition among them, a female can better discriminate the really fit from the pretended fit and thus improve her chances of selecting the fittest. Promiscuous mating increases the number of males on "friendly terms" with a mother chimp. These suitors become less hostile to her offspring (which is important, since male aggression is a major cause of primate infant death).[32] We are socialized to believe that monogamy comes naturally to human females and is a desirable ideal. Yet none of our nearest relatives, the great apes, are monogamous, and few of the many primate species are permanently bonded. Only 20 percent of human societies are considered strictly monogamous.

The point of this detour into promiscuity is to show that the desire for sexual variety may be as natural, as strong, and as beneficial to females as to males. Comparison of the Kinsey Report of 1948 with a *Cosmopolitan* survey of 1980 shows an enormous increase in the number of females buzzing about promiscuously. In the 1980 survey, twice the number of wives reported having had extramarital affairs by age 35, totaling nearly 50 percent of the sample.[33] Beauty asymmetry cannot be explained as part of the natural order of things if women are as eager as men are for fresh-featured partners. Evolution has not fashioned females more "fairly" because males are more promiscuous. Both sexes seem to crave a diet of extra desserts.

Tailored Genes

Biology is not destiny . . . but a fact of nature which enters into the logic of every social system and every cultural ideology.

— Susan Whyte[34]

According to Greek mythology, the prophet Tiresias spent time living first as a woman and then as a man. When asked which sex enjoyed greater erotic pleasure, he announced that females had more fun. The prophet's eyes were eventually put out because he saw too much too clearly. Those who challenge gender myths are often labeled blind fools or traitors to tradition. Culture is reluctant to rewrite old file cards. As Galileo discovered, science is culture and myth as much as it is fact.

Culture and nature are interwoven in the fabric of our genes and in the pattern of our social bonds. Like other human drives for food and sleep, sexuality acquires complex meanings far afield of its original purpose. An overpowering yen for fresh features, big breasts, tiny feet, long blond hair, has social as well as natural origins. Genes are always relevant to human behavior, but theories based on genetic evidence have a way of evolving contrary to women's best interests.

Over the years, genetic determinism has defined females as innately less intelligent, less evolved, less sexually arousable, but more attractive than males. The "neutral" theory of evolution has led men of science to assert that female breasts evolved primarily as long-distance sexual signals for males to notice; that the estrous cycle was lost primarily so that females could continuously satisfy the sexual needs of their mates; that the hymen evolved primarily to ensure female virginity. These genetic "truths" seemed universal and irrefutable (at least for a time).

Science is invariably wed to social doctrine and then used to preserve the status quo. Facts which "prove" women are naturally more attractive because men crave a variety of pretty faces or because men's brains are primed for visual seduction, become secondary to the gender roles that such "facts" support. Since physical traits, including beauty, are viewed as an inherent part of nature, genetic explanations for sex differences are regarded with great respect. Biological truth takes on moral overtones as gender differences become equated with "God" as well as with "good."[35] The Bible is cited to warn men that wearing long hair or putting on women's clothes is sinful and unnatural. Genetic explanations of beauty asymmetry are convenient scapegoats, relieving us of responsibility for gender inequities.

Science often views female sexuality from an androcentric perspective. When biologists refer to androgens as "male hormones" which stimulate sexual desire in both sexes, a woman's sex drive is in effect attributed to her "masculine" components. A "conquest vocabulary" is common in scientific literature. Male monkeys are described as "taking and possessing" a female when it was her hormones and her postures that controlled the encounter. Or we are told about agile sperm that must compete against millions of rivals to win the race and "rape the passive female ovum or die." This same conquest vocabulary pervades the vernacular—for instance, when adolescent males banter in locker rooms, asking each other "What did you get? Did she put out?" Language is important. It matters whether you think of yourself as the wooer or the wooed, the pursuer or the pursued.

Symons suggests that in monogamous marriages, women give

sex for love while men must *give up* promiscuous sex for love. But sex is a form of communication that creates emotional, economic, and reproductive bonds as well as sexual ones. The meaning behind a sexual act is determined by the feelings and needs of the partners. As long as women are relatively more dependent than men, the "giving" of sex and/or affection becomes a more significant aspect of female interpersonal power.

Females may be as naturally responsive to visual cues as males, but their social subordination has forced them to "notice" other qualities. As in the case of Ann, most women are simply not as free to choose or change mates on the basis of attractiveness alone or even on the basis of love alone. Some theorists predict that greater independence will allow women to choose mates mainly for their looks (as men have generally done), and that men will then find themselves "in the meat market strutting and preening in the same way that women have always done."[36]

Such a prediction assumes, of course, that the male pattern is the more natural one; that as women acquire self-determination, they will begin to behave more "normally," that is, like voyeuristic men. Women often do adopt a masculine pattern, not because it is any more natural but because people tend to imitate behavior that is valued as the norm. An equally possible outcome is that greater social and economic independence will liberate women from having to advertise themselves through exaggerated beauty signals. Ann, for instance, might become affluent enough to attract a man who would happily father her children if she could support them. No doubt women will continue to use sex in somewhat different ways than men; for example, to nurture relationships and create intimacy rather than to test their power. As one respondent to a sexual survey commented, "Women don't want to be free to adopt the male model of sexuality. They want to be free to find their own."[37]

Nature arranged the loss of estrus in humans, giving Ann the freedom of sexual choice. Greater freedom increased the burden of sexual responsibility. Ann received few responses to her personal ad. (Men who run such ads get many more answers than women do.) As her thirty-second birthday looms, she is investing more and more in personal adornment in order to send out stronger signals of attractivity. Guthrie concludes in his discussion of body hot spots that our reliance on courtship potential to reinforce social status has grown out of all proportion in the last century. Even in monogamous cultures, people continue their seductive ornamentation after marriage because seductive signals increasingly have become status symbols and adornment provides class identity. The result, he asserts, is an overemphasis on appearance, a loss of intimacy between partners, and a breakdown of the mating bond.[38]

Complex human behavior does not fit neatly into discrete categories. In trying to distinguish the pursuer from the pursued, the charmer from the charmed, we fall into the trap of oversimplification. The public display of a receptive rump or a glamourous face, or an ad that offers a curvaceous, blond-haired, reproductively eager female named Ann is only part of the story. The tango is danced by two, and the signals of the wooer are meaningless without the responses of the wooed. Moreover, sexual duets are never performed on empty stages. They involve personal variations, superimposed on biological themes, that in turn must harmonize with social overtones—including myths that set the stage even as they drown out the natural melodies orchestrated by our genes.

9

Myth America Grows Older

> Everywhere one looks there is this glossy little animal, some-
> times quite young and sometimes a little older, but always
> imagined, always pictured as The Girl.
>
> — C.W. Mills[1]

W OMEN'S bodies are inherently more childlike than men's—
smaller, smoother, weaker. Femininized beauty emphasizes an infantile look, making women increasingly more vulnerable as they mature. Age erases their baby faces, and sets the
stage for a mid-life beauty crisis.

Two categories of natural beauty are distinguished by Guthrie
in an analysis of the biology of beauty.[2] The first type incorporates
juvenile qualities, which appeal to our love of children. We are
automatically attracted to someone who is tiny, helpless, cute,
and cuddly, writes Guthrie, because these childlike traits evoke
care-giving responses. Actresses like Mia Farrow and Goldie Hawn
embody this form of aesthetic appeal. They are eye-catching because they look like adorable needy waifs. The second category
of beauty incorporates more mature sexual signals. Beauties like
Raquel Welch or Sophia Loren are typically taller, darker, fuller-
figured. Their rounded hips and full breasts impact on the viewer,
signaling both eroticism and maternal security.

The key to maximizing one's attractiveness, explains Guthrie,
is to tune up both forms of natural beauty at once, mixing and
balancing signals of modest purity with those of overt sexuality.

Monroe's pouting smile and purring voice, for example, conveyed innocence even as her broad behind swayed seductively.

When juvenile characteristics persist into maturity, they are called neotenic traits (from the Greek *neo*, meaning new, and *tein*, meaning to stretch). Literally, the look of a newborn is stretched into adulthood. Nature fosters neotenic traits through evolution—for instance, as humans evolve from hairy apes into the hairless skin of children. Culture fosters neotenic traits through a variety of cosmetic rituals that mimic the language of nature. Clothing and grooming are used to accent the two categories of beauty. During a certain fashion era, women bind their breasts to look more childish; then during the next era they pad their breasts to look more sensuous. Similarly, men alternately shave their beards to look more boyish, or wax their mustaches to look more threatening. Male attractiveness is more often enhanced by dominance traits, while female beauty generally emphasizes greater neotenic traits. Princes are tall and dark, while the lovely virgins who wait for them are delicate and fair. The bound foot and the wasp waist are extreme examples of the role of culture in fostering an infantile look.

In search of greater beauty, women impersonate the full red lips of a nursing infant; the pink cheeks and smooth skin of a toddler; the wide eyes and blond hair of a cherub; the girlish giggles and impish smiles of a child at play. In turn, babyish nicknames like Dolly, Chickie, and Cookie are pinned on them for life. Clothing designers capitalize on the value of the neotenic look by borrowing from kiddie fashions—pinafores, lacy smocks, babydoll nighties, floppy bows, and pastel shades. Advertisers exploit women's need to look neotenic by asking "Can you compete with your little girl's looks?"—"Which are the mother's hands, which are the daughter's?"—"Are you protecting your schoolgirl complexion and guarding your girlish figure?" One media analyst describes the dominant theme in commercials as "Women shouldn't grow up." In a reverse Lolita phenomenon, women are encouraged to mimic their daughters, which insidiously leads to commercials in which girls are displayed as sensuous women. If females are considered prettier when they look girlish, then girls become more vulnerable to commercial and sexual exploitation, as if they were grown women.

Neotenic beauty traits are portrayed on the frozen face of the cover girl. Untouched by time, her unlined features neither mellow nor mature beyond an adolescent stage. The best fashion models are described as those with the "least faces," and the girls *(sic)* with the more "fetal looks" are often the most successful. These model faces are certainly beautiful in a passive way. Imitations of inanimate objects, they stare blankly, gaze provocatively, or smile simply, but rarely convey the full range of mature adult emotions. A bevy of high fashion models all under 16 years of age and including Brooke Shields ushered in the 1980s with a new image of the child-woman. These beauties are supreme temptresses because they are tabooed as children.

Along with a juvenile look, childlike personality traits are also considered more feminine than masculine. The Bem Sex Role Inventory, for example, lists "childlike" as a feminine characteristic. This test also rates people as more feminine if they are "gentle, shy, gullible, soft-spoken, and fond of children" (traits that originally were rated as feminine by large groups of subjects).[3] Women and children are thereby conceptually linked together not only in terms of looks but also in terms of childish behavior. Furthermore, females and children are both judged to be more attractive as a group than are males or adults.

Andelin devotes a whole chapter of *Fascinating Womanhood* to the subject of how to cultivate the childlike image "that amuses and fascinates men because it's such a contrast to their own superior strength and masculine ability."[4] She describes the ideal wife, from a man's viewpoint, as one who radiates health, happiness, and especially childlikeness. To develop a fascinating facade she suggests the following:

> . . . if you want to create some youthful styles of your own visit the little girls' shops. There you will see buttons and bows, checks, pleats, daisies. . . . Look in the children's section of pattern books . . . girlish hair styles are the traditional long styles, braids, pony tails, curls, with the addition of ribbons, flowers, bows, barrettes. Your husband may not want you to wear these in public, but he will love them at home.[5]

Andelin explains that by looking girlish, a woman can more easily use childish tactics. She can express emotions in an infantile way, looking "adorably angry . . . by stamping her feet, shaking her curls, pouting with an innocent face." Outfitted in buttons and bows it becomes easier to slip into the role of daddy's little girl. One satisfied reader testified that "when I stuck out my lower lip during a fight, my husband said, 'you look so cute when you do that,' and we both forgot the argument."[6]

By cultivating neotenic beauty traits through cosmetic rituals, women alter their access to certain forms of power. For neoteny joins women with children not only in attractive and appealing ways but also in subordinating ways. An immature look conveys a lack of maturity, a lack of self-control, a lack of wisdom and authority. The more women mimic children, the more childish they appear and the more like children they are treated. (Both need to be protected, shielded from harsh language, and kept close to home doing housework or homework.) When the outer image impersonates a child, it becomes harder to take the inner person seriously.

The treatment of women and children as a similar class is inspired by more than mere physical connection. Traditions built on that bond equate women with children both culturally and legally. Since the social control of children is readily justified, then so far as women appear to be childlike, their subordinate social position can be rationalized. There is nothing wrong with looking or acting childlike at times. But to do so most of the time jeopardizes one's chance of being treated like an adult at any time. Clearly, it becomes harder for females to mature into confident grownups when they are called girls, and are called on to look like girls, all their lives.

Guthrie suggests that neotenic traits naturally evolve to encourage care-giving toward helpless youngsters. Moreover, an immature look in an adult can serve as an appeasement gesture by reducing hostile threats from dominants. Adorned like a doll, a female acquires the power to elicit support. Studies confirm, for instance, that doors get opened more often for women dressed in skirts and feminine outfits than for those wearing pants.[7] Neotenic traits are seen as innately attractive in females, explains Guthrie, since they reinforce the social dominance of males. Hence, women learn to amplify the natural language of neotenic beauty because its signals are an important part of the dominance hierarchy. The following section considers hair removal and hair coloring as examples of the power game in which women adorn themselves in the image of a subordinate child.

Preserving Prime Time

We have only one life to live, and Clairol invites us to live it as a blonde. Millions of women accept the invitation, hoping to rinse beauty into their lives. Why does blonder equal prettier? Because in the language of biology, blonder also means younger. One in four American women is born blond, but only 5 percent remain so after puberty casts the shadow of maturity. One way to look younger is simply to stay blond longer. (Since blondness occurs mainly among Caucasians, it also carries with it the high status of the dominant group in a racist culture like ours.) About one out of three Miss America contestants has been blond.

Before 1930, hair dye was uncommon and was considered uncouth. By 1950, the cosmetic industry had convinced us that nice girls could do it too. Ads focused on reconnecting the adult woman with the little girl inside—"She's as much fun as a kid, and just as fresh-looking." By bringing out a woman's youthful highlights, a rinse could bring back the carefree days of childhood.

Blond men look younger too. Fair-haired lads appear more boyish, less macho. Yet few adult males choose to become blonder, since blondness signals subordination. In films and advertisements, blond men are rarely paired with darker women; the power system looks out of kilter with such couples. The swarthy ethnic Othello captures the pale Desdemona, a treasure of "higher and lighter caste."

Blond equals soft and pure; a sunny day; a princess with a golden crown; an angel with a halo. In contrast, dark equals sinister, mysterious, dirty; the fearful shadows of night; the black robes of witches. On the ancient Greek stage, heroes wore blond wigs, villains wore dark ones. Children's dolls are usually blond and blue-eyed, as are most fairy-tale princesses.

Blond stereotypes come in contrasting pairs. Like other myths, they survive best when counterbalanced. The proverbial dumb blonde is beautiful but empty-headed, as if her brains were somehow burnt out by the glow in her hair. A bright and powerful woman can wear her blond curls as a decorative and disarming defense. With the softening halo of gold, she can act shrewd without appearing shrewish. Natural blondes report that their fairness makes others see them as symbols or objects rather than as human beings. They feel as if they are expected to behave in a special way and they must consciously work to shake off the blond stereotype.

On the one hand, a blond pixie like Goldie Hawn is typecast as cute, dumb, and innocent. On the other hand, an adventuress like Goldilocks is the archetype of the loose woman. She wanders unchaperoned into strangers' houses, sleeps in their beds, tries out different "sizes" until she finds one that feels "just right." She is a platinum playgirl, acting on impulse and indulging in one pleasure after another.

Gentlemen prefer blondes, they say, because blondes mean "good times . . . good sex . . . it's easier to score with one." Recall the case of Barbara, the teenager who immediately ran out to bleach her hair when her boyfriend expressed a preference for golden locks. A Clairol executive remarked that "If a woman has a marriage problem, her first response after 'Kill the other woman' is 'I'll become a blonde.' "

Do blondes really have more fun? In *Blond Beautiful Blond*, Lois Wyse concludes that being a blonde is not just a color but a state of mind, an embodiment of romantic dreams.[8] The peroxide that bleaches the hair seems to permeate the brain as well. Studies show that those who rinse in highlights feel differently afterward. They believe that blondes are softer and more feminine, that "there's a blond kind of body, a blond way of dressing." A self-made blonde is seen, by herself and by others, as a mixture of naïveté and sensuality. Like Monroe or Bardot, she is a baby doll ready for action, a ripe fruit in an innocent skin. Wyse suggests that because blondes see themselves as more glamorous, they project an image that makes others respond to them in that way. Consequently, they do indeed have more fun.

Being blond is not enough. One must be silky smooth as well, in order to look childlike. Two thousand years ago, the Roman poet Ovid warned women in his *Ars Amatoria (The Art of Love)* to "let no rude goat find his way beneath your arms, and let not your legs be rough with bristling hair." American women remove more body hair than females in any other western culture. Few dare to venture onto beaches or into beds without first pruning away the unsightly, embarrassing, even repulsive growth. The deep aversion to "excess" hair on a woman's upper lip, chin, underarms, nipples, bikini line, legs, and so forth, only shows how strongly both women and men are socialized to mistrust the natural female form.

Those cursed with an overabundance of body hair are abundantly distressed by it. We hate it, and so we depilate it—bleaching, shaving, melting, plucking, or shocking it into oblivion in what has been called "the classic feminine mopping up operation."[9] A variety of ingenious products are offered by those who profit from this cosmetic "problem." One advertisement warns, "When it comes to looking beautiful, you need more than a miracle cream or a new shade of lipstick . . . because sleek hairfree skin is really where beauty begins." They offer, in one handy package, a complete hair tending kit with "electrolysis for permanent hair removal; roll on wax for long term hair removal; specially formulated creams for short term hair removal; cream lighteners to make fine hair invisible by turning it a pale, skin-matching shade in minutes. . . ." Such products restore to women the smooth skin of a preadolescent. They are part of the cosmetic routine that exaggerates neotenic traits and that preserves the image of woman-as-girl.

Body hair signals sexual maturity as well as dominance. Hair conjures up images of wild beasts and primitive ape-men. As a tool of intimidation, it bristles with anger. We speak of scary moments as hair-raising. One reason that humans as the naked ape have become increasingly more naked, explains Guthrie, is because a less hairy human is a less frightening one. Smooth skin encourages social bonding. To denude oneself helps to delude others with a friendlier looking body. Depilation mimics youth and therefore can serve as a gesture of appeasement for both men and women. In fact, beards, as symbols of power in ancient Egypt, were permitted only for royalty. Queen Hatshepsut wore a goatee to affirm her high status. Today, a few stiff bristles on a lady's chin or the faintest shadow on her upper lip completely negates all other aspects of her feminine charm.

Denuded and tidy, women slip into the stereotype of female neatness. Recall that in the Broverman study mentally healthy women were expected to be preoccupied not only with appearance but with neatness as well. The compositions of second-graders show they already know that "boys like to get messy and don't take baths . . . while girls are pretty and neat." A hairy manly fellow can be casually unkempt, but a pretty gal must look smooth and neatly put together.

Females are socialized to censor body hair, just as they are taught to repress their sexuality. (Dreams and fantasies of hair are often interpreted as symbolic of genitals and of the wish for uninhibited sexual expression.) The silky legs and hairless underarms of a child-woman connote her sexual innocence, even as they make her more sensuous. A proper lady never allows a coarse pubic hair to stray across the bikini line into public view. Such hairs announce too loudly that a sexual organ lies just behind the boundary. A fine line separates the sexually innocent beauty from the sexually active broad: the former lives a tidy contained life; the latter gets into "hairy" situations.

Females begin with less body hair because of hormonal differences. This minor dimorphism then grows into major dimensions when used to distinguish the beauties from the beasts. By inflating the value of a hairless body, then crowning it with golden curls, the beauty myth alters women's appearance to look more childlike.

Shaving legs, bleaching hair, painting on cherubic faces, extends the neotenic look of childhood into womanhood. Because looking good requires looking young, prime time for females peaks in the late teens and early twenties. When people were asked to rate various categories of faces, the white female teenage face was consistently judged more attractive by subjects of all ages, races, and sexes.[10] Susan Sontag observes that:

Only one standard of female beauty is sanctioned: the girl. The great advantage men have is that our culture allows two standards of male beauty: the *boy* and the *man*. . . . Men are able to accept themselves under another standard of good looks—heavier, rougher, more thickly built. A man does not grieve when he loses the smooth, unlined, hairless skin of a boy. . . . while the passage from girlhood to early womanhood is experienced by many women as their downfall—for women are trained to want to continue looking like girls forever.[11]

The first Miss America was only sixteen; the average age of pageant winners is now around twenty-one. College women often have trouble understanding what the beauty myth is all about (or what feminism is about for that matter), since they already enjoy the high status characteristic of a chimp in heat.

While a baby face can charm and captivate, its veneer wears thin with time. Worship of neotenic beauty traits during the first half of the female life cycle leads to a beauty crisis during the second half. Aging women seem all the more unattractive and alien when they no longer can impersonate an infantile illusion. It is hard to admit the connection between a preoccupation with looking younger and a disgust with growing older. Yet the pleasure of being adored as a youthful beauty contributes to the pain of being rejected as an aging ugly. And the anxiety that is felt as the bloom of youth fades is one of the most destructive aspects of the beauty myth.

Premature Obsolescence

A man of about 30 strikes us as a youthful, somewhat un-formed individual whom we expect to make powerful use of the possibilities for development opened up to him by anal-ysis. A woman of the same age, however, often frightens us by her physical rigidity and unchangeability. It is as though . . . the difficult development to femininity had exhausted the possibilities of the person.

— Sigmund Freud[12]

Women's lives are marked by a precipitous drop in social value at mid-life. Prime time ends and they find themselves pushed over the hill into no-man's-land, considered old simply because they no longer look very young. The emphasis on juvenile traits as being essential to feminine beauty means that older women are judged more harshly than men.

Aging is determined by social as well as by biological factors. It is a state of mind as much as a state of matter. Both sexes watch their bodies wear away each year, but time hangs more heavily on female faces, not because women age faster but because they are prematurely devalued. Despite a life expectancy that is now nine years longer than men's, middle-aged women are seen as relatively older than their male contemporaries.

Susan Sontag identified this bias as "the Double Standard of Aging." She emphasized that the differing standards of attractiveness for men and women are a major part of the problem, first because feminine beauty standards stress youthfulness more heavily than masculine standards, and second because these standards of attractiveness are applied more stringently to women than to men.

> Men also care about their bodies and want to be attractive . . . but since the business of men is mainly being and doing, rather than appearing, the standards for appearance are much less exacting. . . . Men are not subject to the barely concealed revulsion expressed in this culture against the female body, except in its smooth, youthful, firm, blemish-free form. . . . The desire to be the "right age" has a special urgency for a woman it never has for a man. . . . A much greater part of her self-esteem and pleasure in life is threatened when she ceases to be young. . . . Most men experience getting older with regret or apprehension. But most women experience it even more painfully with shame.[13]

Research supports the assertion that the double standard of aging is linked with looksism. Attractiveness is judged to decline with age for both sexes, but faster for females. When subjects rated photos of the same people at youth, middle age, and old age, aging women were thought to diminish in attractiveness to a greater extent than aging men. Moreover, ratings of men's masculinity remain fairly constant over the life span, whereas women's femininity is perceived to be in rapid decline between youth and middle age.[14]

Males and females do not approach the starting line of aging on an equal footing. Nor do they run the same course. The Older

Women's League (OWL) originally defined "older" females as those over age thirty. The male life cycle is not cleaved by a thirty-year yardstick. Men are not cut down so early as women are because their attractiveness is neither equated with a neotenic ideal nor inflated to such grand proportions.

Masculinity is measured by strength, which is why aging men worry most about losing their ability to "perform" in the various arenas of life; femininity is measured by attractiveness, which is why aging women worry so much about losing their looks. Many women report a sense of failure as they feel the core of their gender identity slipping away from them.

Losing one's girlish beauty means losing a self-image that has been socialized since birth. Although the French have long recognized that women of a certain age still retain a certain appeal, this brief stage only predicts with certainty that obsolescence is imminent. Anticipation of the fall from grace can be as painful as the fall itself.

Pretty women have the most to lose. A fading face is experienced as an overwhelming assault to someone whose good looks have always brought her instant attention. As noted earlier, studies show that those women who were prettiest in college suffer more adjustment problems during middle age than those who were plainer-looking. Men's adjustment to aging, however, is unrelated to their former degree of attractiveness.[15] On her fortieth birthday, Grace Kelly commented that although forty was a marvelous age for a man, it was torture for a woman, since it meant "the beginning of the end." When the end begins at mid-life, females are robbed of their right to maturity.

In *Mirror, Mirror: The Terror of Not Being Young*, Elissa Melamed describes the anguish that is felt as women anticipate "the beginning of the end." Appearance anxiety, she writes, has its origins in early childhood, when girls are socialized to overvalue their physical appearance. It escalates during puberty and reaches a new peak at mid-life, when flesh can no longer be painted or packaged into the neotenic ideal. Melamed shares her own painful rite of passage out of the security of youthful beauty and into the appearance anxiety of middle age:

As a psychotherapist, I realized that I was obviously dealing with something deeper than some wrinkles and gray hairs. I was feeling divided, divided against myself: a changeless person trapped inside a changing body; a centered person at odds with a needy person; an honest person ashamed of the "me" who wanted to play the youth game. A voice echoed in my head: "No, you are no longer the fairest in the land." . . . While I was young, *because* I was young, I had naively confused recognition of my youth and beauty with recognition of *me*. I had, in fact, identified the "me" with this frozen young personage. Like Sleeping Beauty, I had fallen into a trance around the age of 15 from which I was just beginning to wake.[16]

Women who are chronologically at one stage of life but socially pushed into another suffer a developmental asynchrony. They feel out of step with themselves. The demand for idealized beauty traits distorts the natural process of maturation, causing asynchronies to occur again and again. Except for a brief period in late adolescence and early adulthood, females are constantly prodded into a stage of development that is inappropriate to their actual age. Girls of five are given makeup kits with a ten-year-old on the cover who pretends to be sixteen. Preteen dresses are marketed for children of eight. Fashion magazines peddle night creams and moisturizers to adolescents, warning them that "it's never too early to start worrying about wrinkles." When a group of high school sophomores discussed why they felt they absolutely had to wear makeup to class each day, one explained "because of these ugly bags under my eyes," and another added, "I have to cover up all the lines and the puffiness."

Mothers struggle to look as young as their daughters, while daughters are borrowing their mothers' clothes. Fifty-year-olds pay surgeons to resurrect their forty-year-old faces. By mid-life, nearly every woman has been tempted to lie about her age. Those who do, hope they look as young as the lie. Not telling one's age after a certain point has become a universal joke. For a woman senses that once she tells, she will be treated as though she is older than she feels inside.

The myth of female beauty first pressures young girls prematurely into sexual display, then retards their natural growth into womanhood, and finally denies them the many images and stages of maturity. On the horizon of the female life cycle, middle age flows in like a tidal wave, dissolving juvenile beauty traits and leaving women high and dry on a rather barren beach.

The Vanishing Lady

> We are the same age: I am no longer a young woman. Oh my love, imagine yourself in a few years time as a handsome man in the fullness of your age, beside me in mine. Imagine me, still beautiful but desperate, frantic in my armour of corset and frock, under my make-up and powder, in my young tender colors. Imagine me, beautiful as a full-blown rose which one must not touch.
>
> — Colette[17]

Even before they reach that certain age, most women become aware of a shift in the kind of attention they receive. Being overlooked, ignored, or visually dismissed contributes to appearance anxiety. "We are put into another category by the eyes of others," writes Melamed. "What these eyes tell us is that they will no longer mirror us. The eyes make no contact: they glance and slide off as if they had seen an inanimate object."[18] The silence of being unseen can be devastating after a lifetime of listening for the compliment or searching for the approving glance that confirms one's ability to please. Women even start to miss the street harassment that at least acknowledged their presence. "A whole week in Rome and I wasn't even pinched," complains a friend. Invisible to others, women start to lose track of themselves.

In the *New York Times Magazine*, Charles Simmons writes to a male audience:

> You realize that all your life you have screened women out. Too tall, too short, too fat, too thin, ill dressed. . . . And of course, too mature. The gray hair, the dowager's hump, the stringy arms, you didn't have to *look* actually, not to be interested. A hint in the eye's corner kept the eye moving for the fresh face, the springy hair, the youthful waist between firm hips and bust.[19]

Appearance anxiety increases as women see themselves filtered out. Unconsciously they also contribute to their own effacement.

Like performers who perfect the trick of the disappearing lady, aging women become experts at vanishing:

— *Vanishing* into the woodwork of agoraphobia; banishing ourselves at home because we look too tired, too ill, too unkempt

— *Vanishing* into the taboos against asking a woman her age . . . as if forty-one or fifty-four were obscene

— *Vanishing* into lies that lop off years, making them seem unlived

— *Vanishing* into depression, into a vain attempt at suicide or into hospital wards; drowning in a dose of Valium or alcohol; pulling the covers over our heads

— *Vanishing* in futile efforts to keep time from flooding childlike faces; sandbagging ourselves against a sea of wrinkles and melting away into vanishing creams or age-spot removers

— *Vanishing* into memories; stepping aside as lifelong husbands pursue the younger women we once were

— *Vanishing* into a stack of unanswered letters to men who advertise for good companions but respond only to younger ones

— *Vanishing* from TV ads in which aging women are only seen selling soap or denture cream

— *Vanishing* into the hands of surgeons who peel off our wrinkles and discard them in a plastic bag

Pros at the art of hiding, older women unconsciously deny the fact that they hide. Appearance anxiety is shrouded in embarrassed silence, tucked into the crevices of private thought, so that each women goes on believing that she alone suffers from it.

What do the middle-aged voices of appearance anxiety sound like when they *are* raised?

ANN. "It makes me angry and frustrated to see my looks slipping away from me just when I'm beginning to feel like a whole person."

EMILY. "I try to avoid mirrors. They only make me self-conscious. Getting older isn't so bad, but looking older is really awful."

MARGARET. "Lately I see my aging mother's face in my own. I'm scared that somehow I'll wake up looking as old as she does."

HILDA. "I'm prepared to die but not to look lousy for the next forty years."[20]

ZOE. "Listen to me. Think what it is like to have most of your

life ahead and be told you are obsolete! Think what it is like . . .
to be told . . . that you are not a person but a joke. . . . Don't
you pretend for a minute as you look at me, forty-three, fat, and
looking exactly my age, that I am not as alive as you are and that
I do not suffer from the category into which you are forcing me."[21]

CAROL. "I grew up with a beautiful mother who, in spite of
being a professional woman, sat for hours in front of the mirror
plucking out white hair as it grew in. Watching her demoralizing
fight against aging, I allowed my hair to grow white, but the
threat of 'shriveling up' is nevertheless a reality of my life. When
a wiser friend challenged my fear, I realized that trying to look
attractive (meaning youthful) is part of my 'assumptive' world,
an adolescent commitment that is difficult to relinquish."[22]

The double standard of aging is more than just a set of biased
attitudes that diminish self-esteem. It translates into a set of sober
statistics that describe reality for aging females—higher rates of
singlehood, unemployment, hospitalization. As women lose their
looks with age, they often lose their position in the world as well.
Displaced as beauty objects, they are all too often displaced as
workers, wives, and homemakers.

Aging women are the fastest growing poverty group in this
country. Females comprise nearly three quarters of the elderly
poor, and their impoverished state is often linked with being
unmarried. There are three times as many single women as single
men over age fifty. Four out of five elderly women live alone. In
one third of the second marriages the bride is more than a decade
younger than the groom, and she can expect to live the last ten
years of her life as an aged, often poor widow.[23] Highly respected
men like Justice William Douglas take wives half their age. The
rare older woman who enjoys a young lover must first break a
taboo. Her mate is then ridiculed either as a fortune hunter or as
a neurotic hung up on a mother figure.

Even before mid-life, women find themselves neutered and
sexually disqualified by their loss of beauty. Men can become
craggy and scarred by time with less sexual penalty. Actors age
into distinguished leading men, while actresses find themselves
unemployable once they look sexually implausible. An over-forty

Marlboro man who roams the plains is clearly not yet over the hill. His weathered skin proclaims his virility, his touch of gray adds character.

Women's reproductive capacity does end earlier and more abruptly than men's. But female sexual capacity remains unchanged in middle age and may even increase after menopause. Three quarters of women surveyed who were over seventy reported that they still feel erotic desire. The biggest sexual problem for aging women is not lack of interest or responsiveness but lack of a partner. While this is partially the product of greater female longevity, it is also caused by the decision of many men to marry younger women and by the double standard that brands older women as unattractive and therefore sexually undesirable. (Jane Goodall reports that aging chimps enjoy a more favorable position. "Ugly Old Flo" was the eldest of a chimpanzee group but "despite her decrepit appearance, she had more suitors than any other female.")

Men are expected to display their power by working hard, playing hard, staying hard. The fading face of a matronly mate is sometimes used to explain a man's dwindling potency. Popular magazines warn a wife to keep up her appearance so that her husband can keep up his performance. Medical textbooks even suggest that his loss of lust may be due to her loss of looks. Here again, the double standard links age with gender stereotypes: loss of beauty for women, loss of power for men.

Of course, aging reduces the physical power of both men and women. But the social concept of aging traces a different power curve for each sex. A man's star may still be rising at age forty, even fifty, long after a woman's has begun to set. A woman's maturity, wisdom, and competence cannot compensate for her wrinkles or fat. Life after youth is less terrifying for men because they have many older and even elderly models who are admired and respected—the presidents and professionals who run the business of the world. A comparable group of powerful women over sixty, deciding the fate of nations while wearing sensible shoes, is harder to imagine.

At each stage of life, people need models with whom they can identify. Some of these models are provided by the media. Unfortunately, middle-aged women are hard to find in the typical cast of media characters. Missing from billboards, magazine ads, variety shows, and newscasts, their absence parallels that of other minority groups who were at one time almost totally banned from popular culture. Advertisers cannot use middle-aged women because they represent negative values, one analyst concludes. When they are employed, they are stereotypically cast as "plump, passive, bumbly, comic figures"—such as Edith Bunker buying a headache remedy. Analysis of ads over the past thirty years indicated that three out of four women appeared to be under thirty years of age, and only four percent looked over forty.[24]

A 1982 survey of local news anchorpersons showed that nearly half of the men but only 3 percent of the women were over age forty. Moreover, 18 percent of the men were over fifty, but not a single anchorwoman was that old.[25] Anchorpersons need to be authoritative in order to be believable; and for women, this means being pretty. Russell Baker laments this fact:

> The faces of television newswomen are never wrinkled. Not like the reliable face of Walter Cronkite. . . . [They] always seem to have arrived fresh from the presser two seconds ahead of the camera. Several years ago, to be sure, there was a woman with a wrinkled face on the networks, but they put her aside . . . cut the juice to her camera. I still miss that woman. She was evidence that women who had undergone human experience grew faces like everybody else.[26]

One newswoman optimistically predicts that in the future "they aren't going to get rid of us so easily just because of our wrinkles." However Liz Trotta of CBS claims that looks remain the number-one factor in the careers of female newscasters.

Older women find themselves banished prematurely because they offend a system primed to value females mainly for their childlike beauty and because they threaten a system that fears female power unless it is packaged attractively. In western culture, status is denied to elderly people in general but to aging women in particular. In some societies women do not vanish after childbearing ends but become even more visible, enjoying a dramatic rise in status. (Note, for instance, the great respect shown to the traditional Chinese matriarch.) Isak Dinesen once wrote that "only when women are old enough to have done with the business of being women can they let loose their strength."[27] A second blossoming is possible after the cultivation of children is completed. In a fertile environment, females can grow beyond the constraints of beauty and of motherhood into the full bloom of personhood. Too often, they feel cut down as obsolete just when they have so much to offer.

Monroe gave up at thirty-six. Would she have been able to muster enough courage to live out the second half of her life if she had lived in a world where aging actresses could remain leading ladies? Gloria Steinem observes that a woman whose identity is equated with being blond or smooth or cute becomes dangerous to herself and to others as she begins to age. "Because I have work I care about," Steinem adds, "it's possible that I may be less difficult to get along with when the double chins start to form."[28] Yet, Steinem's fiftieth birthday smile adorned the covers of magazines precisely because her good looks are so enduring and so exceptional (despite her insistence that this is what fifty really looks like). In contrast to Steinem, Betty Friedan is not exhibited as a wonderful example of how to grow old gracefully. Women who outwardly age more slowly—or better yet not at all—are admired as a superior breed.

Aging women have greater value when their image remains pleasing. An over-sixty Nancy Reagan is painfully thin, perfectly coiffed, always packaged in chic. Some applaud her for inaugurating a new wave of glamour for the mature woman. But wealthy women (often the wives or daughters of powerful men) have always enjoyed protracted visibility because their wealth enables them to remain attractive much longer. The First Lady's high style increases the pressure on average women to attain the youthful look that only privileged women can afford.

Some older women do manage to acquire and retain power beyond the limits of beauty and outside the control of others. Throughout history, these women have been branded as troublemakers because they challenged the idea of female subordination. They are the so-called wicked witches, an archetype based on the belief that females grow mean and ugly with age. Stripped of her youthful femininity, the aging woman may be feared as a sorceress, taunted as a hag, or ridiculed as a mother-in-law. Every Halloween, little girls dress up in black to enact symbolically the image of the ugly old lady. Witch phobia, witch hunting, and witch burning are, of course, not merely the fiction of fairy tales but also the facts of life. Sontag observes:

> One of the attitudes that punish women most severely is the visceral horror felt at aging female flesh. It reveals a radical fear of women instilled deep in this culture, a demonology of women that has crystallized in such mythic caricatures as the vixen, the virago, the vamp and the witch. Several centuries of witch-phobia, during which one of the cruelest extermination programs in Western history was carried out, suggest something of the extremity of this fear. That old women are repulsive is one of the most profound esthetic and erotic feelings in our culture. Women share it as much as men do. . . . Like men, they find old age in women "uglier" than old age in men.[29]

Deep down, most females are afraid of turning into one of the ugly witches remembered from childhood fairy tales. And so they devour "magic" potions and professional advice on how to look thirty for the next twenty years.

Buying Time

> When she took off her wet bathing suit at the house she noticed that the dark shine of sunburn was beginning to cover the map of tiny red veins she had on her right leg, near the knee. It could scarcely be seen at all. There was the satisfaction of some small reprieve. She looked over her shoulder at her naked back and backside and legs in the mirror. How long? Five years? Six? (What did the bodies of women in their forties look like?) A few years and she wouldn't be able to look at this anymore.
>
> — Nadine Gordimer[30]

With each passing year, a woman must dip ever deeper into her cosmetic jars to control the "fate of her face." Gradually, she gives up the look of a cover girl for that of a covered girl (or the stereotype of the overly made-up old maid). Beyond a certain age, putting on one's face is tantamount to hiding it. Experts offer an alternative: the face lift. After all, the difference between concealing age with paint and with surgical reconstruction is only a matter of degree. And so, secret visits are paid to the modern witch doctors of youthfulness—the dermatologists, cosmetologists, and aesthetic surgeons who reset the face of time.

The decision whether to have one's face lifted relates to the larger question of how to face up to the aging process. A middle-aged woman peering into her mirror stands at "a philosophic intersection where vanity, vogue, fear of aging and insecurity meet and collide," writes Mary-Lou Weisman in an essay. "The bottom line, the ultimate wrinkle, is the integrity of the self. . . . One must fight for one's self, even though the reward for waging that battle is often no more but never less than the cold consolation of integrity," Weisman observes. "That's why I haven't gotten a face lift—so far."[31] But many women (including many feminists) do decide, at that philosophic juncture, that personal integrity is best maintained by facing the knife.

A look at one patient's profile illustrates how appearance anxiety delivers faces into the hands of doctors. At age forty-nine, Jean is a well-educated mother of three, married to a businessman and content to be manager of his office. She started to think about a face lift when she hit forty, but the final decision was long in coming and difficult to make. In part, Jean felt she was being overly vain; but she eventually became convinced that surgery would reduce her mounting anxiety about looking older and could restore her self-confidence. In a therapy session just before the operation, she made this comment:

> Everyone, including Bob, tells me I'm crazy. After twenty-five years of marriage, he said, what difference can a few wrinkles make? But I'm sure that if I look better, I'll feel better too. You see, somehow, I still think of the real me as looking like I did on my wedding day. I only want to look as young as I feel inside. Why shouldn't I do whatever I can to make myself happier, if only for a few more years?

Jean felt that she was influenced by a barrage of advertisements in newspapers and on TV that made surgery look so simple and so necessary:

> "Take a good hard look at yourself and admit how you feel."

"How is your face in general? Wrinkled? Put your hands to your temples and push up and back. Don't you look better?"

"You *can* do something about the way you look. . . . There's nothing wrong with personal vanity; it keeps people slender, younger, handsomer."

"Some changes are more than aesthetic, they're very necessary for the woman who has aged faster than her years."

Advertisements talk of tucking tummies, sucking fat, bobbing noses, doing eyelids as if a doll was being remodeled instead of a person. Surgeons seem as adept at publicizing the face lift as at performing it. They capitalize on ageism and looksism by setting new aesthetic standards even while selling them. Some surgical texts describe aging as a "degenerative disease" or a "recurring deformity" that should be attacked as early as possible.[32] Surgery thus alters norms, and a lifted face may appear to be a necessity. During her first surgical consultation, Jean secretly hoped the doctor would tell her she looked too young for the operation and should come back in a few years. He didn't.

Appearance anxiety is at its highest level among middle-class women like Jean who have the material means to combat their "deformity" and who consequently find it harder to "let themselves go" into the aging process. Each wrinkle is experienced as an assault on their self-esteem. A hidden agenda often underlies the desire for cosmetic surgery: an unconscious longing to feel physically younger, to cure a husband's impotence, to rival a daughter's beauty, to compete with a younger woman for a man who is older than both of them. Fear is commonly mentioned as a motive for surgery—fear of abandonment, dependency, or loneliness.

Jean's husband is not totally content with his fifty-three-year-old face, but he has not seriously considered lifting it. Surveys show that 30 percent of women, as compared to only 12 percent of men, would have a face lift if they could afford it. Things are changing, however. Wrinkled male faces are not quite as respectable as they once were, and more men are now turning to surgery to gain a competitive edge in the world. Before 1970 only 5 percent of face lifts were performed on males; now the figure has risen to 25 percent.[33] In fact, the growing interest in cosmetic surgery for men has been attributed to the influence of the women's movement. So-called liberated men feel freer to express their concerns over appearance and feel less stigma about self-adornment.

Jean's face lift and eyelid surgery took several hours and cost $7000 in 1984 Like most cosmetic surgery patients she received no insurance benefits and ignored possible complications with the rationalization "It won't happen to me." Problems occur about 15 percent of the time and include hemorrhages, unfavorable reactions to the anesthetic, facial nerve damage, abnormal scarring, and, in rare cases, permanent deformity or even death. Despite the complications and high cost, the number of face-lift candidates increases annually by 10 percent. In California alone, thirty thousand plastic surgeons are kept busy. One of them predicts that in time, having a face lift will become as routine as having a tooth filled. The increasing demand for cosmetic surgery is a result of many factors: longer life expectancy; new advances in medical technology; greater affluence, permitting greater investment in appearance; media portrayal of idealized beauty standards; aggressive promotion by doctors; rising divorce rates and greater numbers of single people; and, finally, the belief that everlasting beauty can be bought for the right price.

Does a face lift accomplish what patients expect it to? The answer is both yes and no. Looking younger does not automatically translate into feeling better. After surgery, there must be a shift in self-image to correspond with the new look. Those who expect the surgeon to deliver a new mate, anchor a wandering one, or fashion a radical new lifestyle are disappointed. A few patients find that they miss their familiar old faces, but the vast majority of face-lift patients feel pleased with the results. Almost all of them believe that they look younger and better. Jean expressed this sense of satisfaction:

> Now I enjoy looking at myself again. I'm more relaxed, and more open to new people. My birthday is coming and I'm not nearly as frightened of the big 5-O. I look much younger; it's as simple as that. My only regret is that I waited so long.

Has Jean's personal integrity been enhanced or compromised

by having a face lift? Would a mentally healthy person endure that much pain, invest that much money, suffer that much trauma for a temporary reprieve from a few wrinkles? She probably would.

At one time, cosmetic surgery patients were considered emotionally unstable, both by professionals and by the public. Textbooks described them as obsessive perfectionists, excessive narcissists, or extremely depressed. A 1960 report, for instance, concluded that one third of cosmetic surgery patients had personality trait disorders, 20 percent were neurotic, and 16 percent were psychotic.[34] Such patients are viewed less critically today because cosmetic surgery is now regarded as a valid psychotherapeutic tool. It is accepted as an augmentation rather than a mutilation—a chance to take "authorship of one's own appearance." One study found a 64 percent success rate in improvement of personality characteristics after cosmetic surgery.[35]

In fact, the face lift is being sought by many psychologically healthy females who take an active problem-solving approach to life; by career women who decide they need it for professional survival; and by single women who feel they need it for social survival. These women want to get rid of their self-conscious preoccupation with a cosmetic distraction in order to turn their attention to more important things. Camus observed that after 40 we become responsible for our faces. Women who seek a surgical solution to the double standard of aging may be making a healthier response than those who withdraw into a depressive state. Clearly, the pressure on females to preserve one of their greatest assets— a youthful face—is enormous. The face lift has been described as a mid-life passage that leads regressively backward rather than progressively forward. More and more women are choosing this rite of passage in the reverse direction because it is so rewarding.

A woman's decision to have cosmetic surgery must be viewed in its cultural context; a culture that measures her against an unfair standard that is not applied to men; that labels her sexually obsolete when she still experiences sexual desire and feels sexually desirable; that teaches her from childhood on that female beauty is the equivalent of an adolescent image. She may be trying unrealistically to escape from the reality of aging, but she may also be using a rational defensive strategy. Cosmetic surgery is her antidote to appearance anxiety—an answer that is not meant to defeat nature but rather to defend herself against a cultural stereotype and against the myth of female beauty.

Ignoring the Clock

. . . the unfinished beams in the roof are veiled by cobwebs. They are lovely, I think, gazing up at them with new eyes. They soften the hard lines of the rafters as grey hairs soften the lines on a middle-aged face. I no longer pull out grey hairs or sweep down cobwebs.

— Anne Morrow Lindbergh[36]

Can we revise the double standards and the gender myths that push both men and women into ill-fitting roles? Can we reconstruct an image of aging that will permit those who have wrinkled in the face of time to look more sympathetically at the map etched on their skin? Can we trace with pleasure rather than erase with fear the lifelines of experience, allowing our bodies to tell the truth about where we have been?

Are there models of women who successfully resist the neotenic beauty ideal? Who grow unself-consciously from childhood into adolescence, mature securely into womanhood, and finally move gracefully into middle and advanced old age? Who have enjoyed their reflections without hesitation and have accepted their aging bodies without appearance anxiety?

Such models do exist. They are masters at the art of healthy narcissism. Laurie Lisle has painted the portrait of such an artist.[37] Her biography of Georgia O'Keeffe reveals intimate images of the woman that are as startling as O'Keeffe's canvasses. These images, which span nearly a century, confirm that beauty can bloom continuously from within, outside the boundaries of a myth.

Right from the start, Georgia O'Keeffe seemed determined not only to live distinctively, but to look distinctive as well. "From the time I was a little girl," she recalls, "if my sisters wore their hair braided, I wouldn't wear mine braided. If they wore ribbons, I wouldn't. I'd think they looked better without it too." Because she was so totally unconcerned about looking unconventional, her distinct style was tolerated rather than teased. A high school classmate recalls:

> The most unusual thing about Georgia was the absolute plainness of her attire. . . . Georgia's hair was drawn smoothly back from her broad, prominent forehead, and she had no bows. . . . Her features were plain—not ugly—for each one was good, but large and unusual looking. She would have made a strikingly handsome boy.[38]

Devoted to painting, O'Keeffe refused to be diverted from achievement toward adornment. Her yearbook describes her as "a girl who would be different in habit, style and dress; a girl who doesn't give a cent for men. . . ." Lisle concludes that O'Keeffe was fiercely proud of being a woman throughout her life and rejected the traditional subordinate role assigned to her gender.

At the age of thirty, O'Keeffe met and eventually married the world-famous photographer Alfred Stieglitz. He became as entranced with her appearance as with her mind and photographed her intensely during their long marriage. O'Keeffe seemed to see herself in a new way through the eye of his lens. Past ninety when she finally published a volume of these pictures, she wrote, "I was photographed with a kind of heat and excitement and in a way wondered what it was all about. . . . You see, I'd never known what I looked like or thought about it much. I was amazed to find my face was lean and structured. I'd always thought it was round. . . . I could see myself, and it has helped me to say what I want to say in paint."[39]

Stieglitz's photographs portray the artist in her thirties and forties, yet she looks older than her years. Her expressions are grave, as we see in the illustration. The contrast between her flowing body and her forbidding face is dramatic. As one critic commented, "She isn't mugging or impersonating; she's entrancing herself. She may be wearing masks, but they have been brought up from within—they are her own."[40]

The camera captured every detail. In Lisle's description:

> She wore no makeup and did not tweeze or shave a hair from her body. The down on her upper lip and belly was delicately recorded as well as the fuzz in her armpits. Her mouth often turned down

at the edges into a scowl, whereas her heavy, unplucked eyebrows flew up like inquisitive wings. . . . Her classic chiseled profile rivets the eye. . . . She looked like a spirit, weighted down by womanhood, trying to take flight.[41]

Georgia O'Keeffe was named one of the twelve outstanding women of the century at the 1939 World's Fair and subsequently received the Presidential Medal of Freedom. After her husband's death, she worked in relative solitude for twenty years, continuing to look and live distinctively. She broke the rules once more in her ninth decade by forming an intimate alliance with Juan Hamilton, a man almost sixty years her junior. "Their relationship consisted of many elements: man-woman, parent-child, artist-artist . . . roles all inspired by sincere respect and genuine affection," writes Lisle. At Hamilton's urging, O'Keeffe, who had worn nothing but black and white since early adulthood, began to wear colors. His affection and encouragement helped her to start painting again. When asked to identify the happiest stage of life, O'Keeffe replied, "There is no happiest stage, there are only happy moments." She is described at ninety as sweeter and more feminine than at any time before.

Georgia O'Keeffe created some of the world's most captivating images, but her own personal beauty required no formal composition. In her we have a model who seems to have moved securely through life without appearance anxiety. Why was she able to mature with so much strength and dignity? Was it because she viewed herself from her own perspective? Because she ignored all pressures to cultivate an ill-fitting facade? Because she claimed the right to look old long before she aged? Of course, not everyone is a genius like O'Keeffe. Most of our self-portraits will not be as unique as hers. But perhaps we can learn from her and from similar models to be more courageous in our concepts of personal attractiveness, more honest in facing ourselves and others.

Women generally live long lives, but they do not age with as much strength as they might. What would it look and feel like to grow old in a world where females were accorded an equal place in society for their whole lives? We all have the right to look mature. As Sontag concludes, the challenge is to be seen and treated as full human beings, not only as women. She suggests that "Instead of being girls, girls as long as possible, who then age humiliatingly into middle-aged women and then obscenely into old women, we can become women much earlier—and remain active adults, enjoying the long erotic career of which women are capable, far longer."[42] It may be hard to change the way others see us. But we can try to see ourselves differently by turning a more compassionate eye on our own faces; by letting go of obsessive thoughts of youthful beauty; and by rejecting idealized standards that are not applied to men.

The so-called golden years lose their luster in light of the double standard of aging and in face of the myth of female beauty. Women hasten their own obsolescence by clinging too long to an adolescent ideal. Beauty is not universally equated with blondness or smoothness. Other choices are possible. Growing up means shaking off the childish mask. Coming of age with dignity means looking as mature as we really are and still seeing ourselves as sensuous human beings.

10

Loosening the Bonds of Beauty

To gild refined gold, to paint the lily,
To throw a perfume on the violet,
To smooth the ice, or add another hue
Unto the rainbow, . . .
. . . .
Is wasteful and ridiculous excess.
— Shakespeare, *King John*[1]

A RTISTS sometimes rework a canvas by painting over it. The older conception, called pentimento, is replaced with a fresh choice. To reassess the influence of beauty, we have to stand back from our mirrors for a broader perspective. Considering beauty as a social construct, we can see more clearly what has been retouched, what needs to be wiped clean, and where to begin anew. In the end, it is not the physical body alone that is important but also the way it reflects back to the self, mirrored by myth into one's own eyes.

"Yes, I'm really looking at myself," says Laurie. "What do I see? My hair is nice and I like my eyes, but my hips are still much too heavy. If I lost another few pounds over here, I think I'd be just right." Thus an eighty-pound anorectic responds to her therapist's question while standing before a mirror. Her body sends signals that it is suffering, but they go unheeded. Hunger

goes unfelt, emaciation goes unseen. Mind and body are dissociated, for Laurie has learned to "disattend" by turning off her
feelings and denying her pain. In order to overcome anorexia,
she must be taught to acknowledge natural sensations and to
experience her body more accurately.

In the quest for feminine beauty, women become obsessed with
their flesh while forced at the same time to deny its sensations.
As these feelings are sealed off, the divided self may acquire the
conquering mentality of mind against body. The physical self
becomes an obstacle to be overcome. Of course, mind and body
were not designed as adversaries but rather as natural allies. Anatomy cannot be dismissed in the search for a new destiny, nor can
a woman fully enjoy her body by constantly blocking it out.

A first important step in loosening the bonds of the beauty
myth is to recognize these repressed sensations by tuning in to
body messages and by consciously studying them. We can learn
to admit to feelings of hunger, satiation, lethargy, anxiety, exhaustion; to recognize the hyperactivity and insomnia caused by
diet schemes; to observe awkward postures and loss of balance;
to notice compulsive rituals of running to the mirror or climbing
on the scale; to question the hours spent creaming, brushing,
tweezing, outlining, examining, counting, covering, coloring, and
agonizing over each inadequacy; to sense when pain is felt in
connection with the daily cosmetic routine—soreness, stinging,
aching, pinching, itching, burning, numbness.

As part of her treatment program for anorexia, Laurie was given
a series of exercises to reconnect her to her body sensations.
Standing for long periods with her arms outstretched, she became
more aware of internal pain. Drawing her silhouette on a wall,
she compared her real proportions to the distorted image she had
projected and could actually touch and measure the difference
between the two.

Through such simple exercises, the body can be experienced
in new ways that heighten the awareness of beauty's burden—
for instance, by eating whatever is desired for a week or fasting
for a day; by boycotting mirrors, banishing razors, or going without makeup. Guided imagery is being used successfully by therapists in helping weight-obsessed women develop a more accurate
view of themselves. They are taught first to create vivid body

images and then to alter those images at will: to inflate or deflate them, to view them from different angles, to project them forward or backward in age. This valuable technique can promote a more flexible and more realistic self-perception.[2]

If we listen attentively to natural signals, the body itself can teach us how to respect its delicate physical balance and how to live more comfortably within our skin. Flesh has its own laws of loveliness. Females do have more fat than males; breasts and hips come in many shapes; not all women are a size eight. The body can serve as a resource rather than as a scapegoat. It is programmed to speak authentically for itself. Many bulimics, for instance, find that when they finally give up vomiting and purging and pay attention to natural hunger pangs, proper weight can be maintained without difficulty. Listening carefully to body messages is a first step in learning to break down the wall of silence that surrounds the female world.

Breaking Silences

An unnamed problem is like an undiagnosed disease. By guarding the secret conflicts of living as one of the fair sex, each woman becomes a carrier of illness. Tillie Olsen ticks off the silent ailments of women like the items on a grocery list:

> Unclean; taboo. . . . The three steps behind; . . . burned alive on the funeral pyre, burned as witch at the stake. . . . Purdah, the veil. . . . Denied vision. . . . Bound feet, corseted, cosseted, bedecked; denied one's body. . . . Fear of aging. Fear of expressing capacities. Soft attractive graces; the mirror to magnify man . . . flattering, manipulating, appeasing . . . the harms of instilling constant concern with appearance; the need to please, to support . . . hours agonizing over appearance; concentration shredded into attracting.[3]

As long as women refuse to tell, the world can never know the truth about the female experience.

Silence is the compatriot of subordination: a tacit message that we accept and approve of what we are. Breaking silence is a key to stripping off masks. By naming names and telling tales we can chip away at ill-cast roles. Humans are, after all, the talking animals. A single shout can sometimes start a riot. Breaking silences means lifting the quarantine for the "sickies" who hide behind closed doors; the bulimics who vomit their lives away; the closet eaters and diet cheaters who cower under cover; the cosmetic junkies who live in terror of withdrawal, pretending youth and fearing truth. No more silence means naming the unmentionable, proclaiming the existence of stretch marks, age spots, varicose veins, flat chests, and all the rest. Fat is a fact of life. No more silence means discovering new unmentionables even as we "keep harping away on the old ones, because their unmentionability grows back."[4] Breaking silence means an end to the illusion of fairy-tale loveliness. It means rejecting the role of fair damsel and taking responsibility for one's own distress.

My trips to the electrologist as a teenager were physically painful and made me terribly self-conscious about my "problem." But the greatest impact of that cosmetic ritual was made by the secrecy surrounding it. "Don't tell your father; he won't approve. Don't tell anyone; they don't need to know." The message was that having "unwanted" hair was shameful and removing it was equally shameful. Such secrecy prevents both women and men from recognizing the full burden of feminine beauty.

Myths can swallow up reality but only in limited quantities. A chorus of voices eventually is heard. A chorus of voices breaks the taboo of silence, putting an end to private guilt and getting us used to the sound of shared pain. Speaking out can be an antidote for unnamed ailments. In the voices of others, one's own unvoiced symptoms are recognized and diagnosed. A chorus of voices can transform a private pain into a public issue. Things do change when women begin to tell it like it is, the way they see and feel it:

ANN. Last spring I let the hair grow under my arms and put on a sleeveless T-shirt. My boyfriend asked me whether I was trying to turn into a man.

ELIZABETH. I love to wear really tight jeans. But I can't stand the way they cut in at the crotch. Now I've learned to wear a sanitary pad and don't have to suffer so much.

GENA. I'm five feet one inch with 34DD breasts. I had deep grooves in my shoulders from the pressure of my bra straps, continuous neck and shoulder pains, lower back pains, sore and swelling breasts every menstrual period, and a lifetime spent searching for clothes that were dark enough, covering enough, and high-cut enough not to call attention to my pendulous breasts; the humiliation of walking down streets to a never-ending chorus of hoots and whistles; and a series of job interviews and work situations where attention was so riveted on my bosom that whatever I was proposing was totally lost and irrelevant.[5]

Replaying the voices of history, we can recall the origins of our vulnerability:

> My foot binding began when I was seven, with a ceremony on the lucky day of the month. That night mother wouldn't let me remove the shoes. My feet felt on fire and I couldn't sleep. . . . Beatings and curses were my lot for loosening the wrappings. . . . Mother would remove the bindings and wipe the blood and pus which dripped from my feet. She said that only with removal of the flesh could my feet become slender.[6]

In my clinical practice I have learned to ask direct questions about body conflicts. Many women are so used to preserving silence that even in therapy they neglect to mention important problems or feel too ashamed to discuss them. Janet had been a patient for over two years. Her major difficulty was a physically abusive husband who was also a chronic gambler. At twenty-eight Janet had no children and was securely employed. She kept insisting that she wanted a divorce but could never bring herself to the point of leaving her husband. One day in the middle of a session, she leaned forward and barely whispered that she had something important to say—something she had never mentioned and that was a big factor holding her in this unhappy marriage:

> I've never been able to tell this to anyone. Only my sister and my husband know. It's hard to say but . . . I've had breast implants. I was still in college when I had them done, just a few months before I met Brian. They were a failure from the start. They felt so unnatural. I thought I had come to terms with my breasts but I know that if this marriage ends, I'll have to face being single again. I don't see how I could ever let a man touch me. I'm ashamed I ever had the surgery. I'm ashamed of how my breasts look and feel. I'm even ashamed that I never had the courage to tell you this before.

A dramatic improvement often occurs when a patient finally claims the right and musters the courage to say out loud what she has never dared to admit. In Janet's case, doing so changed the focus of her therapy and freed her to end a destructive relationship.

Speaking out means sharing the joy of giving up painful rituals in the search for comfort and authenticity:

BRENDA. Now that I'm fifty, I've become more relaxed about my appearance. I've settled on a routine which requires a minimum of time and energy. Low maintenance is essential for me. My hair is strictly wash and wear. Comfort and color are what I think of first when shopping for clothes.

CORINNE. I was a big baby, an overweight child, and a fat teenager. I grew up wearing "chubby" dresses and was put on a diet even before I started school. I have tried every diet imaginable, been to clinics, fasted, tried hypnosis and hated myself every time I lost weight and then gained it back. Finally I decided that I'd had it, and gave up dieting altogether. It hasn't made much difference in the way I look, but I've stopped fighting myself and feel content for the first time in years.

Speaking out means finding new ways to discuss appearance without deprecating it. A physician once described a patient of mine as "slightly obese." At five feet five inches with a large frame and weighing one hundred and thirty pounds, this patient by current standards was about ten pounds overweight. *Obese* means excessively fat. The expression "slightly obese" contains a contradiction and in this case represents a gross exaggeration. When terms like *obese* are used too loosely, they cloak a normal body with pathology. What should we call a woman who is ten pounds overweight? Plump? Stout? Full-figured? Magazines for the happily heavy are creating a new vocabulary, calling them well stacked, weighty women, hot and hefty, queen-sized, big mamas. New labels fill a linguistic void, making it easier to speak out about the reality of female bodies.

Praise can be a powerful tool that shapes body image. "You look fat and fresh today" is a complimentary greeting for a Punjabi Indian. We can practice speaking out by giving healthier compliments to our friends and, equally important, to ourselves:

You look confident, content. . . . Your body seems relaxed, comfortable, agile. . . . Your face is animated, alive, serene. . . . Your hair is great for sports, the gray looks stately. . . . It's wonderful to see you eating with pleasure. . . . Your face seems softer, more casual without makeup; you look natural, more like yourself.

Many of us innocently fall into the trap of telling little girls how pretty they look, how cute their dresses are, how lovely their hair is. Such compliments bubble out to my nieces from some deep well within me, in effect, momentarily turning these girls into beauty contestants. Compliments can reach beyond the confines of appearance. Our daughters, along with our sons, might be told that their eyes are shining, their legs look strong, their voices sound happy.

Breaking silence can also mean asking sympathetic questions. Why does your nose bother you so much? Will you miss it if you change it? How might you accept it as it is? What does your husband, mother, lover think? This kind of dialogue encourages others to share beauty conflicts and to ask for support.

Speaking out about beauty means addressing men as well as women in a different voice. Men also suffer from the fear of being unattractive. They struggle with balding heads and bulging bellies. Short men know all too well the problems of looking like a subordinate. Speaking out can mean returning a man's compliments and comments—remarking on his eyes, his outfit, and his cute behind and giving him gifts of adornment such as corsages, sexy underwear, and jewelry. Men are beginning to enjoy hedonic display. They too are having facials and face lifts, and they are buying more cosmetics every year. Commercials featuring star athletes have legitimized the use of hair spray, cologne, and skin toners and have convinced some men that vanity is not strictly a female affair. (Men's cosmetics—boxed in manly colors, smelling of the great outdoors, and named after savage brutes—are still marketed to the macho image, however.)

Men can be asked to try some exercises in feminine beauty awareness, such as walking down a flight of stairs in high heels while carrying a tray of drinks, or sitting in a short skirt with feet crossed at the ankles, imagining that people are trying to look up your legs. Sensitized by such exercises men may view feminine beauty with different eyes.

Speaking Out

As we have listened for centuries to the voices of men and
the theories of development that their experience informs, so
we have come more recently to notice not only the silence of
women but the difficulty in hearing what they say when they
speak. Yet in the different voice of women lies the truth of
an ethic of care, the tie between relationship and responsibility and the origins of aggression in the failure of connection.

— Carol Gilligan[7]

Carol Gilligan's book, *In a Different Voice*, suggests that for
women, more than for men, identity is built through a history
of relationships. Women's self-images are not distinct from intimacy but are fused with it, she writes. Thus, women are especially afraid of rejection, since loss of love is equated with loss of
self.

Hoping to preserve relationships, women avoid conflict and
falsely assume that harmony can be achieved through silent conformity. But unsolved issues translate into hidden agendas; and
hidden conflicts are not very useful ones. No doubt there will be
a backlash directed against women who question their image as
beauty objects and proclaim their right to a different role. Because
we are so used to females whose faces and voices are always
smiling or composed, the look and sound of conflict is especially
frightening. Anger is not very pretty, as Brownmiller observes
in her analysis of femininity:

An angry woman is hard, mean and nasty, she is unreliably,
unprettily out of control. Her face contorts into unpleasant lines,
the jaw juts, the eyes are narrowed, the teeth are bared. Anger is
a violent snarl and a hostile threat, a declaration of war.[8]

Fearing reprisal for any display of anger, women tend to repress
it and to redirect it inward. This is the unspoken rage that causes
depression, that drives the anorectic to self-starvation, or pushes
the beauty queen to suicide.

Gilligan urges women to use their well-developed powers of
sensitivity and relatedness to focus back on their own needs. She
warns that we must attend to our inner voice and to our body

signals, and not allow the male "voice over" to drown us out. Only by turning up the volume of the different voice of women, can it become audible.

When subordinates start speaking out, dominants are first surprised or confused, and then they too grow angry. If one side breaks the rules of the gender game, it cannot go on as planned, and both sides feel at a loss. Most men still want to give things to women—presents, compliments, flattery, jewelry, identity, permission. They feel threatened by a woman who does not wait for what a man wants to give and instead speaks up about what she wants and starts to take it for herself. An outspoken woman who rejects the conventional trappings of femininity may find herself ridiculed or ignored; she may lose a job, a promotion, or a loved one. A professor of dermatology who ran a conference on the psychology of cosmetics declared:

> I don't want anything to do with women who don't wear makeup. . . . First of all, it's a social statement that says "I'm not going to conform." . . . Some people who won't wear makeup can become big leaders, I suppose, and valuable persons in society, but I don't like them.[9]

In his view, a woman who refuses to make herself up in beauty is delivering a loud defiant message—that she does not wish to please others primarily through appearance.

If we reject the beauty images that make others love us, they may stop loving us. Well then, declares one writer, "Let us be ourselves and good riddance to those who are repulsed by us."[10] But things are not so simple, egos not so strong. We somehow miss even those "professors of beauty" who reject us. More painful still, we may find such a person within our own heads. Often we ourselves turn out to be the person most repulsed by our own heavy thighs or baggy eyes. To live without the acceptance of those whom we need and care about is hard enough. To live without self-acceptance is even more tormenting.

Speaking out in a different voice will generate various kinds of conflicts—with others, with our own history, with our self-perception, and with the new beauty fads continuously being promoted. Reclaiming the open expression of conflict as legitimately feminine is a necessary step in beauty reform. Piaget has shown that people grow wiser by challenging the world through action. Probably women can tolerate more conflict and backlash than we suppose. By questioning the role of fair lady, we can grow strong in new ways. We may feel less need of the critical men who find us less attractive, and we may feel more comfortable with tolerant men—the sympathetic, generous, encouraging men who feel free to love us for the same strengths we love in them.

Fashion and Feminism

Maybe I'm sick of the masquerade, I'm sick of pretending eternal youth . . . sick of peering at the world through false eyelashes, so everything I see is mixed with a shadow of bought hairs; . . . I'm sick of the powder room. I'm sick of being a transvestite—I refuse to be a female impersonator. I am a woman, not a castrate.

— Germaine Greer[11]

Over the years, feminist voices have influenced the popular image of beauty and the personal choices of beauty. Feminism challenges us to unlock the doors that divide man's space from woman's space. It calls for an end to "woman as the Other" and for her readmission into the realm of full personhood. But territory is rarely given up freely by those who control it. More often, it must be captured through acts of rebellion.

The war between fashion and feminism has long been fought on a variety of grounds—health, mobility, sexual and commercial exploitation. Feminists are often accused of being antibeauty. There is a difference, however, between protesting the damaging effects of a beauty myth and opposing the value of beauty in itself. The first form of protest is a valid feminist issue; the second is counterproductive.

The widespread belief that feminism is antibeauty translates into a bias suggesting that feminists themselves are ugly creatures hiding in a philosophy that excuses their flaws. Gloria Steinem notwithstanding, feminists of the 1970s were often stereotyped as homely libbers; (just as the suffragettes a century earlier were described as "unsexed women, entirely devoid of personal attraction"). After a lecture on feminism, a student once came up to me and said, "You look and sound too feminine to be a feminist. Your image doesn't fit your ideology."

What should a feminist look like? People think they know. When college students were asked in 1975 to select supporters of feminism from a group of photos, they chose the less attractive women.[12] "Real" feminists were found to be as likely as anyone else to sort feminists from nonfeminists on the basis of attractiveness in a photograph. In another study, subjects were asked to select reasons why women in a series of pictures had become feminists. Positive, flattering reasons were chosen for the pretty women, and negative, unflattering reasons were chosen for the less attractive ones. Subjects believed that homely women "needed feminism more" and that pretty women become feminists for humanitarian rather than personal reasons.[13] Such stereotypes produce a corollary belief that if a woman is pretty enough she does not need to be "liberated." In fact, research suggests just the opposite: women who rate themselves as more attractive hold more profeminist views. (As feminism has become more widely accepted in recent years, there has been a reduction in the belief that feminists are ugly females.)

Historians note that the oppression of women recurs in cycles, as does the resurgence of resistance to it. Likewise, would-be dress reformers rise and fall like hemlines. Feminists of the nineteenth century opposed current fashion, believing it to be both dangerous and frivolous. Elizabeth Cady Stanton put on a pair of bloomers and advised exercise and clean living to achieve a healthy glow. At the same time, antifeminists dismissed the natural look as unattractive and warned women to avoid all physical and emotional strain that would lead to wrinkles and premature aging.

Early in this century, feminists tried to democratize beauty by defining it in ways that were within every woman's grasp. Ironically, their theme was adopted by the then-fledgling cosmetic industries, which were much more successful than the feminists were in democratically selling cosmetics to anyone who could pay the price. For the most part, the suffragists were committed to voting reform, not beauty reform. They marched to jail wearing immense feathered bonnets. Hecklers would pull off the protesters' hats and yank down their hair to humiliate them. After winning the right to vote, feminists retreated into silence for nearly forty years, during which time cosmetics were not only legitimized but became essential to the happy housewife–gracious hostess image that peaked in the 1950s.[14]

Prudence Glynn, former fashion editor of the *London Times*, notes that "despite irrefutable proof that followers of fashion would catch pneumonia, displace their inner organs, risk miscarriage, heart attacks, bunions . . . the reformers hell-bent on hygiene have been dismally unsuccessful in alerting society to obey their very sensible suggestions, right down the ages."[15] Why? Because, the attempts at reform have disregarded women's need for glamour, vanity, narcissism, and eroticism, explains Glynn. A woman does want to be pretty, to attract others, to feel at times elegant, erotic, or irresistible. Beauty does provide wonderful fringe benefits. Indeed, narcissism can be healthy. It signals a desire to enjoy oneself, to develop one's potential to the fullest, to overcome handicaps and eliminate flaws that distract others from seeing us favorably.

Looks do count, in love and in work. Reformers must begin with this premise, in order to meaningfully challenge the beauty myth. There is no denying the power of beauty to influence others. Its absence, whether real or imagined, threatens the ego. Hence women will continue to pursue beauty in their search for self-esteem. Humans are naturally primed to enjoy certain tastes and smells. A pretty profile is a potent stimulus. To deny these built-in human dynamics is to become antibeauty, a position that will invariably remain unpopular, unwise, and ineffective. However, the value of attractiveness has been exaggerated and has been unequally assigned to the feminine role. This is the problem that can legitimately be protested. It is not beauty per se that corrupts, but the assumption that beauty is imperative to femininity.

Physical attractiveness is a human trait, neither masculine nor feminine. The ultimate challenge is to shift the perception of beauty into a neutral territory so that neither sex will bear the greater burden of it or receive the greater benefit from it.

That feminists across the centuries have faced the same questions only proves that there are no easy or permanent answers. Nevertheless, as Gertrude Stein observed on her deathbed, posing the right questions can be as important as finding the right answers. If women don't want to be regarded as decorative dolls, can they still delight in self-display? Is the ultimate goal to be accepted for oneself—uncoiffed, unadorned, and, therefore, in the eyes of many, unkempt? How should we respond to a mother's desire for a face lift, to a friend's longing for a fuller bosom, to a daughter's request for a new nose, to our own inner yearning to wash away the gray? When are cosmetic transformations a negative act of self-rejection, and when are they a positive act of self-enhancement? To whom do our bodies belong, if not to ourselves? Many feminists have difficulty finding personal answers to such questions, for they, too, experience the conflict between conviction and convention, between the utopian ideal of natural beauty that includes all, and the actual ideal of cultured beauty that excludes so many. College women who today describe themselves as feminists report that they do not view beauty rituals as symbols of female dependence upon male approval. Rather they regard looking pretty as part of the feminist mandate to project confidence, to utilize assets, and to feel good about oneself.

History proves that social problems rarely fade away; they simply reemerge in new forms. One thing does seem clear: While there may be no ultimate truce in the war between fashion and feminism, new weapons are required as time erodes old constraints and technology creates contemporary ones. The victims of anorexia are dying at an alarming rate. Stiletto heels are as popular as ever. Surgeons are offering exotic solutions to the "problem" of looking too mature.

Although old issues resurface, old answers are not always old hat. As long as women are expected to masquerade as the fair sex, there will be continuing need for counterpressure. Girls of each generation become mesmerized anew by their mirrors and need to have the vital issues of health and comfort rephrased in a modern idiom. Since beauty will no doubt remain tied to femininity in the foreseeable future, its definition cannot be abdicated to others—not to the fashion industry, not to the media, not to men, not even to other women. Every woman has a right (and a responsibility) to consciously decide for herself how she wishes to be seen. She has the right to be judged and to judge herself according to realistic standards; she has the right to like and enjoy her own body. Feminism is concerned with protecting these rights. Ultimately, the value of beauty reform is not in its rhetoric but in its ability to reinterpret experience and to offer solutions that enhance the quality of life for both women and men.

How much responsibility can we take for changing the images that constrain us? To some extent, the beauty myth is fashioned by forces outside our personal control. Yet, in the end, we are the ones who buy and apply the products, who make and keep the appointments, who encourage each other to enact the mythical ideal.

If we reject the premise that anatomy is destiny, and if we resist the temptation to conclude therefore that socialization is destiny, we are left with the alternative belief that people themselves are at least partly in control of the myths that control them. Though obsessed with beauty as a feminine ideal, we do have the option to challenge our obsession. If we recognize that option, we can begin to use it.

In Her Own Image

> He is playing masculine, she is playing feminine. . . . He is playing the kind of man that she thinks the kind of woman she is playing ought to admire. She is playing the kind of woman that he thinks the kind of man he is playing ought to desire.
>
> — Betty Roszak and Theodore Roszak[16]

Myths drape gender in the stark black-and-white costumes of a bride and groom. Placed side by side, the bridal couple create maximum contrast. Males and females have been color-coded, like pawns lined up across a chessboard, moving in prescribed patterns. Some people still argue that sexual attraction requires the tension of polarity, just as positive and negative charges are required for electrical impulses to flow. "Vivre la différence!" they shout.

Admittedly, extremes are stimulating. In the optical art of Victor Vasarely, for example, maximum contrast enchants the eye with vibrant illusions. Vasarely explains, however, that black and white are used as symbols that complement each other. "I am striving for a world view in which good and evil, beautiful and ugly . . . are joined in a fertile notion of androgyny," he writes.[17]

Some feminist psychologists have offered androgyny as a bridge to the black and white of gender cleavage. This ancient archetype integrates traditionally masculine and feminine traits (such as beauty or strength) and redefines them as being appropriate to either sex. Androgyny is "an attempt to free individuals from the confines of the appropriate" so that they can choose their place from the full range of human experience.[18] The Greeks coined the term *androgyny* from *andro* (male) and *gyne* (female), and they called androgyny the third sex. Androgyny also flows from the Greek conception of beauty as a unity of inner and outer qualities, a fusion of the masculine and feminine elements that comprise the total person.

As a model of psychological unity, androgyny assumes that maximum contrast can coexist within the same person; that anyone can be at once both highly masculine and highly feminine, both beautiful and strong, both gentle and aggressive. Jung considered the androgynous fusion of the masculine animus and the feminine anima as essential to a well-balanced personality. Androgyny is not meant to disguise or deny sex differences but rather to provide a fertile climate in which individuality can flourish. Androgynous men and women are not conceived of as carbon copies of each other, nor as "blurred bodies" fashioned into a freak form of sexual neutrality. The vision of a third sex was created to increase human diversity, not to reduce it to a single mode. Extremes of black and white coexisting in the same individual allow for infinite shades of gray.

Can an androgynous model provide an alternative to the beauty myth? If beauty became less essential to femininity and more equally valued in both sexes, we would certainly have moved in an androgynous direction. From time to time a unisex look has been adopted. Often it reflects and fosters a lifestyle in which males and females learn, earn, and yearn in similar ways. Androgynous style can combine masculine and feminine elements, as it did in the late 1960s when long hair, jewelry, and flashy colors were worn with jeans, vests, and boots by both sexes. Unisex images are still common today in nursery schools, on college campuses, and on the streets of modern China. Androgynous fashions reduce the perception of woman as the Other. Consequently they also reduce her need for beauty as a compensation.

Freud considered our fundamental bisexual nature a source of psychological conflict. He concluded that the "same-sex" component of the personality must vanquish or repress the opposite-sex component in a well-adjusted person. In effect, the stronger side must take over the weaker side. This psychoanalytic solution typifies a masculine approach to conflict resolution. A more feminine approach, according to Gilligan's research, is one of integration and cooperation. By seeking peace through alliance rather than victory through conquest, inner harmony between one's masculine and feminine components becomes possible. Moreover, why must we assume that the so-called masculine and feminine parts of the self are at war? There is strength in unity. The model of androgyny encourages integration and free expression of one's full potential. Whole men and whole women are more, not less, than the stereotypic halves that gender roles traditionally prescribe and that Freud espoused. As long as females remain the fair sex, androgynous behavior becomes difficult—for men are then forced to repress the healthy aspects of self-adornment, while women become obsessed with them.

The idea that beauty can be androgynous tends to evoke both discomfort and suspicion. Resistance stems in part from the greater value still accorded to masculine characteristics. When these traits command greater respect, they remain the model for "normal" behavior.

Androgyny threatens men; first because men lose status if they embrace feminine traits (i.e., by adorning like women); and second, because men lose status when women adopt masculine traits (i.e., by ignoring beauty and seeking direct power). Recognizing the fundamental inequality between the male animus and the female anima, Jung warned women to repress the stronger animus and not to encroach on man's territory. As long as masculine traits are considered the norm, femininity is in danger of being swallowed up by androgyny. We see women putting on pants and flocking to gyms or to assertiveness-training courses to expand their androgynous potential, but where are the men clamoring for courses on how to be patient, gentle, compliant, and graceful?

When Henry Higgins complains, "Why can't a woman be more like a man?" and then glibly recounts woman's flaws, we sense that deep down he also revels in these flaws, for they ensure the gap that preserves his position as mentor. Hidden behind a mythology of differences, the similarities between men and women go unnoticed.

Men fear and resist androgyny as a threat to male dominance. And women are also afraid. They don't want to be masculinized by androgyny any more than men want to be femininized by it. Women worry that if they adopt a more androgynous image, they will be seen as less feminine and therefore less lovable. They hesitate to cast off "the crutches of the cripple," for without the feminine "handicap" women will have to test their real strengths and admit their limitations. Idealized beauty is part of the barrier that keeps women confined but makes them feel safe. In a well-defined space, elevated onto a pedestal, and smiling from behind a made-up face, women feel secure, knowing what must be given in exchange for what they need (even if the price is high).

Beauty provides women with a ready-made identity. To shake loose from that old familiar myth is akin to cutting off an old friend, someone who has shared and shaped one's life. Without that myth or that friend as a frame of reference, a painful void is left. Without our mirrors to provide an identity, what will we look like? Without beauty to define us, how can we be women?

This explains, in part, why feminist attempts at fashion reform have been met with so much resistance from both women and men. The beauty myth is deeply rooted in the psychology of gender and in the politics of power. Women cling to the beauty role because they feel they have much to gain from it: the security of a familiar image; the pleasure of flattery; an achievement arena that does not evoke fear of success; a rationalization for failure; a source of power to attract and influence others; a pleasant diversion and a way to fill time; an excuse to postpone decisions while waiting for Mr. Right. These are the rewards that keep us wed to a mythical beauty ideal. These are the losses we fear when faced with the challenge of change.

What can we expect to gain by facing that challenge? What benefits would derive from a social system in which both sexes shared more equitably in the burdens and delights of beauty?

First, a gain in freedom—freedom from the pressure of pretending something exists that is merely imagined. Freedom from chronic self-consciousness and from constant appearance anxiety. Freedom to grow stronger through more direct modes of power and to grow older with confidence. Freedom to move with greater strength, speed, and security, unconstrained by ladylike posturing.

Second, a gain in comfort and health. An endless number of illnesses are attributed to cosmetic causes. They include serious eating disorders (anorexia, obesity, bulimia, chronic dieting, weight obsession, binging), spinal and foot deformities, agoraphobia, depression, back pain, eye infections (and even blindness from contaminated mascara), acne, skin cancer, allergic reactions, deaths from anesthetics, migraines, insomnia, amphetamine addiction, and others.

Third, a gain in resources. When less energy, time, and money are invested in dressing, combing, coloring, buying, adorning, displaying, and doing everything else required to enact the myth of female beauty, more of these resources become available for working, loving, playing, creating, and everything else that life has to offer.

Fourth, a gain in authenticity. Myths are based on a distortion of reality. They protect people from the unknown and the overwhelming, but they also prevent us from seeing ourselves and others realistically. We will never know what the natural components of masculinity and femininity are until the cultural constraints have been lifted. By moving beyond the boundaries of beauty, we may explore our androgynous potential and discover who we really are.

It takes courage to seek a new image of femininity. But females do have some special strengths that will help. In the first place, a woman lives with constant physical change and learns to cope with it. The tides of her life flow in and out in measured waves— menarche, menstruation, pregnancy, birth, lactation, menopause. These cycles are further washed by the coming and going and yearly growing of her children. In such rhythmic waves, self-image dissolves over and over and she must reconstruct it anew. Familiarity with handling change can help her cast off an outworn beauty image and recast herself in a more comfortable mold.

Other so-called feminine traits are helpful, too—qualities such as patience, compliance, gentleness, sensitivity, and concern. Patience to let the body set its own proper weight; compliance with the natural process of aging; gentleness with living flesh; sensitivity to feelings of pain; a tender concern for skin, for eyes, for breasts. These assets can keep a woman stable as she works to loosen the bonds of beauty.

Relationships are another potential source of strength. Carol Gilligan's research shows that women feel a basic sense of connectedness to others, whereas men operate more often from a premise of separateness. In friendship, women can support each other (as they are used to supporting men) by encouraging, complimenting, admiring, nurturing, sustaining, celebrating. In effect, sisterhood can provide a "bulwark against foot binding."[19]

New support groups are beginning to form. Overweight women are gathering together not just as "weight watchers" but to proclaim that they, too, are beautiful just as they are. By working out in special exercise groups, hefty women are reclaiming a sense of dignity in being big. The potential for beauty support systems is virtually unlimited. Imagine groups for the large-breasted or the flat-chested; for clothes and cosmetics addicts; for the truly disfigured and the handicapped (who want to be beautiful as much as anyone else does); for those terrorized by age anxiety; for the exceptionally pretty who also suffer because of their looks. Many of my patients, who agonize privately over their bodies, emphasize how isolated they feel. Support groups end isolation. They provide sound practical solutions to beauty problems and generate new attitudes about attractiveness that feel more authentic. In groups, women learn to identify with each other and to recognize their common response to the myths that misshape them. Mutual sharing transforms beauty competitors into allies.

In her studies of primates, Sarah Blaffer Hrdy reports that although competition among females is a fact of life, companionable behavior like grooming, huddling together, and sharing infant care is far more common on a daily basis than competitive behavior. Great apes are social creatures, and mutual grooming is one of their favorite activities. They reach out to touch each other, to express affection or fear, to make up after fights. Hours are spent combing, picking over fur, scratching, and stroking.

Grooming serves primarily as a social ritual that maintains group cohesiveness.[20]

Ironically, humans have dehumanized grooming rituals, separating them from the social aspects that are so important to other primates. In western cultures we rarely use grooming to communicate affection or to satisfy our need for skin contact. Mutual grooming has been largely replaced by the lonely process of personal adornment. To be a well-groomed woman is to be neat and tidy, not well cared for by others. In contrast to the "lower animals" we buy grooming from the manicurist or the beautician, paid for and scheduled by appointment.

Among chimps, females are the ones who usually initiate grooming. While females occasionally groom children and males, most often they groom each other. Mutual grooming seems to serve as nature's way of fostering the bonds of sisterhood. Human females might follow their example by washing and arranging each other's hair; by giving massages or manicures; by playfully using cosmetics to decorate one another, as adolescent girls often do. Such grooming rituals would be especially meaningful to the ill, the elderly, or the handicapped, who may view their bodies negatively and who often yearn for human touch. Grooming others can expose us to the realities of aging, to racial differences, and to the great variety of human bodies. Women have concentrated for too long on using grooming to attract male attention or appease male aggression while neglecting its value in drawing women together. In effect, we can demythologize the look of beauty through the touch of friends.

A basic function of the beauty myth has been to separate the haves from the have nots and thereby to divide women. But it is possible to expand the ideal from a tool of exclusion to one of inclusion. The narrow boundaries of beauty can be stretched to make room for the stouter, older, plainer, flatter, freckled, and funny-faced among us. Simply by reinforcing others for nonconventional beauty choices, we can alter the norm. The broader the concept of beauty, the greater the possibility of self-acceptance, since everyone's body changes with time. As we judge others, so will we be judged and so will we judge ourselves.

In the sixties, "Black is beautiful" became a rallying cry for ethnic pride, helping people of color to regain a sense of personal worth from their appearance. The normative Caucasian beauty image was gradually infiltrated by Afros, corn braids, and other ethnic influences, until eventually the Miss America crown came to rest (for the first time in half a century) on the head of a dark-skinned model. Which shows that beauty images can expand to include those who were formerly excluded.

Gender myths are sustained as much by behavior as by beliefs. When more women began wearing makeup at the end of the last century, the attitude shifted from "Nice girls don't" to "Nice girls do" and then to "Nice girls *should*." If enough women flaunt a new look, an old norm gets nudged over. Eventually the scale tips and a new standard is set (sometimes better and sometimes worse than the old one). The questions we need to ask now are, What norms need a push and in what direction? What changes would enhance the enjoyment of beauty? What alternatives might free femininity from its constraints? Equally important, how do we develop the confidence to enact the necessary changes?

Myths are sustained by simple acts. We can begin by questioning everyday behavior. An important process begins when we ask ourselves, Is this particular prop needed? What would happen if it was given up or shared equally with men? Questioning an old habit is tantamount to breaking it. Enough questioners loosening their corsets, flushing away their diet pills, and kicking off their tight shoes, and the world is not quite what it was before.

We can ask, Is chronic dieting effective? Are lacquered nails imperative? How much is really spent on grooming? Can I think of my face, my breasts, my hips more compassionately? Can I look at other women differently? Am I motivated to display myself out of fear or out of pleasure? What will happen if I abandon one item or one attitude of cosmetic pretense and live without it momentarily? How could I become more content with my looks? What can I leave unchanged that makes me distinctive?

When several women were asked to describe cosmetic decisions that helped them define their personal image, one said, "I decided not to get a nose job." Indeed, an authentic style can be achieved as much by what we don't do to ourselves as by what we do do. Some faces are memorable because their "flaws" remain unfixed. Think of Barbra Streisand's nose, Eleanor Roosevelt's mouth, or the unplucked brows of Georgia O'Keeffe. It takes strength to step outside a myth and seek a new identity in personal differences.

Questioning even one cosmetic convention that feels constraining is a gesture of courage and rebellion. Small acts do create a new reality. Small steps do set us on a different course. Everyday acts of reform are readily available to every woman. They can tip the scale toward a less oppressive social system.

Identifying the myth of female beauty as both a treasured legacy and a tragic liability is my way of interrupting silence. The beauty myth has many facets, wears many faces, and bears many names: the tyranny of glamour; the cult of beauty asymmetry; the pedestal plot; looksism; false femininity; fair but unfair; seen but unseen; oppressive objectification; obsessive narcissism; cosmetic slavery; beauty as a beast and a burden. To break a personal silence, each of us must identify the myth in a personal voice.

For so long, women have viewed their bodies as blurred reflections, heard their voices through muffled echoes, touched only those parts of their destiny that others placed in the hands of "pretty girls." To the extent that females are beauty bound in a decorative corner, society is denied their full contribution.

If the myth of female beauty is a by-product of female deviance and subordination, as I have tried to show, then the pretty postures of oppression will diminish as sex roles are equalized. "The more women assert themselves as human beings, the more the marvelous quality of the Other will die out in them," predicts Simone de Beauvoir.[21] Giving birth to a new self-image entails work, risk, and commitment. Undoubtedly, independence is woman's greatest asset. An economically, emotionally, and sexually independent woman is armed to be a myth slayer. She is less likely to embrace the static image of a mannequin; less likely to use her body as a gesture of appeasement; less likely to depend on appearance as her primary source of power. As women gain access to the institutions that control society, they gain the means to shift beauty off the back of femininity and onto the gender-neutral position where it belongs. We will be released from the bonds of the beauty myth when women can look as ordinary as men, and still be valued as normal, lovable human beings.

Notes

INTRODUCTION

1. Sexton, A., "Little Girl, My String Bean, My Lovely Woman," 1966, 62.

1. THE FAIR SEX

1. Bettelheim, B., 1976, 62.
2. Abeel, E., 1981, 143–50.
3. Kalick, M., 1978.
4. Madar, T., as cited in Unger, R., 1985.
5. Berscheid, E., & Walster, E., 1974.
6. Dion, K., et al., 1972.
7. Dion, K., 1974.
8. Wilson, G., & Nias, D., 1976.
9. Chesler, P., 1972.
10. Adams, G., 1977.
11. Snyder, M. et al., 1977.
12. Tagore, R., as cited by Wald, C., 1975.
13. Unger, R., 1985.
14. Rubin, J. et al., 1974.
15. Joffe, C., 1971.
16. Ford, C., & Beach, F., 1951.
17. Reis, H. et al., 1980. Also see Cross, J., & Cross, J., 1971.
18. Unger, R., 1979, 211.
19. Deutsch, F. et al., 1983.
20. Mathes, E., & Kahn, A., 1975.
21. Miller, A., 1970.
22. Berscheid, E. et al., 1971. Also see Krebs, D., & Adinolfi, A., 1975.
23. Walster, E. et al., 1966.
24. Coombs, R., & Kenkel, W., 1966.
25. Bar-Tal, D., & Saxe, L., 1976.
26. Symons, D., 1979, 204.
27. *New York Times*, Dec. 21, 1983, C–11.
28. Sigall, H., & Landy, D., 1973.
29. Elder, G., 1969.
30. Harrison, A., & Saeed, L., 1977.
31. Gilligan, C., 1982, 30.
32. Ephron, N., 1975, 3.
33. Broverman, I. et al., 1970.
34. de Beauvoir, S., 1953, Introduction, xv.
35. Firestone, S., 1970, 132.
36. Clifton, A. et al., 1976.
37. de Beauvoir, S., 1953, 246.

2. LOOKING GOOD AND FEELING BAD

1. Rossner, J., 1983, 376.
2. Rubin, L., 1979.
3. Hutchinson, M., 1982.
4. Miller, T. et al., 1980. Also see *Glamour*, Jan. 4, 1984, 198–202.
5. Ephron, N., 1975, 198.
6. Sanford, L., & Donovan, M., 1984, 5–6.
7. Ibid., 370.
8. Cash, T. et al., 1983.
9. Adams, G., 1977, 227–28. Also see Lerner, R. et al., 1973.
10. Murstein, B., 1972.
11. Noles, S. et al., 1985.
12. Berscheid, E., & Walster, E., 1974.
13. Lott, B., 1981, 378.
14. Broverman, I. et al., 1970.
15. Alta, 1971, 3.

16. *Time*, May 2, 1983, 45.
17. Shulman, A.K., *Memoirs of an Ex-Prom Queen*, New York: Alfred Knopf, 1972, as cited in Ephron, N., 1975, 19.
18. Lucker, G. et al., 1981.
19. Wilson, G., & Nias, D., 1976.
20. Berscheid, E., & Walster, E., 1974.
21. Jong, E., "Alcestis on the Poetry Circuit," 1973, 25.
22. Sanford, L., & Donovan, M., 1984, chapter 8.
23. As cited in Pierre, C., 1976, 156.
24. Henley, N., 1977, 167.
25. Griffin, S., 1982, 36.
26. Kenrick, D., & Gutierres, S., 1980.
27. Stannard, U., 1971, 122.
28. Kane, E., findings reported at the National Council on Family Relations annual meeting, as cited in *Cornell University Human Ecology News*, February 1983.
29. *New York Daily News*, March 30, 1980, 9–C, as cited in "How ads woo women," *Social Issue Resources Series*, vol. 2, art. 26.
30. Combs, M., 1982.
31. Hutchinson, M., 1982, 67.

3. PROPS AND PAINT

1. Bruner, J., 1973.
2. As cited in Perutz, K., 1970, 137.
3. Perutz, K., 1970.
4. Henley, N., The American way of beauty: Of parlors, beauty and/or funeral, in *The Paper*, vol. 1 (15), reprinted by KNOW Press, P.O. Box 10197, Pittsburgh, PA 15232.
5. Hays, H.R., 1964, 274.

6. Goffman, E., as cited in Janeway, E., 1980, 247.
7. Janeway, E., 1980, 243.
8. Ibid., 245.
9. Banner, L., 1983, 3.
10. de Beauvoir, S., 1953, 688.
11. Kunzle, D., 1977, 577.
12. Stannard, U., 1971, 122; 128.
13. Guthrie, R.D., 1976.
14. Bernard, J., as cited in Williams, J., 1977, 121.
15. Dickinson, E., "Witchcraft Was Hung in History," 1951.
16. Brain, R., 1979, 184.
17. Ibid., 136–137.
18. Sontag, S., as cited in Pierre, C., 1976, 106.
19. Brain, R., 1979, 12.
20. Hays, H.R., 1964, 142.
21. Jong, E., 1981, 66.
22. Andelin, H., 1965. Also see Morgan, M., 1973.
23. Flügel, J.C., 1930.
24. Banner, L., 1983, 9–10.
25. As cited in Banner, L., 1983, 23.
26. Banner, L., 1983, 205.
27. As cited in Brain, R., 1979, 12.
28. Bettelheim, B., 1976.
29. Ibid., 265.
30. Dowling, C., 1981, 20.

4. ACTING AND ATTRACTING

1. Woolf, V., 1929, 35–36.
2. Lips, H., 1981, see chapter 1.
3. Ibid., 9.
4. Ibid.
5. Morgan, E., 1972, 200–201. Also see Chance, M., & Jolly C., 1971.
6. Lips, H., 1981, 55.
7. Ibid., 62.
8. Ephron, N., 1983, 148.
9. Brownmiller, S., 1984, 29.
10. Barron, S., 1984, 29.
11. Henley, N., 1977. Also see

Lips, H., 1981. Both present research comparing gestures of gender and of power.
12. Henley, N., 1977, 176.
13. Chesler, P., and Goodman, E., as cited in Henley, N., 1977, 145.
14. Morris, J., 1974, 149.
15. Andelin, H., 1965, paraphrased from pp. 240–41.
16. Yeats, W.B., "For Anne Gregory," 1983, 245.
17. Kinzer, N., 1977, 108.
18. Guthrie, R.D., 1976, 59.
19. Deut. 22:5.
20. Britain, S., as cited in Lips, H., 1981, 77.
21. Flügel, J.C., 1930, 162.
22. Schreiner, O., cited in Partnow, E., 1978, 4.
23. Levy, H., 1966, 248.
24. Guthrie, R.D., 1976, 101.
25. Levy, H., 1966, 88.
26. Woolf, V., 1929, 52.
27. Janeway, E., 1980, 3.
28. Ibid., 240.
29. Steinem, G., 1983, 205.

5. IS ANATOMY DESTINY?

1. Brownmiller, S., 1984, 228.
2. Waters, J., paper presented at the First International Symposium on the Psychology of Cosmetic Treatments, September 1983, Philadelphia.
3. Von Baeyer, C. et al., as cited in Snyder, M., 1982.
4. Cash, T. et al., 1977.
5. Heilman, M., & Saruwatari, L., 1979. Also see Dipboye, R. et al., 1975.
6. Bowman, A., as cited in Pogrebin, L.C., 1983. Also see Heilman, M., & Stopeck, M., 1985.

7. Washington Post, Sept. 10, 1981, 4.
8. McGowan, B., as cited in McGuigan, D., 1976, 144.
9. Olsen, T., 1978, 29.
10. Jong, E., 1975, 261.
11. Cash, T., & Janda, L., 1984.
12. As cited by Stannard, U., 1971, 125.
13. Sherman, J., 1983.
14. Terman, L., & Oden, M., 1959.
15. Miller, J.B., 1976, 49.
16. Tyler, F., Rafferty, J., & Tyler, B., as cited in Dowling, C., 1981, 256.
17. Rossi, P. et al., 1974.
18. Lips, H., 1981, 162.
19. Touhey, J., 1974.
20. Brownmiller, S., 1984, 212.
21. Parsons, T., as cited in Bernard, J., 1981, 476.
22. Veblen, T., 1934, 130–46.
23. Shakespeare, Julius Caesar, act 1, sc. 2, lines 51–57.
24. Freud, S., as cited in Roszak, B., & Roszak, T., 1969, 22.
25. Reik, T., as cited in Firestone, S., 1970, 66.
26. Freud, S., 1974.
27. Freud, S., as cited in Roszak, B., & Roszak, T., 1969, 27, 80.
28. Wagman, M., 1967.
29. Janeway, E., 1975, 97.
30. Kolbenschlag, M., 1979, 41.
31. Griffin, S., 1982, 203.
32. Horney, K., 1979, 62–70.
33. Binder, P., 1954, 120.
34. Caplan, P., 1984.
35. Thompson, C., 1973, 76.

6. MYTH AMERICA GROWS UP

1. Shepard, S., "My Mother Was Pregnant," in Stanford, B., 1974, 42.

2. Rubin, J. et al., 1974.
3. Seavy, C. et al., 1975.
4. Hoffman, L., 1977.
5. Coombs, C. et al., 1975.
6. Bernard, J., 1981, 479.
7. Lamb, M., 1976.
8. Maccoby, E., & Jacklin, C., 1974, 329.
9. Joffe, C., 1971.
10. Weitzman, L. et al., 1972.
11. Williams, J., 1977, 176.
12. Vespa, M., 1975 and 1976.
13. Author's unpublished data.
14. Unger, R., & Madar, T., as cited in Unger, R., 1985.
15. Dion, K., 1973.
16. Simmons, R., & Rosenberg, F., 1975.
17. Fried, B., 1979, 37.
18. Hyde, J. et al., 1977.
19. Williams, J., 1983, 161.
20. Ibid., 161.
21. Sexton, A., "Little Girl, My String Bean, My Lovely Woman," 1966.
22. Bohan, J., 1973.
23. Offer, D. et al., 1981.
24. Musa, K., & Roach, M., 1973.
25. Offer, D. et al., 1981.
26. Dacey, J., 1979.
27. Kleinke, C., & Staneski, R., 1980.
28. Fulton, J., & Black, E., 1983.
29. *New York Times*, Sept. 13, 1983, editorial page.
30. Umiker-Sebok, J., 1981, 226.
31. Tan, A., 1977.
32. Firestone, S., 1970, 151.
33. Richard Rodgers and Oscar Hammerstein, lyrics from "Sixteen Going On Seventeen," from *The Sound of Music*, 1959.
34. Erikson, E., 1968, as cited in Lott, B., 1981, 82.
35. Erikson, E., 1968, as cited in Lott, B., 1981, 77.

36. Nin, A., 1967, as cited in Lott, B., 1981, 77.
37. Coleman, J., as cited in Bernard, J., 1981, 478.
38. Lott, B., 1981, 79–83.
39. Kolbenschlag, M., 1979, 28.
40. Horner, M., 1972.
41. Heilbrun, C., 1973, 3.
42. Jackaway, R., & Teevan, R., 1976.
43. Douvan, E., & Adelson, J., 1966.
44. Condry, J., & Dyer, S., 1976.
45. Sherman, J., 1983.
46. Solano, H., 1976.
47. Williams, J., 1983, 186.
48. Maccoby, E., & Jacklin, C., 1974, 161.
49. Landy, D., & Sigall, H., 1974.
50. Lanier, H., & Byrne, J., 1981.

7. SHAPING DOWN AND SHAPING UP

1. Chernin, K., 1981, 18.
2. Millman, M., 1980, 235.
3. *Glamour*, February 1984, Feeling fat in a thin society. pp. 198–201.
4. Halmi, K. et al., 1981.
5. Millman, M., 1980, 240.
6. Fallon, A., & Rozin, P., 1985.
7. Banner, L., 1983, 112.
8. Garner, D. et al., 1980.
9. Ibid.
10. Perutz, K., 1970.
11. Millman, M., 1980, 230.
12. Bruch, H., 1973, 195.
13. Millman, M., 1980, 100.
14. Orbach, S., 1978, 21.
15. Bruch, H., 1973, 96.
16. Orbach, S., 1978, 52.
17. Ibid., 78.
18. *Newsweek*, March 7, 1983, 58, and *People*, Feb. 21, 1983, 52.
19. Bennett, W., & Gurin, J., 1982.

20. Garner, D. et al., 1983. Also see Crisp, A., 1981.
21. Boskind-Lodahl, M., 1976, 346.
22. Faust, M., 1979.
23. Canning, H., & Mayer, J., 1966.
24. Brooks-Gunn, J., & Petersen, A., 1983, 115.
25. Umiker-Sebok, J., 1981.
26. Bruch, H., 1973, 304.
27. Levenkron, S., 1982.
28. Sanford, L., & Donovan, M., 1984, p. 379.
29. Branch, C., & Eurman, L., 1980.
30. Halmi, K. et al., 1981. Also see Pyle, R. et al., 1983.
31. Levenkron, S., 1979.
32. Gains, C., & Butler, G., 1983, 65.
33. Dwyer, J. et al., 1967.
34. Snyder, E., & Spreitzer, E., 1978.
35. Garner, D. et al., 1983.
36. *Time*, June 16, 1958, 86.
37. *Time*, Aug. 30, 1982, 72.
38. Greer, G., 1971, 202.
39. Snyder, E., & Kivlin, J., 1975.
40. Rosen, T., 1983, 62.
41. Rindskopf, K., & Gratch, S., 1982.
42. Sanford, L., & Donovan, M., 1984, 379.
43. Gornick, V., 1971, 83.
44. Combs, M., 1982, 17.
45. MacLeod, S., as cited by Scarf, M., 1982.

8. ATTRACTION AND SELECTION

1. Goodman, E., 1981, 216.
2. Beach, F., 1976.
3. Hrdy, S., 1981.
4. Beach, F., as cited in Symons, D., 1979, 354.
5. Sarty, M., 1975.

6. Rosenblatt, P., 1974.
7. Mead, M., 1967, 196–97.
8. Wilson, E., 1975, 376.
9. Harrison, A., & Saeed, L., 1977.
10. Bernard, J., 1981, 476.
11. Dawkins, R., 1976, 177–78.
12. de Beauvoir, S., 1953, 682.
13. Darwin, C., as cited in Bernard, J., 1981, 475.
14. Ploss, H., & Bartels, M., 1965.
15. Teitelbaum, M., 1976, 191.
16. Spencer, H., as cited in Teitelbaum, M., 1976, 185.
17. Morgan, E., 1972, 3–4.
18. Symons, D., 1979, chapter 7.
19. Ibid.
20. Ibid., 198.
21. Kinsey, A. et al., 1948.
22. Ibid.
23. Symons, D., 1979, 170–75.
24. Morgan, E., 1972, 155.
25. Brackley, J., 1980, 69.
26. Haviland, J., & Malatesta, C., 1981, 183.
27. Symons, D., 1979, 208.
28. Morgan, E., 1972, 248.
29. Morgan, M., 1973, 92.
30. Sherfey, M., 1973.
31. Hrdy, S., 1981, 160–88.
32. Ibid., 174.
33. Wolfe, L., 1980, 4.
34. Whyte, S.R., as cited in Ardener, S., 1978, 63.
35. Lambert, H., 1978.
36. Rosenblatt, P., 1974.
37. Hite, S., 1976, 303.
38. Guthrie, R.D., 1976.

9. MYTH AMERICA GROWS OLDER

1. Mills, C.W., as cited in Bernard, J., 1981, 142.
2. Guthrie, R.D., 1976.
3. Bem, S., 1974.
4. Andelin, H., 1965, 264.
5. Ibid., 297–98.

6. Ibid., 278.
7. Eagle, S., & Snodgrass, S., 1984.
8. Wyse, L., 1980.
9. Brownmiller, S., 1984.
10. Cross, J., & Cross, J., 1971.
11. Sontag, S., 1979, 473.
12. Freud, S., 1965, 134.
13. Sontag, S., 1979, 469, 474, 476.
14. Deutsch, F. et al., 1983.
15. Berscheid, E., & Walster, E., 1974.
16. Melamed, E., 1983, 11–12.
17. Colette, "The Vagabond," as cited in Symons, D., 1979, 192.
18. Melamed, E., 1983, 75.
19. Simmons, C., 1983.
20. Melamed, E., 1983, 42.
21. Moss, Z., 1970, 173.
22. Heckerman, C., 1980, 164.
23. Melamed, E., 1983.
24. England, P. et al., 1981.
25. National Organization for Women, *National Times*, October 1983.
26. Baker, R., 1981.
27. Dinesen, I., as cited in Heilbrun, C., 1981, C–2.
28. Steinem, G., 1983, 12.
29. Sontag, S., 1979, 474, 475.
30. Gordimer, N., 1960, 202.
31. Weisman, M., 1983.
32. Melamed, E., 1983.
33. McMahon, J., 1981.
34. Edgerton, M. et al., 1961.
35. Kalick, M., 1978.
36. Lindbergh, A., 1955, 33.

37. Lisle, L., 1980.
38. Ibid., 32–33.
39. Ibid., 131, 135, 136.
40. Ibid., 135.
41. Ibid., 131, 133.
42. Sontag, S., 1979, 478.

10. LOOSENING THE BONDS OF BEAUTY

1. Shakespeare, *King John*, act 4, sc. 2, line 11.
2. Sanford, L., & Donovan, M., 1984, suggest exercises designed to improve body image and self-esteem.
3. Olsen, T., 1978, 26–29.
4. Morgan, R., 1977, 49.
5. Vandestienne, G., 1982, 13.
6. Levy, H., 1966, 26.
7. Gilligan, C., 1982, 173.
8. Brownmiller, S., 1984, 210.
9. *Philadelphia Inquirer*, Sept. 22, 1983, C–1.
10. Shulman, A.K., 1980, 595.
11. Greer, G., 1971, 58.
12. Goldberg, P. et al., 1975.
13. Jacobson, M., & Koch, W., 1978.
14. Banner, L., 1983, 14.
15. Glynn, P., 1982, 95.
16. Roszak, B., & Roszak, T., 1969, vii.
17. Vasarely, V., 1978.
18. Heilbrun, C., 1973, Introduction, x.
19. Bernikow, L., 1980, 147.
20. Hrdy, S., 1981, 180.
21. de Beauvoir, S., 1953, 132.

Bibliography

Abeel, E. (1981). *I'll Call You Tomorrow*. New York: William Morrow.

Adams, G. (1977). Physical attractiveness research: Toward a developmental social psychology of beauty. *Human Development, 20,* 217–239.

Alta (1971). Pretty. In V. Gornick & B. Moran (Eds.), *Woman in Sexist Society* (p. 3). New York: Basic Books.

Andelin, H. (1965). *Fascinating Womanhood*. New York: Bantam.

Ardener, S. (1978). (Ed.), *Defining Females: The Nature of Women in Society*. New York: John Wiley.

Baker, R. (1981, March 8). Wrinkles on T.V. *New York Times Magazine*, p. 20.

Banner, L. (1983). *American Beauty*. New York: Alfred Knopf.

Barron, S. (1984, Jan. 15). Reviving the rituals of the debutante. *New York Times Magazine*, pp. 26–36.

Bar-Tal, D., & Saxe, L. (1976). Physical attractiveness and its relationship to sex-role stereotyping. *Sex Roles, 2* (2), 123–133.

Beach, F. (1976). Sexual attractivity, proceptivity and receptivity in female mammals. *Hormones and Behavior, 7,* 105–138.

Bem, S. (1974). The measurement of psychological androgyny. *Journal of Consulting and Clinical Psychology, 42,* 155–162.

Bennett, W., & Gurin, J. (1982). *The Dieter's Dilemma: Eating Less and Weighing More*. New York: Basic Books.

Bernard, J. (1981). *The Female World*. New York: Free Press.

Bernikow, L. (1980). *Among Women*. New York: Harmony Books.

Berscheid, E., Dion, K., Walster, W., & Walster, G. (1971). Physical attractiveness and dating choice: A test of the matching hypothesis. *Journal of Experimental Social Psychology, 7,* 173–189.

Berscheid, E., & Walster, E. (1974). Physical attractiveness. In L. Berkowitz (Ed.), *Advances in Experimental Social Psychology: Vol. 7* (pp. 158–216). New York: Academic Press.

Bettelheim, B. (1976). *The Uses of Enchantment: The Meaning and Importance of Fairy Tales*. New York: Alfred Knopf.

Binder, P. (1954). *Muffs and Morals*. New York: William Morrow.

Bohan, J. (1973). Age and sex difference in self-concept. *Adolescence, 8,* 379–384.

Boskind-Lodahl, M. (1976). Cinderella's stepsisters: A feminist perspective on anorexia nervosa and bulimia. *Signs, 2* (2), 342–356.

Brackley, J. (1980, Nov.). Male strip shows: Where women are finding laughs, gasps, and a night out. *Ms.,* pp. 69–71.

Brain, R. (1979). *The Decorated Body*. New York: Harper & Row.

Branch, C., & Eurman, L. (1980). Social attitudes towards patients with anorexia nervosa. *American Journal of Psychiatry, 137,* 631–632.

Brooks-Gunn, J., & Petersen, A. (Eds.). (1983). *Girls at Puberty*. New York: Plenum.

Broverman, I., Broverman, D., Clarkson, F., Rosencrantz, P., & Vogel, S. (1970). Sex-role stereotypes and clinical judgments of mental health. *Journal of Consulting and Clinical Psychology, 34,* 1–7.

Brownmiller, S. (1984). *Femininity*. New York: Linden Press/Simon and Schuster.

Bruch, H. (1973). *Eating Disorders*. New York: Basic Books.

Bruner, J. (1973). *On Knowing*. New York: Atheneum.

Canning, H., & Mayer, J. (1966). Obesity: Its possible effect on college acceptance. *New England Journal of Medicine, 275,* 1172–1174.

Caplan, P. (1984). The myth of woman's masochism. *American Psychologist, 39 (2),* 130–139.

Cash, T., Cash, D., & Butters, J. (1983). Mirror, mirror on the wall . . . ? Contrast effects and self evaluations of physical attractiveness. *Personality and Social Psychology Bulletin, 9,* 351–358.

Cash, T., Gillen, B., & Burns, S. (1977). Sexism and "beautyism" in personnel consultant decision making. *Journal of Applied Psychology, 62 (3),* 301–310.

Cash, T., & Janda, L. (1984, Dec.). The eye of the beholder. *Psychology Today,* pp. 46–52.

Chance, M., & Jolly, C. (1971). *Social Groups of Monkeys, Apes and Men*. New York: E.P. Dutton.

Chernin, K. (1981). *The Obsession*. New York: Harper & Row.

Chesler, P. (1972). *Women and Madness*. Garden City, N.Y.: Doubleday.

Clifton, A., McGrath, D., & Wick, B. (1976). Stereotypes of women: A single category? *Sex Roles, 2 (2),* 135–148.

Combs, M. (1982, Feb.). By food possessed. *Women's Sports,* 12–17.

Condry, J., & Dyer, S. (1976). Fear of success: Attribution of cause to the victim. *Journal of Social Issues, 32,* 63–83.

Coombs, C., Coombs, L., & McClelland, G. (1975). Preference scales for number and sex of children. *Population Studies, 29,* 273–298.

Coombs, R., & Kenkel, W. (1966). Sex differences in dating aspirations and satisfaction with computer-selected partners. *Journal of Marriage and the Family, 28,* 62–66.

Crisp, A. (1981). Anorexia nervosa at normal body weight: The abnormal/normal weight control syndrome. *International Journal of Psychiatry in Medicine, 11,* 203–233.

Cross, J., & Cross, J. (1971). Age, sex, race, and the perception of facial beauty. *Developmental Psychology, 5,* 433–439.

Dacey, J. (1979). *Adolescents Today*. Santa Monica, Calif.: Goodyear.

Dawkins, R. (1976). *The Selfish Gene*. Oxford: Oxford University Press.

de Beauvoir, S. (1953). *The Second Sex*. New York: Bantam.

Deutsch, F., Clark, M., & Zalenski, C. (1983). *Is there a double standard of aging?* Paper presented at the annual meeting of the Eastern Psychological Association, Philadelphia.

Dickinson, E. (1951). *The Poems of Emily Dickinson.* T.H. Johnson (Ed.), Cambridge, Mass.: Belknap Press of Harvard University Press.

Dion, K. (1973). Young children's stereotyping of facial attractiveness. *Developmental Psychology, 9,* 183–188.

———. (1974). Children's physical attractiveness and sex determinants of adult punitiveness. *Developmental Psychology, 10,* 772–778.

Dion, K., Berscheid, E., & Walster, E. (1972). What is beautiful is good. *Journal of Personality and Social Psychology, 24,* 285–290.

Dipboye, R., Fromkin, H., & Wiback, K. (1975). Relative importance of applicant, sex, attractiveness and scholastic standing in evaluation of job applicant resumés. *Journal of Applied Psychology, 60,* 39–43.

Douvan, E., & Adelson, J. (1966). *The Adolescent Experience.* New York: John Wiley.

Dowling, C. (1981). *The Cinderella Complex.* New York: Simon & Schuster.

Dwyer, J., Feldman, J., & Mayer, J. (1967). Adolescent dieters: Who are they? *American Journal of Clinical Nutrition, 20,* 1045–1056.

Eagle, S., & Snodgrass, S. (1984). *Beauty seen through open doors.* Paper presented at the American Psychological Association, Toronto.

Edgerton, M., Jacobson, W., & Meyer, E. (1961). Surgical-psychiatric study of patients seeking plastic surgery. *British Journal of Plastic Surgery, 13,* 136–145.

Elder, G. (1969). Appearance and education in marriage mobility. *American Sociological Review, 34,* 519–533.

England, P., Kuhn, A., & Gardener, T. (1981). The ages of men and women in magazine advertisements. *Journalism Quarterly, 58,* 468–471.

Ephron, N. (1975). *Crazy Salad.* New York: Alfred Knopf.

———. (1983). *Heartburn.* New York: Alfred Knopf.

Fallon, A., & Rozin, P. (1985). Sex differences in perception of desirable body shape. *Journal of Abnormal Psychology, 94* (1), 102–105.

Faust, M. (1979). Physical growth of adolescent girls: Patterns and sequences. In C.B. Kopp (Ed.), *Becoming Female: Perspectives on Development* (pp. 427–447). New York: Plenum.

Firestone, S. (1970). *The Dialectic of Sex.* New York: William Morrow.

Flügel, J.C. (1930). *The Psychology of Clothes.* New York: International University Press.

Ford, C., & Beach, F. (1951). *Patterns of Sexual Behavior.* New York: Harper & Row.

Freud, S. (1969). Anatomy is destiny. In B. Roszak & T. Roszak (Eds.), *Masculine/Feminine* (pp. 19–29). New York: Harper & Row.

———. (1933, 1965). *New Introductory Lectures on Psychoanalysis, Vol. 22.* J. Strachey (Ed.). New York: W.W. Norton.

———. (1974). Some physical consequences of the anatomical distinction between the sexes. In J. Strouse (Ed.), *Women and Analysis*. New York: Viking.

Fried, B. (1979). Boys will be boys will be boys. In R. Hubbard, M. Henifin, & B. Fried (Eds.), *Women Look at Biology Looking at Women* (pp. 37–60). Boston: G.K. Hall.

Fulton, J., & Black, E. (1983). *Dr. Fulton's Step ɤ Step Program for Curing Acne*. New York: Harper & Row.

Gains, C., & Butler, G. (1983, Nov.). Iron sisters. *Psychology Today*, pp. 64–69.

Garner, D., Garfinkel, P., & Olmsted, M. (1983). An overview of sociocultural factors in the development of anorexia nervosa. In P. Darby (Ed.), *Anorexia Nervosa: Recent Developments in Research* (pp. 65–82). New York: A.R. Liss.

Garner, D., Garfinkel, P., Schwartz, D., & Thompson, M. (1980). Cultural expectations of thinness in women. *Psychological Reports, 47*, 483–491.

Gilligan, C. (1982). *In a Different Voice*. Cambridge, Mass.: Harvard University Press.

Glynn, P. (1982). *Skin to Skin: Eroticism in Dress*. New York: Oxford University Press.

Goldberg, P., Gottesdiener, M., & Abramson, P. (1975). Another put-down of women? Perceived attractiveness as a function of support for the feminist movement. *Journal of Personality and Social Psychology, 32*, 113–115.

Goodman, E. (1981). *At Large*. New York: Summit Books.

Gordimer, N. (1960). *Occasion for Loving*. New York: Viking.

Gornick, V. (1971). Woman as outsider. In V. Gornick & B. Moran (Eds.), *Woman in Sexist Society* (pp. 71–74). New York: Basic Books.

Greer, G. (1971). *The Female Eunuch*. New York: McGraw Hill.

Griffin, S. (1982). *Pornography and Silence*. New York: Harper & Row.

Guthrie, R.D. (1976). *Body Hot Spots*. New York: Van Nostrand Reinhold.

Halmi, K., Falk, J., & Schwartz, E. (1981). Binge eating and vomiting: A survey of a college population. *Psychological Medicine, 11*, 697–706.

Harrison, A., & Saeed, L. (1977). Let's make a deal. *Journal of Personality and Social Psychology, 31*, 257–264.

Haviland, J., & Malatesta, C. (1981). The development of sex differences in nonverbal signals: Fallacies, facts and fantasies. In C. Mayo & N. Henley (Eds.), *Gender and Nonverbal Behavior* (p. 183). New York: Springer-Verlag.

Hays, H.R. (1964). *The Dangerous Sex*. New York: Putnam.

Heckerman, C. (1980). *The Evolving Female*. New York: Human Sciences Press.

Heilbrun, C. (1973). *Toward a Recognition of Androgyny*. New York: Harper/Colophon Books.

———. (1981, Feb. 5). Hers Column. *New York Times*, p. C-2.

Heilman, M., & Saruwatari, L. (1979). When beauty is beastly. *Organizational Behavior and Human Performance, 23*, 360–372.

Heilman, M., & Stopeck, M. (1985). Attractiveness and corporate success:

Different causal attributions for males and females. *Journal of Applied Psychology, 70* (2), 379–388.

Henley, N. (1977). *Body Politics: Power, Sex, and Nonverbal Communication.* Englewood Cliffs, N.J.: Prentice-Hall.

Hite, S. (1976). *The Hite Report.* New York: Macmillan.

Hoffman, L. (1977). Changes in family roles, socialization and sex differences. *American Psychologist, 32,* 644–657.

Horner, M. (1972). Toward an understanding of achievement-related conflicts in women. *Journal of Social Issues, 28,* 157–176.

Horney, K. (1979). The problem of feminine masochism. In J. Williams (Ed.), *Psychology of Women: Selected Readings* (pp. 62–70). New York: W.W. Norton.

Hrdy, S. (1981). *The Woman That Never Evolved.* Cambridge, Mass.: Harvard University Press.

Hutchinson, M. (1982). Transforming body image: Your body, friend or foe? *Women and Therapy, 1* (3), 59–67.

Hyde, J., Rosenberg, B., & Behrman, J. (1977). "Tomboyism." *Psychology of Women Quarterly, 2,* 73–75.

Jackaway, R., & Teevan, R. (1976). Fear of failure and fear of success: Two dimensions of the same motive. *Sex Roles: A Journal of Research, 2,* 283–293.

Jacobson, M., & Koch, W. (1978). Attributed reasons for support of the feminist movement as a function of attractiveness. *Sex Roles, 4,* 169–174.

Janeway, E. (1975). *Between Myth and Morning: Women Awakening.* New York: William Morrow.

———. (1980). *Powers of the Weak.* New York: Alfred Knopf.

Joffe, C. (1971). Sex role socialization and the nursery school: As the twig is bent. *Journal of Marriage and the Family, 33,* 467–475.

Jong, E. (1973). *Half-Lives.* New York: Holt, Rinehart and Winston.

———. (1975). *Here Comes and Other Poems.* New York: Signet Book/New American Library.

———. (1981). *Witches.* New York: H. Abrams.

Kalick, M. (1978). Toward an interdisciplinary psychology of appearances. *Psychiatry, 41,* 243.

Kenrick, D., & Gutierres, S. (1980). Contrast effects and judgments of physical attractiveness: When beauty becomes a social problem. *Journal of Personality and Social Psychology, 38,* 131–140.

Kinsey, A., Pomeroy, W., & Martin, C. (1948). *Sexual Behavior in the Human Male.* Philadelphia: W.B. Saunders.

Kinzer, N. (1977). *Put Down and Ripped Off: The American Woman and the Beauty Cult.* New York: T.Y. Crowell.

Kleinke, C., & Staneski, R. (1980). First impressions of female bust size. *Journal of Social Psychology, 10,* 123–124.

Kolbenschlag, M. (1979). *Kiss Sleeping Beauty Good-Bye.* New York: Doubleday.

Krebs, D., & Adinolfi, A. (1975). Physical attractiveness, social relations, and personality style. *Journal of Personality and Social Psychology, 31,* 245–254.

Kunzle, D. (1977). Dress reform as anti-feminism. *Signs, 2* (3), 570–579.

Lamb, M. (1976). (Ed.), *The Role of the Father in Child Development.* New York: Wiley.

Lambert, H. (1978). Biology and equality: A perspective on sex difference. *Signs, 4* (1), 97–117.

Landy, D., & Sigall, H. (1974). Beauty is talent: Task evaluation as a function of the performer's physical attractiveness. *Journal of Personality and Social Psychology, 29,* 299–304.

Lanier, H., & Byrne, J. (1981). How high school students view women: The relationship between perceived attractiveness, occupation and education. *Sex Roles, 7,* 145–148.

Lerner, R., Karabenick, S., & Stuart, J. (1973). Relations among physical attractiveness, body attitudes, and self concepts in male and female college students. *Journal of Psychology, 85,* 119–129.

Levenkron, S. (1979, July 27). *Reporter Dispatch.* White Plains, N.Y., p. B-1.

———. (1982). *Treating and Overcoming Anorexia Nervosa.* New York: Scribner.

Levy, H. (1966). *Chinese Footbinding.* New York: W. Rawls.

Lindbergh, A. (1955). *Gift from the Sea.* New York: Vintage Books.

Lips, H. (1981). *Women, Men, and the Psychology of Power.* Englewood Cliffs, N.J.: Prentice-Hall.

Lisle, L. (1980). *Portrait of an Artist: A Biography of Georgia O'Keeffe.* New York: Pocket Books.

Lott, B. (1981). *Becoming a Woman.* Springfield, Ill.: Charles Thomas.

Lucker, G., Beane, W., & Helmrich, R. (1981). The strength of the halo effect in physical attractiveness research. *Journal of Psychology, 107,* 69–75.

Maccoby, E., & Jacklin, C. (1974). *The Psychology of Sex Differences.* Stanford, Calif.: Stanford University Press.

McGuigan, D. (1976). *New Research on Women and Sex Roles.* Ann Arbor, Mich.: University of Michigan Press.

McMahon, J. (1981). *Plastic Surgery for Men.* New York: Everest House.

Mathes, E., & Kahn, A. (1975). Physical attractiveness, happiness, neuroticism and self-esteem. *Journal of Psychology, 90,* 27–30.

Mead, M. (1967). *Male and Female: A Study of the Sexes in a Changing World.* New York: William Morrow.

Melamed, E. (1983). *Mirror, Mirror: The Terror of Not Being Young.* New York: Linden Press/Simon & Schuster.

Miller, A. (1970). Role of physical attractiveness in impression formation. *Psychonomic Science, 19,* 241–243.

Miller, J.B. (1976). *Toward a New Psychology of Women.* Boston: Beacon Press.

Miller, T., Coffman, J., & Linke, R. (1980). A survey on body image, weight, and diet of college students. *Journal of the American Dietetic Association, 17,* 561–566.

Millman, M. (1980). *Such a Pretty Face: Being Fat in America.* New York: W.W. Norton.

Morgan, E. (1972). *The Descent of Woman.* New York: Stein & Day.

Morgan, M. (1973). *The Total Woman.* Old Tappan, N.J.: Fleming H. Revell.

Morgan, R., (1977, Sept.). The politics of body-image. *Ms.*, pp. 47–52.

Morgan, R. (Ed.). (1970). *Sisterhood Is Powerful: An Anthology of Writings from the Women's Liberation Movement*. New York: Random House.

Morris, J. (1974). *Conundrum*. New York: Harcourt Brace.

Moss, Z. (1970). It hurts to be alive and obsolete: The aging woman. In R. Morgan (Ed.), *Sisterhood Is Powerful* (p. 173). New York: Vintage Books.

Murstein, B. (1972). Physical attractiveness and marital choice. *Journal of Personality and Social Psychology, 22* (1), 8–12.

Musa, K., & Roach, M. (1973). Adolescent appearance and self-concept. *Adolescence, 8*, 385–394.

Noles, S., Cash, T., & Winstead, B. (1985). Body image, physical attractiveness and depression. *Journal of Consulting and Clinical Psychology, 53* (1), 88–94.

Offer, D., Ostrov, E., & Howard, K. (1981). *The Adolescent: A Psychological Self-Portrait*. New York: Basic Books.

Olsen, T. (1978). *Silences*. New York: Delacorte.

Orbach, S., (1978). *Fat Is a Feminist Issue*. New York: Berkley Books/Paddington Press.

Partnow, E. (Ed.). (1978). *The Quotable Woman*. New York: Anchor Press/Doubleday.

Perutz, K. (1970). *Beyond the Looking Glass*. New York: William Morrow.

Pierre, C. (1976). *Looking Good*. New York: Readers Digest Press.

Ploss, H., & Bartels, M. (1965). *Femina: Libido Sexualis*. New York: The Medical Press.

Pogrebin, L. (1983, Dec.). The power of beauty. *Ms.*, pp. 75–79.

Pyle, R., Mitchell, E., & Eckert, E. (1983). The incidence of bulimia in freshman college students. *International Journal of Eating Disorders, 2*, 75–85.

Reis, H., Nezlek, J., & Wheeler, L. (1980). Physical attractiveness in social interaction. *Journal of Personality and Social Psychology, 38* (4), 604–617.

Rindskopf, K., & Gratch, S. (1982). Women and exercise: A therapeutic approach. *Women and Therapy, 1* (4), 15–26.

Rosen, T. (1983). *Strong and Sexy: The New Body Beautiful*. New York: Delilah.

Rosenblatt, P. (1974). Cross cultural perspectives on attraction. In T. Huston (Ed.), *Foundations of Interpersonal Attraction* (pp. 79–95). New York: Academic Press.

Rossi, P., Sampson, W., Bose, C., Jasso, G., & Passel, J. (1974). Measuring household social standing. *Social Science Research, 3*, 169–190.

Rossner, J. (1983). *August*. Boston: Houghton Mifflin.

Roszak, B., & Roszak, T. (Eds.). (1969). *Masculine/Feminine*. New York: Harper & Row.

Rubin, J., Provenzano, F., & Luria, Z. (1974). The eye of the beholder: Parents' views on sex of newborns. *American Journal of Orthopsychiatry, 44*, 512–519.

Rubin, L. (1979). *Women of a Certain Age*. New York: Harper & Row.

Sanford, L., & Donovan, M. (1984). *Women & Self-Esteem*. Garden City, N.Y.: Anchor Press/Doubleday.

Sarty, M. (1975, Sept.). *Human Behavior*, p. 45.

Scarf, M. (1982, Aug. 8). A hungry way of saying no. *New York Times Book Review*, p. BR-7.

Seavey, C., Katz, P., & Zalk, S. (1975). Baby X: The effect of gender labels on adult responses to infants. *Sex Roles*, *1*, 103–110.

Sexton, A. (1966). *Live or Die*. Boston: Houghton Mifflin.

Sherfey, M. (1973). *The Nature and Evolution of Female Sexuality*. New York: Vintage Books.

Sherman, J. (1983). Girls talk about mathematics and their future. *Psychology of Women Quarterly*, *7* (4), 338.

Shulman, A. K. (1980). Sex and power: Sexual bases of radical feminism. *Signs*, *5* (4), 590–604.

Sigall, H., & Landy, D. (1973). Radiating beauty: Effects of having a physically attractive partner on person perception. *Journal of Social Psychology*, *28*, 218–224.

Simmons, C. (1983, December 11). The age of maturity. *New York Times Magazine*, p. 114.

Simmons, R., & Rosenberg, F. (1975). Sex, sex-roles, and self-image. *Journal of Youth and Adolescence*, *4*, 229–258.

Snyder, E., & Kivlin, J. (1975). Women athletes and aspects of psychological well-being and body image. *Research Quarterly*, *46* (2), 191–199.

Snyder, E., & Spreitzer, E. (1978). Correlates of sports participation among adolescent girls. *Research Quarterly*, *47*, 804–808.

Snyder, M. (1982, July). Self-fulfilling stereotypes. *Psychology Today*, pp. 60–67.

Snyder, M., Tanke, E., & Berscheid, E. (1977). Social perception and interpersonal behavior: On the self-fulfilling nature of social stereotypes. *Journal of Personality and Social Psychology*, *35*, 656–666.

Solano, H. (1976). *Teacher and pupil stereotypes of gifted boys and girls*. Paper presented at the annual meeting of the American Psychological Association. Washington, D.C.

Sontag, S. (1979). The double standard of aging. In J. Williams (Ed.), *Psychology of Women: Selected Readings*, (pp. 462–479). New York: W.W. Norton.

Stanford, B. (1974). *On Being Female*. New York: Pocket Books.

Stannard, U. (1971). The mask of beauty. In V. Gornick & B. Moran, (Eds.), *Woman in Sexist Society* (pp. 118–130). New York: Basic Books.

Steinem, G. (1983). *Outrageous Acts and Everyday Rebellions*. New York: Holt, Rinehart & Winston.

Symons, D. (1979). *The Evolution of Human Sexuality*. New York: Oxford University Press.

Tan, A. (1977). TV beauty ads and role expectations of adolescent female viewers. *Journalism Quarterly, 56*, 283–288.

Teitelbaum, M. (1976). *Sex Differences: Social and Biological Perspectives.* Garden City, N.Y.: Anchor Press/Doubleday.

Terman, L., & Oden, M. (1959). *The Gifted Group at Mid-Life.* Stanford, Calif.: Stanford University Press.

Thompson, C. (1973). Cultural pressures in the psychology of women. In J. Miller (Ed.), *Psychoanalysis and Women* (pp. 69–84). New York: Penguin.

Touhey, J. (1974). Effects of additional women professionals on rating of occupational prestige and desirability. *Journal of Personality and Social Psychology, 29*, 86–89.

Umiker-Sebok, J. (1981). The seven ages of women. In C. Mayo & N. Henley (Eds.), *Gender and Non-Verbal Behavior* (pp. 220–239). New York: Springer-Verlag.

Unger, R. (1979). *Female and Male.* New York: Harper & Row.

———. (1985). Personal appearance and social control. In M. Safir, M. Mednick, D. Izraeli, & J. Bernard (Eds.), *Women's Worlds: The New Scholarship.* New York: Praeger.

Unger, R., Hilderbrand, M., & Madar, T. (1982). Physical attractiveness and assumptions about social deviance: Some sex-by-sex comparisons. *Personality and Social Psychology Bulletin, 8*, 293–301.

Vandestienne, G. (1982, Feb.) Breast reduction: When less is more. *Ms.*, p. 13.

Vasarely, V. (1978). *Vasarely.* New York: Alpine Fine Arts.

Veblen, T. (1934). *The Theory of the Leisure Class.* New York: Modern Library.

Vespa, M. (1975, Feb. 9). The littlest vamps. *New York Sunday News.*

Vespa, M. (1976, Sept.). A two year old in false eyelashes. *Ms.*, pp. 61–63.

Wagman, M. (1967). Sex differences in types of daydreams. *Journal of Personality and Social Psychology, 7*, 329–332.

Wald, C. (1975). *Myth America.* New York: Pantheon.

Walster, E., Aronson, V., Abrahams, D., & Rottmann, L. (1966). Importance of physical attractiveness in dating behavior. *Journal of Personality and Social Psychology, 4*, 508–516.

Weisman, M. (1983, Nov. 3). Hers Column. *New York Times*, p. C-2.

Weitzman, L., Eifler, D., Hokada, E., & Ross, C. (1972). Sex role socialization in picture books for preschool children. *American Journal of Sociology, 77*, 1125–1150.

Williams, J. (1977). *Psychology of Women* (First Edition). New York: W.W. Norton.

———. (1983). *Psychology of Women* (Second Edition). New York: W.W. Norton.

Wilson, E. (1975). *Sociobiology: The New Synthesis.* Cambridge, Mass.: Belknap Press of Harvard University.

Wilson, G., & Nias, D. (1976, Sept.). Beauty can't be beat. *Psychology Today*, pp. 96–103.

Wolfe, L. (1980, Sept.). The sexual profile of that *Cosmopolitan* girl. *Cosmopolitan*, pp. 254–265.

Woolf, V. (1929). *A Room of One's Own*. New York: Harcourt Brace.

Wyse, L. (1980). *Blond Beautiful Blond*. New York: M. Evans.

Yeats, W.B. (1933). *The Poems of W.B. Yeats*. R. Finneran (Ed.). New York: Macmillan.

Copyright Acknowledgments

T HE author and publisher are grateful to the following for permission to reprint portions of copyrighted material and to reproduce photographs.

TEXTUAL MATERIAL

Pp. viii and ix: From "Little Girl, My String Bean, My Lovely Woman," in *Live or Die*, by Anne Sexton. Copyright 1966 by Anne Sexton. Reprinted by permission of Houghton Mifflin Company.

P. 11: Copyright © 1983 by The New York Times Company. Reprinted by permission.

Pp. 36 and 37: From *Half-Lives*, by Erica Jong. Copyright © 1971, 1972, 1973 by Erica Mann Jong. Reprinted by permission of Holt, Rinehart and Winston, Publishers.

P. 58: Reprinted by permission of the publishers and the Trustees of Amherst College from *The Poems of Emily Dickinson*, edited by Thomas H. Johnson, Cambridge, Mass.: The Belknap Press of Harvard University Press, Copyright 1951, © 1955, 1979, 1983 by the President and Fellows of Harvard College.

P. 82: Reprinted with permission of Macmillan Publishing Company from "For Anne Gregory," by W.B. Yeats, in *W. B. Yeats*, edited by Richard J. Finneran. Copyright 1933 by Macmillan Publishing Company, renewed in 1946 by Bertha Georgie Yeats.

P. 117: Copyright © 1972 by Boulder Community Women's Center.

P. 136: Copyright © 1959 by Richard Rogers and Oscar Hammerstein II. Williamson Music Co., owner of publication and allied rights throughout the Western Hemisphere and Japan. International Copyright Secured. ALL RIGHTS RESERVED. Used by permission.

P. 184: Judith Brackley, for permission to reprint material from "Male Strip Shows where Women Are Finding Laughs, Gasps, and a Night Out." *Ms.*, November 1980.

Pp. 200, 201, 210, and 218: Susan Sontag, "The Double Standard of Aging,"

PHOTOGRAPHS

(Credits for photographs following page 82)

(Credits for photographs following page 178)

Index

About the Author

For many years a professor of psychology and women's studies, Dr. Rita Freedman now maintains a clinical practice in Scarsdale, N.Y. A graduate of Cornell University, she received her Ph.D. from the State University of New York at Albany. She writes and lectures on topics related to the psychology of women. She has two children.